Books of Merit

CABIN FEVER

CABIN

THE BEST

NEW CANADIAN

NON-FICTION

FEVER

EDITED BY MOIRA FARR

AND IAN PEARSON

The Banff Centre
inspiring **creativity**

THOMAS ALLEN PUBLISHERS, TORONTO

Library and Archives Canada Cataloguing in Publication data
available on request.

Editor: Janice Zawerbny
Jacket design and photography: Bill Douglas
Map illustration: Daniel Cristini

Published by Thomas Allen Publishers,
a division of Thomas Allen & Son Limited,
145 Front Street East, Suite 209,
Toronto, Ontario M5A 1E3 Canada

www.thomas-allen.com

The publisher gratefully acknowledges the support of
the Ontario Arts Council for its publishing program.

We acknowledge the support of the Canada Council for the Arts,
which last year invested $20.1 million in writing and publishing
throughout Canada.

We acknowledge the Government of Ontario through the
Ontario Media Development Corporation's Ontario Book Initiative.

We acknowledge the financial support of the Government of Canada
through the Book Publishing Industry Development Program (BPIDP)
for our publishing activities.

The Banff Centre would like to thank Rogers Communications Inc. for their
generous support of the Literary Journalism Program.

13 12 11 10 09   1 2 3 4 5

Printed and bound in Canada

Contents

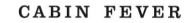

CABIN FEVER

Introduction

Marni
Jackson

The entrance to the Leighton Artists' Colony is easy to miss. First, you have to walk past the small, mysterious sheds where the visiting musicians practise. Stray violin notes or piano phrases drift out of these sheds, at all hours. Just beyond them, a path leads into a forest that shelters eight studios. Elk occasionally nap in the shade, and the rakish peak of Mount Rundle is visible through the trees. The studios are highly distinctive: one is spiral shaped and secretive, another is nearly all windows, a third is a former fishing boat. (The joke being, perhaps, that writing, like fishing, is a faintly irrational form of patience.) As soon as you step into one of these spaces, you begin to rethink your creative boundaries: obviously the architects didn't hold back—and neither should you.

The thirteen non-fiction stories in this anthology are examples of the remarkable writing that has come out of Banff, and this secluded corner of the Canadian Rockies. Officially, the collection represents the best work from the last six years of the Literary Journalism program at the Banff Centre, and marks its twentieth anniversary. (Four previous anthologies have been published by the centre.) Unofficially, I would venture that this is some of the best non-fiction writing around, I can imagine coming across any of these stories in *Granta*, *Brick*, or *The New Yorker*. These writers are breezily adept at storytelling, and well equipped with the documentary skills of the journalist. They tell us things we didn't know, and take us places we've never been. Their narratives ignore the usual roadblocks, and escort us into new terrain, whether it's an exploration of the consciousness of whales, a visit to a rural bar in France where the real absinthe is stashed, or a broken-hearted expedition into the jungles of Suriname. They share with us the dirty, addictive, lucrative pull of tree planting in British Columbia, the perils of riding a bike in the city, and they turn rapturous on the subject of Colville Bay oysters. Jeremy Klaszus, a twenty-five-year-old Edmonton journalist, patiently elicits his grandfather's memories of life in a Prussian refugee camp. Penney Kome remembers what it was like to be ten years old in Chicago, when family friends became the target of the McCarthy witch hunts. Megan Williams, a Canadian living in Rome, turns a story about learning how to drive in Rome into a stylish comedy about civic corruption and Italian history. And there's romance; Deborah Ostrovsky, a young Anglo woman, marries a Québécois man, enrols in French class, and discovers a whole new grammar of relationships.

Over the years, the title of the Literary Journalism program, along with the genre itself, kept changing; it began as "Arts Journalism," then became "Cultural Journalism and Creative Nonfiction," and could well undergo name surgery again in the future. But the focus has remained the same: to offer journalists and other non-fiction writers a chance to develop their craft during a month-long residency at the Banff Centre. Apart from taking advantage of the peace and privacy at Banff, the participants benefit from the company of visiting artists, the guidance of faculty editors, and the music-facing rigours of workshops with the other writers.

There are any number of bucolic writers' retreats, in Vermont or Tuscany, some with picnic lunches gravely left on the stoop, but they are reserved for novelists, scholars, or poets. Only the Banff Centre has extended this kind of creative support to working journalists and non-fiction authors, who are usually too busy trying to pay their bills to focus on deepening their craft.

In the year 1996, when I was a writer in the program, I had the pleasure of working with editor Don Obe, whose pencil marks (2HB, invariably) in the margins of my essay were highly intrusive, and correct. I worked in the Davison studio that July, which is equipped with a baby grand piano—a novel and welcome form of procrastination. I was writing an essay about television versus print, and having trouble with it. Don would arrive at my door with the orange pencil slanted over his ear. As I glumly turned the pages of my manuscript he would pencil a question mark beside certain foggy bits, while at the same time convincing me that I was "a draft away" from being done. The on-site editor is a wonderful luxury for writers more accustomed to the solitary trudge.

The LJ program has had many distinguished faculty members. For most of a decade, Don Obe worked alongside the late Barbara Moon, another legendary editing talent. For the past eight years of the program, Moira Farr and Ian Pearson have guided more than sixty writers through their doubts, multiple drafts, and occasional despair to the last sentence of their stories. They have selected and edited the pieces in this anthology; their presence in particular has kept the standards at Banff very high.

The setting deserves some credit too. Mountains are the most ambitious of landscapes, a geological text of time and change that tunes us in to the environment. Every time I make my way back to Banff, and the mountains come into view, the ragged flow of the horizon reminds me of a cursive line of writing. The beauty and aplomb of the mountains can't help having an impact on any artist who spends time at Banff. For one thing, it's hard to entertain petty thoughts in their company. No doubt the mountains are responsible for a certain amount of overwriting but it's true, they make you dream, and reach.

Every summer, the LJ program asks international authors to deliver public lectures at Banff. In the past, these speakers have included such estimable practitioners of non-fiction as Richard Rodriguez, Deidre Bair, Lawrence Wechsler, Ron Wright, Eleanor Wachtel, and the Mexican writer and political activist Elena Poniatawksa. This anniversary summer, authors Susan Swan and Michael Ondaatje will come to Banff to talk about (or around) their work.

Among the alumni of the program are some familiar Canadian bylines and many distinguished book award nominees: Erna Paris, Sandra Martin, Taras Grescoe, Mark Abley, Patricia Pearson, Rick

Salutin, Stan Persky, Philip Marchand, Camilla Gibb, Katherine Govier, Charles Foran, and Don Gillmor, as well as energetic new voices, such as Alex Hutchinson, Chris Tenove, Richard Poplak, Charlotte Gill, Anita Lahey, Chris Koentges, and Jonathan Garfinkel. In 1989, Canada's veteran cultural journalist Robert Fulford launched the LJ program, and began the ongoing process of defining—and redefining—exactly what "literary journalism" means. As Rogers Communication Chair, it's an honour for me to join a list of accomplished essayists and authors that includes Alberto Manguel, Alberto Ruz-Sanchez, Rosemary Sullivan—and Michael Ignatieff.

I'm not suggesting that a month in Banff necessarily prepares someone for the leadership of the Liberal Party. But it has happened.

This collection reflects the new vitality of the non-fiction narrative. For a long time, the line between fiction and non-fiction was clear, and so was their respective status: "serious writing" meant a work of pure imagination; journalism involved the worthy but pragmatic work of delivering the facts. Memoirs, historical narratives, essays, and biographies could be artful, depending on the skill of the author, but that didn't necessarily come with the territory. Novelists and poets were the aristocrats of the written word, while journalists played the role of faithful butlers. The job of non-fiction was to serve.

But in the past few fifty years, the boundaries between the genres have shifted, along with just about everything else in the publishing world. The world of writing is now clamorous with different voices, and newspapers have not only died and gone to hell, they've started to come back again. One young "publisher" is gathering up the best online blogs, and printing them as a newspaper. Print is dead as a doornail; print is being reborn. Novels are being written on cellphones, and the word "column" has been retired. The book review pages of newspapers now include more non-bookish content, such as author interviews. Calling a writer a self-promoter, as Margaret Atwood recently pointed out, used to be an insult. Now self-promotion is a necessity.

People are still reading, perhaps more than they ever have if you count eyeballs on screens, but their reading appetites are changing.

Non-fiction now outsells fiction, and there are more new book awards, with sizable cheques attached, for non-fiction writing. The heated debate over the "truthiness" of memoirs, sparked by the James Frey debacle, shows no signs of losing steam. And the precise point where the charms of a well-told narrative cross over into deliberate deception remains difficult to pin down. *Caveat lector.*

For works of non-fiction, there used to be a reader's compass we could trust, with a needle that always swung round to the true north of fact. But the closer you get to the magnetic poles, the more unreliable a compass becomes—the needle begins to swing about wildly. Something of the same thing has happened in non-fiction writing. We live in a disoriented time, where truth is a kind of magnetic pole; from a distance it behaves like a stable point of reference, but the closer you come to it—in the intimacy of a memoir or the imagined details of an historical narrative—the more its precise location blurs. (The comic writer David Sedaris has hedged his bets regarding truth and facts in personal narrative by calling what he does "real-ish.") All writing, imagined or scrupulously reported, represents a series of personal choices and omissions.

There is, of course, one guaranteed way to identify non-fiction at a glance: by the colon in the title. *Outliers: The Story of Success* by Malcolm Gladwell. This is the helpful, butlerish side of journalism, giving us the bottom line even before the book begins. But I wish we could give non-fiction titles a colonectomy, and banish the servile subtitle. It belongs to the old days of genre-bound writing.

Luckily, writing is a free-range activity. The boundaries between fact and fiction will probably continue to blur, encouraging writers to play in the intertidal zone between the two. Memory, after all, is not a tape recorder or a lie detector. It often functions more as inner novelist, reshaping the landscape of the past according to selective regrets and desires. As the poet, bon vivant, and novelist Jim Harrison has remarked, quoting his fellow American author Andrei Codrescu, "The only source of reliable information is poetry."

In a post-Google world, we are all digital researchers, all Wiki experts. But what we still crave from our storytellers and essayists, regardless of genre or voice, is the "shape" of truth—the come-hither contours of a well-crafted narrative or an elegant argument.

The hardest of facts can coexist with the wildest of imaginings, as anyone who reads David Foster Wallace can attest.

It all comes down to the writing. As publishing evolves and struggles to reinvent itself, I'm optimistic that novels will find new ways to capture distracted, overtasking, blog-weary readers, and that non-fiction will continue to evolve in fruitful ways. The genres will flirt with one another, and the result will be vital new work.

Here are some compelling examples of where non-fiction story-telling may be headed.

Eating Dirt

Charlotte Gill

WE TUMBLE OUT from pickup trucks like clothes from a dryer. Earth-stained on the thighs, the shoulders, around the waists with muddy bands, like grunge rings on the sides of a bathtub. *Permadirt*, we call it. Disposable clothes, too dirty even for the laundry.

Just two hours ago we fell out of bed and into our rags, still crusted with the grime of yesterday. Now here we are, spilling from one day into another, as if by accident, with unbrushed hair, stubbled faces, sleep still encrusted in the corners of our eyes. We drink coffee from old spaghetti-sauce jars, gnaw at protein bars dressed in foil. Cigarettes are lit before feet hit the ground, and the smoke drifts up in a communal cloud.

We tighten the laces of our tall, spike-soled boots, strap on soccer shin pads. We dig through rubber backpacks for Marigold gloves and duct tape and knee braces made out of hinged aluminum and neoprene. We tug it all out in preparation for a kind of battle. We're proud, and yet ashamed.

There is something bovine about us, our crew. We let ourselves be steered this way and that by the barks of our supervisors. At the same time we hate to be told what to do. We slide waxed boxes from the backs of the trucks and fling them down at the road. *Handle With Care*, the boxes read. *Forests for the Future*. Nothing about this phrase is a lie, but neither is it true.

Young planted forest dots the valley the way hair grows in after a transplant. Loggers crawl the mountains. Their trucks climb in the distance, like white bars of soap carried by ants. Trucks going up, trucks going down. The tidal motions of bush work, up to the peaks in the morning, down to the mainlines in the evenings. Logging roads crosscut the landscape like old surgical scars. Few residents but plenty of business. Every crag and knoll cruised, engineered, divvied, high-graded, surveyed from the air. *Creamed*, as we are fond of saying.

"Damn cold," we mutter, rubbing our palms together. We're in shadow, and the air has the stale, uncirculated feel of a cold-storage room. A preserved chill. There is nowhere to hide from it. No inside to duck into for warmth. Ancient forest surrounds us at the far edges of the clearing. Wind-beaten underdog trees with flattened bonsai crowns. Douglas-fir with the tops blown off. Gnarled cedars with bleached wood tusks protrude from lofty, lime-green foliage. Trees with mileage, like big old whales with harpoons stuck in their flanks.

A buzz develops all at once and out of nothing at all, the way bees begin to vibrate when they're about to flee the hive. A box of seedlings is ripped open. A paper bag torn. Bundles of plastic-wrapped seedlings jumble out. The stems are as long as a forearm, the roots grown in Styrofoam tubules to fit in the palms of our hands. We like this thought, it lends a kind of clout—trees grown to our ergonomic specifications.

Boot spikes crunch around in the gravel. A runaway seedling rolls down the road. We jostle around one another, hungry for the day that awaits us. We throw down our treeplanting bags and kneel down next to them and cram them with trees. We do it with practised slapdash, as cashiers drop groceries into white plastic bags. We bump shoulders, quick-fingered and competitive, like grannies at a bargain bin.

Treeplanters—one word instead of two. Little trees plus human beings, two nouns that don't seem to want to come apart.

Pierre is fifty-five, the oldest among us. Jake likes to call him "Old Man." Jake is the youngest. He calls himself "Elfie" in the third person. Rose is a child of treeplanter parents. Her middle name is Blue-flower. Wherever she goes she brings a coffin box full of wardrobe changes. Nick is red-headed, like Richie Cunningham. He doesn't drink, though he used to. Some call him "Risky," like the business. Melissa is an Australian with a constant smile, a spray of brown freckles, buxom lips. She arrived late. Heads turned. There were bouts of sudden shaving. There is John, our Jack of Spades. When he smiles his eyes are empty. And there's me, forgetting to take notes. I push myself into the huddle and switch off my thinking mind.

Before long we've abandoned the scene, an explosion of litter, brown paper and Saran Wrap snaking around on the road. We stomp out in every direction, right and left, up and down the mountain. We lean into the next minute and the next like runners in blocks. We don't know how to work without pitting ourselves against one another, without turning it into an amazing race. Otherwise piecework is grindingly relentless, countless tiny things passing negligibly through human hands. An inaudible gun goes off over our heads and the day begins. The sun is our pace clock in the sky.

We came as one, and now the space between us stretches like the filaments of a web. Soon there will be wind, but for now all the moisture has crystallized and fallen out of the air. We see the puffs of our breath. Our nostril hairs crisp with each inhalation. Our treeplanting bags ride heavily on our thighs. Human saddlebags, one pouch in the back and one on each side. In our daydreams they have sentient, subservient lives. They fill themselves up, we whistle them to life, and they trot out to do the job on their own.

Until someone invents a treeplanting robot, a plane that shoots seedlings from the sky, it's just us and our speed spades—gardening trowels with long wooden necks, plastic handles, blades like over-sized coke spoons.

We size up the weather and shake the cold out of our hands and scope out the massive job that looms before us. We eye it up the way rock climbers stand at the bottom of cliff faces pondering spatial puzzles of slope and texture and rock. How many people are doing just this right now, somewhere in the world? Planning and plotting and procrastinating chores many times their size? A hundred boxes of file folders. A great wall of dirty dishes. A graduate thesis. A long row of toilets to attack with just a scrub brush and a can of cleanser.

The body recoils. It feels wrong in our cells. Our neck hair stands up on end.

Clear-cuts are illogical landscapes, lunar in their barrenness yet bristling with big texture. The bucked limbs, the twisted trunks and the rotten heartwood. The massive stumps. The logs worth less than the cost of the haul to market. Travelling through clear-cuts is an unstable, three-dimensional affair. Imagine a field piled thick with car parts, knitting needles, coat hangers. Imagine climbing through hurricane wreckage. Add slope and cliffs and waterfalls and weather. Slash is a forest's post-mortem revenge, a sharp-toothed terrestrial sea. It's not our fault but it might as well be. Every day the land takes a bite out of us.

There is a clear-cut in the Bowron River valley southeast of Prince George that's the size of a small nation. The evidence could be seen from space. When we fly over the province we witness shaved slopes. When we drive, slash and stumps are a highway blur through the windshield. In B.C. we live among clear-cuts like people of the tropics live in the sugar cane. *Cutblocks*, they are called in the logging trade, like something you could snip at with scissors.

In our first years as treeplanters, the wooden carnage was shocking. The skin of the earth pulled back, underneath a sad, organic gore. A cutblock is monotonous, an endless field of broken and sun-bleached wood. Monster homes, coffee tables, telephone poles, boat hulls, coffee-shop stir sticks, firewood, magazines, Kleenex. Half the world seems made out of wood, but a clear-cut is still dead boring. We wanted to cry, but couldn't. Said we would quit, but didn't. A numbness of attention crept over us, of the sort induced by mega-mall parking lots. There was nothing to jazz our rods and cones. We were growing up, paying taxes, burning holes in our own pockets. We were learning to see without seeing.

Who talked us into this? Who gave us our first taste of treeplanting? A brother, an old roommate, a friend who slept on the couch—it's always someone else's fault. Whoever it was, they hooked us, poured it into us with their stories of pay dirt and adventure. We let it slip down the back of our throats. We hopped buses to Thunder Bay. We drove rust-chewed jalopies west through the flatlands. We practised with Popsicle sticks in the flower beds of our parents' backyards. We were young and impressionable. We needed a one-to-ten list of instructions to roll a joint. We needed maps just to find our way back home.

Now we could plant trees blindfolded in a pair of flip-flops. *Lifers*, we call ourselves, as junkies talk about one another. Where is the friend, where is the pusher now? He's a real estate agent. Or she's a mom behind the wheel of an SUV, with scars on her shins to remind herself how she could bend and yet be strong.

A horseshoe of mountains, checkered with clear-cuts. A finger of inlet pushes into the land. Vancouver Island. Or just "the island," as people call it, as if the world already knows its name. The northern tip, with its rugged folds and its light dusting of residents, its history of abandonment. A century ago the Danes arrived and ten years later, they fled. Then Europeans, Canadians, Americans. A hundred years of coming and going, waves of settlers failing in their various ways to scrape a living from the rain-soaked land and the broody, cold ocean. Here nothing wants to grow but trees. Even the Aboriginal peoples have dwindled down, done their own kind of surviving. They are called the Nahwitti, at least by anthropologists. What would they say if we called this our office, our corner of the world to bash around in?

Far from glinting steel buildings and espresso foam and the breath of a million zipping cars. The trip from Vancouver involves a ferry, four hours of driving, and finally a long, winding gravel road over a mountain pass, pocked with holes in the summer and clotted with snow in winter. A dune of white to climb with tire chains and snow tires. On the other side is Holberg, a tiny village of woodcutters. Their houses nudge up to the jutting inlet amid the tall firs. Trees, trees, trees. From snowy peaks right down to the tideline, where seaweed often dangles from the lower branches. You could feel pushed out to the edge of the storm-hammered shore. You could lose yourself amongst them.

There is no place big enough to house us all, so we're billeted, like a sports team. We live in the motel and in the old logging barracks for a month that stretches into two. These accommodations feature lumpy mattresses with synthetic spreads. Our toilets flush with disposable razors tied to string. Mouse poo in all the cupboards. But there is TV, always good satellite TV, no matter where in the wilds we find ourselves. We wander around opening and closing doors, turning *Survivor* on and off. What are we doing besides looking for an escape hatch? The ceilings look spackled with crushed popcorn. The curtains are the colour of Pringles.

On the road to Holberg, where the line on the map turns from solid to dotted, there is a cedar snag nailed with thousands of shoes. It commemorates the footwear with which hikers have made the journey to Cape Scott, as if the old soles exhausted themselves on the voyage. As if these visitors had climbed up, over, and become different people, grew new footprints on the other side.

Airliners glide the skies on their way to Asia. We vanish like fleas into the fur of the land. We look for moss and signs of dirt, searing holes in the ground with our eyes. We find spots, and we stab as if to wound them, throwing our weight behind. If we're lucky our blades penetrate slickly, as a knife slides into melon. If not, we've got roots, rock, wood, grass—barriers to chip at with the blades of our shovels in search of elusive earth. We dig around in our left-hand bags and come out with the trees, one by one by one. Douglas-firs with slick, wet needles, dangling between our thumbs and forefingers, twigs dressed in green whiskers. Drooping cedars with their young fronds the shade of tennis balls. Twenty-five cents a tree.

We lean into our shovels, pushing forward as if to open a heavy door. Rectangular holes break open at our feet. They sigh a mouldy breath. We bend at the waist and slide the roots down the back of the spade. We've found these trees new hundred-year homes, though we seldom think of it that way. We tuck them in with a punch of our fists. We haven't stood up and we're already walking. Bend. Plant. Stand up. Move on. Our work is simply this, multiplied by a thousand, two thousand, or more. Goodbye, little bastard. Have a nice life.

Bend. Plant. Stand up. Move on. The work is crushing—one could claim almost literally back-breaking. But while the hands are busy the mind is free to wander. Old thoughts float up through the murk of consciousness, like dirt from the bottom of a washing machine. Memories unfurl. We smell the imaginary aromas of childhood. We feel ghost emotions with fuzzy outlines, like the nerves of phantom limbs. Some days we're like bugs crawling around in Velcro. Grubbers in the soil, incapable of dreams. We feel small and insignificant, like we could flake away from the curve of the earth and splash down in the open ocean. Sweat trickles between our shoulder blades. We do a lot of gazing down.

"Do you like work?" we ask one another in the moments in between.

"Not really," we agree.

We can't say what makes the job so addictive, but it must be more than the money. Here no one minds if we're weird and introverted, if we cut our own hair with nail scissors. No one cares if we're chronic stoners. We could plant trees naked if we wanted to, and indeed, some of us have. Here there's no limelight to hog, no way to weasel out from toil. The work is either done or it isn't.

Our hands are scratched and scabbed, our fingerpads etched with dirt. They feel to us, our own digits, swollen and pulsating, like the hands of cartoon characters when they bash themselves with hammers. We came chubby and pale at the end of the winter. We shrank down and hardened, like boot leather dried too fast. We have calluses on top of calluses, piled up on our palms and soles. Farmer's tans. Six-packs. Arms ropy, muscled and veined. We consume 6,000 calories every day. Food goes down without much chewing—not so much eaten as garburated. At night we nosedive into sleep with our engines still gunning, to the sound of our own venous hum.

A rain forest, minus the forest. Naturally, it rains more than it doesn't. On wet days our lives are tinged with dread, a low-grade Sisyphean despair. We've seen moisture come down in every degree of slushiness. In every shape from mist to deluge, so loud we had to shout over its pattering din. We've seen it descend sideways, seen it slither in long strings. We've even seen rain blow up. The wetness envelops, it slides down the skin. Our boots fill up with water.

But not today. The storms have crashed in and rumbled out, and there's a crack of blue in the sky. Glorious white sunlight knifes through bulbous clouds, the kind accompanied by choirs of angels. "What is that glowing orb thing burning up in the sky?"

"I don't know," we joke, "but, goddamn, it hurts my eyes."

The fog slinks away, and we can see the mountain peaks all the way down to the ocean where the waves glitter coldly. We hear low rollers throwing themselves on bergs of black rock, sliding back down the pebbled beaches.

In between cold fronts, our toil feels rhythmic and Zenlike—for hours at a time, almost easy. We aren't shivering or clenching, and we aren't watching raindrops tremble from the tips of our noses. In rare sun our world looks burnished and magical, like the pages of a giant-sized storybook. Even the clear-cuts. We're punch drunk on fresh air.

On fine days there isn't anything in life—no crisis, challenge, no mission impossible—that we couldn't conquer with just a deep, dark sleep, a few cheese sandwiches, and the hot, steady steam of will-power. We look out, at the end of the day, at our fields of seedlings. They shimmy in the wind. *There,* we say, *we did this with our hands.* We didn't make millions and we didn't cure AIDS. But a thousand new trees are breathing.

The days go by in intricate visuals and bodily sensation and zooming clouds and hundreds of schlepping movements accompanied by five-second shreds of thought. None of these with a beginning or an end.

If this mountain had a face, some of us would be toiling away on its forehead, where everything has a funny way of travelling up. Sound, wind, birds. Other planters slip over the brow ridge and down the cheeks, and we hear them crooning out to one another. We hear snatches of a male baritone singing "Sweet Transvestite" from *The Rocky Horror Picture Show*. Someone has lit a joint, and the smoke wafts up in notes of skunk and mouldering grass. Perhaps we hear others badmouthing us, and we're surprised to find ourselves bruised. It's the work that does it to us. The repetition is like psychic sandpaper. We're too tired to front, a little stonewashed around the heart.

Our foremen traverse the cutblocks on foot, or they cruise the roads in trucks. Checking, maintaining, shepherding us through the day. Ravens soar by with their heads and tail flaps swivelling, in search of lunches to attack with their intelligent beaks. Wings swish through the air overhead.

On the road below, Adam unloads seedling boxes from the back of the truck and then stops to blow snot out of one of his nostrils.

He's our captain, a nimble-minded Polish dude, built like an ox, with shrewd blue-green eyes. The diesel engine gurgles. Sweat glistens on the top of his head where a lean V-shaped tuft of hair grows. He smokes furiously, flipping tree box after tree box down to the ground while issuing tactical directives into his walkie-talkie. In another century he'd be a Slavic warlord in fur and jackboots, poring over maps in a tent with snow blowing in through the flaps.

Adam peers over the edge of the road to where Carmen works, knitting at the land.

"Carmen," Adam calls down. She stoops to plant a tree, ignoring him the way people on buses pretend not to hear by armouring themselves with iPods. She stoops and climbs some more.

"Carmen," he calls again, cupping his mouth with his hands. "You've got to wear your high-viz." Day-Glo orange vests, the kind worn by traffic herders. Requisite bush couture. In case we fall and crack ourselves open, so a helicopter can find our pieces from the air.

Carmen stops to glare at him. "Go fuck yourself," she says. She puts her head down and goes back to work. She kills herself in the field as the single moms do—fevers pushed to the ends of thermometers. Fast and yet slow, at the speed of someone hunting for a set of house keys, something small but vital and lost.

Who knows what this grudge is about? It doesn't seem to need a reason. We discover vendettas the same way we learn about everything: breakups, crushes, rumours of hiring and firing. Information, around here, circulates like airborne particles, like microbes passed skin to skin. In the end we know too much about one another, yet never the whole picture.

Carmen and Neil orbit around each other in tighter and tighter circles. The romance unfolds before our very eyes. It blossoms at night in the kitchen, amidst puddles of olive oil and husks of garlic peelings. Huddled chats on the steps with cigarettes and cans of Lucky Lager. Love: we creep up to it with our hands outstretched as if to the heat of a wood stove. What we are expands and contracts like a rubber band, encircling us, crushing us all together.

We fall from the trucks at dawn. Nine hours later we crawl back in, stooped like gorillas. Our bodies feel rusted—even our armpits are sore. It's as if we've been pummelled by small, firm objects. Lemons in a pillowcase. A fatigue so thorough it bungles speech, so deep the whole world gleams.

We travel in a convoy of four pickup trucks, each one screaming around bends, kicking up flumes of beige dust. Adam conveys his crew to their off-duty comforts. Beers, joints, bags of potato chips eaten with dirty fingers. The weary anticipation is palpable. The sound track for the moment is Emily Haines singing: *Tu sais que je n'aime pas ma réalité.* Over and over again. The CD has been wedged in the drive for days, and no one has been able to coax it out.

As our truck hits the road bumps we settle into a nearly comfortable formation, like anchovies dovetailed into a can. We can't wait to arrive at the place we call home, let a hot shower melt us away. Nowhere beyond the village is there a single paved road. There are no bed-and-breakfasts. No cellphone reception. No signs to tell us to slow down for the children. No one wears seat belts. We don't care. Our cheeks are hot pink. Twigs and fir needles nestle in our hair. We are stunned and tired and indestructible.

Dirt. We're striped with it, smeared down the sides of our necks. We've found mud in all our crooks, washed it from every cranny. We've eaten it by accident and even on purpose, just to see how it tasted. On our tongues it felt like sand stirred into cold butter. It tasted just like money.

What have we learned in all this time? How are we improved after a million stooping acts? We've cried in frustration, seen pain so brilliant it glowed. We've sobbed with laughter, submerged ourselves in paroxysms so violent, our ribs were sore the next day. Does this happen elsewhere, in cubicles, in elevators. Is it possible in ironed attire? We know how to climb landslides. How to walk on the guts of the earth so our feet never touch the ground. We know how to hang on by the fingernails and toe spikes. We know how to fall down backwards and forwards, and also how to get up. Where will we take these skills at the end of our tenure? When we quit this miserable, beautiful life.

A
House
Divided

*Jonathan
Garfinkel*

THE MCDONALD's in central Jerusalem might not be the best place to meet a Palestinian in a gold Mercedes. After all, the Golden Arches are a prime terrorist target. Surely the Mysterious Mustaffah will be eyed suspiciously by the Israeli security forces standing in front of McDonald's, frisking and unzipping the bags and clothes of the breakfast customers.

I do my best Jean-Paul Belmondo. It's a survival technique I've picked up the past few days in Jerusalem. Leaning cool against a bus post, smoking nonchalantly, following the curve of lips with thumb, I try not to let my terror get the best of me. The driver I'm waiting for will take me to a Qalandia checkpoint to meet Samer, a Palestinian cameraman from Ramallah. The Israelis won't let him leave the West Bank for "reasons of security." I have never met Samer nor Mustaffah, though I did talk to Samer on his mobile yesterday evening. I told him I wanted a "tour of Palestinian life," to get a sense of the day-to-day in the West Bank. "A crash course," I explained, "on the realities of the occupation."

Go to the McDonald's near Ben-Yehuda. Wait outside discreetly. At 10 a.m. a gold Mercedes will arrive to take you to the checkpoint. The driver's name is Mustaffah. He is a trustworthy man.

At 9:59 a.m. a black Mercedes grinds to a stop in front of my black sandals. Now the black window rolls down with elegance and grace—beautiful, tinted, and electric.

"Mustaffah?" I ask.

"No," says the driver, "I am Muhammad." He wears black-tinted sunglasses. I think my mind is becoming tinted. "Get in the car."

"But what about—"

"Shut up and get in."

I comply, Muhammad puts his foot to the floor and we careen down the street, screeching around tight city corners, terrifying both myself and the stone of Jerusalem. I want to know what happened to Mustaffah, but Muhammad is too busy talking on his cellphone-CB in rapid-fire Arabic.

We speed out of the city. I had forgotten that the maps we used to draw in Bialik Hebrew Day School in Toronto neglected an important detail: Israel is really damn small. Within five minutes we're on a highway. Muhammad takes time away from his CB to point to Beit Hanina to the left, the so-and-so settlement to the right. Within fifteen minutes we're stuck in a mess of traffic going nowhere.

"Where are we?" I ask.

"Checkpoint," he says, lighting up a cigarette.

"Are we really going to drive through this?" I ask.

A blue BMW pulls up next to us. Muhammad rolls down his window and proceeds to swear at the driver in Arabic. I know they're swearing because the only Arabic I know is curses. The two immediately become engaged in a wicked screaming match. Muhammad closes his window.

"What are you fighting about?" I ask.

"We do not fight," he says. "We scream only because we love each other very much. We are brothers."

I have grown quite comfortable in the plush leather seats. I have even begun to like Muhammad, although I have no idea who he is, as we have not said more than these thirty-four words to each other. But I have a good feeling about this bearded man with sunglasses. There is a photograph of his two children on the dashboard wearing Adidas and Nike outfits, and one of his wife in a traditional Palestinian wedding dress, framed in a band of red-and-yellow elastics in the shape of a heart.

"Get out," Muhammad suddenly commands.

"Where am I going?" I ask.

"Do you have a passport?" Muhammad asks.

"Yes." I'm holding on to it for dear life.

"There," he says, pointing to a group of four soldiers, seventeen, eighteen years old, M-16s and eyes scanning bags and ID badges. "You walk through. There you will find Samer."

"How the hell am I going to find Samer?" I ask. I don't even know what he looks like. And while there is an hour of traffic trying to get through the checkpoint to the West Bank, there are at least three hours on the other side trying to return to Israel. And those are just the cars.

"You'll know Samer when you see him," he says.

I want to say to Muhammad: I've never been to the West Bank. I don't want to end up like one of those two mutilated Israeli soldiers lost in Ramallah four years ago, whose hands and feet were paraded by the citizens of that city like piñatas at a Mexican birthday bash. I'd rather not become a decapitated moron, a limbless news item. And besides, I promised my mother I wouldn't do anything dangerous on this trip. *You had to wait until the fourth year of the worst intifada to make your first journey to the Holy Land? You had to go* now *of all times?* Muhammad looks at me, now tilting his sunglasses down towards the end of his nose, revealing two black eyes, swollen with pus and bruises. My fears dwindle, and I close the door. Before I can even say *shukran* (thank you), Muhammad has reversed the Mercedes onto the highway and sped off south towards Jerusalem.

March 12, 2004. I have come to Israel to write a play about a divided house. A director in Tel Aviv has even expressed interest in the story, which began when a Palestinian friend in Toronto, Rana, was living in the house in question. It was 1998, while Rana was in Jerusalem, studying Israeli land assessment laws. She was, ironically, renting a room in a house that was under dispute between an Israeli and Palestinian family. According to Rana, in 1967 the Abu Dalo family fled their house on account of the Six Day War—they were afraid of the advancing Israeli army. When the Abu Dalo family returned after one month's time, they found Shimon and his wife—two Israeli

Jews—had occupied the "empty" house. Hassam Abu Dalo was so incensed he locked himself in his former bedroom for a month and refused to leave. He would sneak out of the bedroom at night to steal supplies from neighbouring construction sites in order to build a shelter for his family. Afraid of getting caught in the logistics of the Israeli legal system, Shimon did not complain to the authorities, and the two families, according to Suha, had managed to live together from 1967 until today. Suha and I often talked about the situation in Israel, and whether a peaceful solution would ever come about. One day she said to me: "You want to understand the situation? Go to Jerusalem, see this house for yourself." She wrote down the address.

I bought my ticket to Tel Aviv. And after this tour of the West Bank, I thought I would catch a ride back to Jerusalem, and visit the house where Palestinians and Israelis somehow live in peace.

I walk through the maze of cars and people towards the checkpoint. Someone sells chai from a silver pot. At the checkpoint an Israeli flag proudly flaps above a mess of concrete, camouflage, and barbed wire. Soldiers check cars and their occupants, slowly, slowly. There hasn't been a suicide bombing in two months, and tensions are supposedly low, making this one of the "better" days at Qalandia. I pass tables with fake Levi's, *Kelvin Klein* T-shirts, homemade Coca-Cola. Walking down the dirt road, my feet stumble on potholes, landmarks of activity and movement, of borders crossed and lives exchanged. A tin-roof-covered walkway marks the pedestrian passageway between the Occupied Territories and Israel, and I walk through with other Palestinians. The Israeli soldiers don't ask for anyone's passport—who's going to bomb Ramallah? On the opposite side of the checkpoint people have stopped bothering to honk. *What's the point?* their eyes say. *Life is this waiting.* Behind the cars lies an open field of broken glass, blown-out tires, and rusted metal. Home is this junkyard: the West Bank, prologue to a nation.

Amidst this rubble and chaos stands a man well over 6 feet in height with a completely shaved head, wearing a blue-and-white Reebok track suit with red vertical stripes. He spots me immediately and approaches to shake my hand. He smiles goofily.

"Fucking shit," he says. "Let's get the hell out of this mess."

I do not argue with the man they call Samer.

The West Bank. Say its name and it conjures images of boys throwing stones at slightly older boys with guns that shoot rubber bullets, tear gas, or grenades. Say "West Bank" and you see American and Israeli flags doused in gasoline, an effigy for the West. Men wearing kaffiyehs spraying bullets straight into the air. Mothers weeping for their martyred sons, coffins carried through cascades of crowd and howl. When one hears "West Bank," one thinks settlements, checkpoints, and curfews. One thinks poverty, humiliation, missile assassinations, and a stateless nation's leader pummelled in his compound. One imagines a breeding ground of terrorists, of bombers, of fanaticism.

The West Bank: the end of the world. The edge of sanity. The big mess everybody and nobody wants.

Samer's Land Rover is equipped with white armour and bullet-proof glass windows. With blue hockey tape he has pasted the word "TV" four times around the vehicle. I feel at once reassured and nervous.

"Are we expecting snipers?" I half joke as he opens the door for me. He doesn't smile.

"This place is hell, my friend. Welcome. Can I smoke?"

I pull out a fresh pack of Lucky Strikes and offer him one.

"Finally. A fucking Canadian who smokes. Today is already full of miracles."

I don't tell him I am new to the habit, that I only started smoking my first night in Jerusalem three days ago. Cigarettes keep you sane, keep you breathing in the here and now.

Samer pulls the Land Rover out of the mess that is Qalandia checkpoint. Soon enough the tour begins. "This is the refugee camp," he says, pointing to the falling ramshackle concrete disasters on our immediate right, "and this is the settlement." He points farther up the road towards a hill. The settlement houses are what we'd call suburban townhouses in North America. The buildings are monotonously replicated row upon row; white stucco facade, cookie-cutter windows, red-shingled roofing. There is an eeriness to their architecture. The quiet, conservative suburbs of North America have been transplanted into an occupied war zone. Certain media buzzwords don't translate into reality; the idea of "dismantling" a settlement, for one. How the hell are they going to dismantle these brick monstrosities? What are they going to do, *give* them to the Palestinians? Bulldoze them?

"This road is the one the army uses to go from the settlement to start their shooting in the camp," Samer says, pointing at a road leading up a hillside.

"When does this happen?"

"Whenever they feel like it."

We turn up the road and Samer parks the TV tank in front of the Muqata, Arafat's compound. Yasser Arafat's compound! We hang out with a couple of Palestinian soldiers who guard the inner gate to where Arafat and Company are holed up. Samer's the life of the party, cracking jokes, smoking cigarettes, and high-fiving the guys. They know Samer because he's a cameraman who has been hired out by many North American TV stations, including CTV, CBC, and NBC. If there's anything going on in the West Bank, he's there—Jenin, Hebron, Nablus—all the hot spots.

The compound is a ghastly sight of ruined buildings. Rebar dangles everywhere, creating a surreal image: the foundation for concrete now resembles a frozen waterfall that might start to flow downstream at any moment. Behind us, Palestinian soldiers conduct feeble military exercises in the courtyard. They remind me of the Woody Allen film *Bananas*; the clothes don't fit the soldiers, and I'm suspicious as to whether or not the guns they have at their feet actually function. Not that it matters. There is so little left to guard here.

I have no idea what we're talking about, but I'm one of the guys: "The Canadian Writer" is how Samer introduces me. I excuse myself and head off in search of a bathroom but discover the building that might have once housed a toilet has been blown to smithereens. I sidle up beside a broken stone wall and proceed to piss discreetly. Gazing up at Arafat's bunker, I spot a haggard face behind a small window. The face wears—am I imagining this?—a black-and-white kaffiyeh. He looks down at me and sees my golden stream of urine. This makes him laugh. I quickly zip up my pants. Did I just see *the man* himself? That is: Did Yasser Arafat just watch a Jewish tourist piss on his compound?

"Ramallah," Samer explains as we get back into the Land Rover, "is the paradise of the West Bank. It is quiet. Here there are no problems. Except at the compound."

I can't tell if he's serious or not. He lights up our cigarettes with a gold Zippo lighter. I ask him where he got it.

"At the store," he says, annoyed by my question. As if they don't have stores in the West Bank or Zippo lighters.

When we stop at a café for lunch, I am embarrassed about the Zippo question. Sitting down on a plastic chair at a wooden table, ordering a Thai chicken sandwich with french fries, I realize I hadn't expected to encounter the "normal" in the West Bank. A sign for the Palestinian beer Tabyeh advertises *on tap by the pint*. People sit, talk, read the newspaper, drink coffee. The banal life that isn't talked about in the media. And yet this is the banality that everyone dreams of—and fights for.

Samer and I discuss politics, sneaking in bites of food between arguments. He launches into his analysis: "Freedom is a very complicated situation. You have to understand that's all we're asking for here. The soldiers don't make decisions easy for us. Ours lives are always in their hands."

When Samer talks, he looks at you in the eyes. His words are weary, exhausted from overuse—the same arguments for too many years. "Before this intifada, they used to bother people randomly in the streets. If there was a checkpoint it would be small and temporary. They would put one up if Israel had an intelligence source saying there was something going to happen. It was also easier to go anywhere; you could be sitting in your house, drinking coffee, and say, 'Let's go to Bethlehem,' and you could, just like that. Now to go to Bethlehem you need special permission to cross with your own car. I have a friend, he went from Ramallah to Bethlehem to cover a story. On the way in, the soldiers said it's okay, you go in, no problem. On the way back, he wasn't allowed to return to Ramallah—where he lives. It took him four days to get permission to return home. The bottom line is the power is out of our hands. Some soldiers are easy, some are strict. You don't know who you're going to encounter."

I ask, "What about the need for security, for Israel to defend itself against terrorist attacks? Doesn't Israel have a right to do this?"

"The justification is bullshit. It's about controlling a people and keeping them in one spot, isolated, helpless and dependent. Some days the Qalandia checkpoint is only open until seven at night. Other days it's until midnight. And others it's twenty-four hours. It's whatever they want. They make life impossibly unpredictable. We live with complete uncertainty." Samer adds, "If this wall was about security, they'd build it at the pre-'67 borders. Instead, Israel puts it in strategic places to get good farmland and more water."

I ask him if the average Palestinian supports suicide bombers. I mention the television images of families being honoured when their children choose to be martyrs.

"Listen: when you see a mother on TV saying I am so happy my fucking son blew himself up, this is bullshit. She is saying this is something she supports in order to feel OK about the tragedy she has to live with."

I don't completely buy it.

"Look, we made a film and interviewed the family of a bomber. The kid was brilliant. He was going to the University in Nablus and was thirteen days away from graduation. The kid was top in his class, and the first in his family to be in the university. Do you think his parents were happy when he blew himself up? It took us two hours just to calm them down so we could ask any questions. They live with an emptiness inside them. You can feel it when you walk into their house. Nobody wants this situation."

We're headed into murky territory here. Food ought to pacify the discussion, distract us from the issue. But I can't separate the images on the TV screen from the scene Samer is painting, and Samer must set the record—or his version of it—straight. "Why aren't more Palestinian intellectuals speaking out against the violence?" I ask. "Where are the peaceful demonstrations?"

"The first intifada, 1987 to 1993, was something like this. It was rooted in the universities, and many students and intellectuals spoke up. Since then most of the intellectuals have been either arrested or deported by Israel." Samer dips a french fry into some Heinz ketchup and holds it in front of me like a teacher holds a ruler, or a policeman a baton. "You have to understand that this intifada is very different than the first. The bombings help advance the political agendas of groups like Hamas. Most Palestinians, myself included, don't support the suicide attacks. But some Palestinians believe there is no other choice. The circumstances are terrible. Since Rabin there is no hope whatsoever. Sharon—a war criminal—is leading their country. The 'peace process,' Oslo, bullshit: it's nothing more than Israel dictating the rules. This is what we live with: the army closes down Bir Zeit [the university in Ramallah] constantly. All the good water in the territories goes to the settlements. Our olive trees are cut down by settlers. We aren't allowed to leave the West Bank or Gaza, and soon we won't be allowed to leave our own cities or villages. They are building a cage around us, this 'separation fence.' Think about it: people are blowing themselves up to get a fucking country. Do you think we want this situation? It's the last act of a Shakespearean tragedy. It's shit man, total shit." Samer pauses, puts down the uneaten french fry, and opts for a Lucky Strike instead.

"Look, I know you're a Jew. When you called me from that apartment in Jerusalem, I could tell from the numbers." Samer lights up. Nobody is paying attention to us in the busy café. I shift in my seat. "Am I going to kill you because of this?" He takes a long drag of his cigarette and stares me in the eyes. He exhales and starts to laugh, "Fucking shit, man, of course not. What matters is whether or not you're a good person. Which I think you might be." He throws me his lighter and laughs some more.

I feel like I've just passed through another checkpoint, only this time it's Samer who is checking my identification. The difference here is that once I have crossed this border there is hope for trust, the possibility of friendship. After paying for my lunch Samer takes me to his apartment, which overlooks a valley where more apartment buildings are being constructed. In spite of the hopelessness of the situation, people are building their futures, however uncertain they might be. I try to imagine the house in West Jerusalem, and wonder if the Palestinian or the Jew takes care of it. What kind of shape are the walls in? Do Abu Dalo and Shimon fight over the small things, domestic issues like where a plant should go, whether or not a room should have carpeting or hardwood floors?

Samer speaks in a different tone now, quieter, as he looks out into the valley, "If I didn't believe in peace, I wouldn't be here with my family. It won't happen tomorrow. But when it does, it will be because Israelis and Palestinians have learned to see each other as human beings. As equals."

Sitting with his wife and two daughters, we drink one pot after another of something I will come to know and love—Arabic coffee—loaded with cardamom and sugar. While we sit contemplating the beautiful view and the apartments being built in the valley, we steer clear of the issue of our religions, beliefs, and backgrounds. Life feels utterly fragile at this particular moment, too precious to pollute with ideology, politics, and history. Samer takes his youngest girl, Sama, onto his lap. She laughs the way a two-year-old laughs, with her entire body, trembling with joy.

Bialik taught me the borders of Israel as understood by its former citizens—my teachers. We drew one map of the country after another each day in class: for Bible studies, geography, literature, or history. These borders never varied—they were learned by rote as the teacher outlined the country on the blackboard and we were expected to draw the same map in our books. They were minimally labelled: Jerusalem in the centre, Tel Aviv to the west, Lake Kinneret in the north, the Dead Sea in the south. What were clear were the borders: Sinai and the Red Sea in the southwest, the Mediterranean in the west, Eilat in the south, Lebanon in the north. The eastern border was always the Jordan River.

Shortly before I left Canada, my mother asked me why it took me seventeen years to take a trip to Israel, and I think part of the answer is to be found in those maps. I could draw the country by heart. I had dreams of these illustrations, my ballpoint pen tracing paper, ink transforming itself magically into landscape. Borders were imprinted into notebooks, my cramped right hand, adolescent dreams. In a way I felt as if I'd already been to Israel. As though maps could replace the smell of almond blossoms, the colour of Jerusalem stone, the sound of rubber bullets sprayed through a crowd.

It's a sunny, spring Jerusalem day as I set off to search for the house. The almond trees are in bloom, and the smell of apricots and oranges sedate the air. Hyacinth and iris bloom in the parks, while security guards holding bomb-checking devices smile in front of the cafés as I walk along Betzalel over to the neighbourhood of Katomon. Earlier this morning I received an e-mail from Rana with the name and address of the street the house is on: 83 Mekhor Chayim.

When I reach Mekhor Chayim, I feel like I'm on the outskirts of town, even though it is only a twenty-minute walk from the centre of the city. The street is quiet and unpaved—the road cradles the sun in its rocky hands. I walk to the end of the street but the numbers only go up to sixty-six. I ask a young woman if she knows where I might find eighty-three, and she looks at me like I've asked whether two plus two might equal five. A young man passes by on his way to work, and I stop him to inquire if any Arabs live in the area—he shakes his head and continues walking. A middle-aged man who runs a corner store, selling soda pop, used electronics, and seeds for gardens, has never heard of any Arabs living on this street. Finally I come to a cream-coloured stucco house with olive-green trim at the end of the road. An elderly couple are sitting outside in their garden drinking lemonade. These people, if any, will know.

"I am looking for a man named Abu Dalo," I say. "Have you heard of him?"

"Abu Dalo?" asks the woman, stirring sugar into her lemonade. "It's an Arab name?"

"Yes."

"Arabs haven't lived here since the 1950s."

"Most of them left in '48 or '49," adds the man. He rubs his fingers on the lining of his yellowed gums, picking food from his teeth with his fingernail.

"Where did they go?" I ask.

"Beit Tzafafa," the woman answers. Her hands are tough and fleshy. "It's an Arab village. Just follow the railway tracks south for 500 metres and you're there."

I'm perplexed. Rana would've made a point of telling me she lived in Beit Tzafafa. "I have a friend who lived in an Arab house owned by a man named Abu Dalo. She said it was on Mekhor Chayim."

"That's this street. And we're telling you, no Arabs have lived here for fifty years."

I'm getting a little frustrated when the man says to his wife, "Why doesn't he go to Ketter ?"

"Who's Ketter ?" I ask.

"Ketter's lived on this street forever. He knows everything that has ever happened here," she answers, stirring more and more sugar into her lemonade. "Ketter knows *everything*."

David Ketter's house is hidden behind a wall of ivy and cast iron. He greets me suspiciously, standing on the other side of a 2-metre fence, trying to catch me in the eyes and decide if my mission is indeed trustworthy. *Who sent you? What do you want?* ask Ketter's eyes.

Ketter is a soft-spoken man. When I say I am in search of a house shared between an Arab and a Jew, Ketter raises his right eyebrow. When I mention that the neighbours claim no Arabs have lived in the area since the early fifties, Ketter simply nods his head and strokes his grey moustache, thin above the lip. He wears prescription sunglasses and runs his long fingers through some eucalyptus leaves.

"I don't know what house you are talking about, but perhaps you could come inside and we could look at some maps together and figure this out," he says more to the flowers than to me.

Behind the fence Ketter's garden is a meticulous work of symmetry. Tulips complement daffodils and iris, weaving colour and shape like Japanese calligraphy weaves ink onto paper. Stones carefully placed, cacti growing between the artful footsteps.

I sit in the backyard and Ketter brings out maps and tea. We speak Hebrew, and he encourages me by correcting my grammar, teaching me the words I've forgotten since I was a child. Ketter was born in this house in 1931, and has fought in every war since. He is now retired and spends his days writing a book about the history of his street—a book no one will ever read.

Ketter is a Zionist from the old school—firm in his ideals, a socialist, hard-working, and a great believer in Israel as the locus for Jewish culture and life. He is secular, detests the extreme religious that are coming to Jerusalem from America, and has a fascination with maps, weapons, and gardening. After various maps from the past five decades reveal no clues, his wife comes outside with a plate of sesame-seed cookies. He takes me to his collection of artifacts in the tool shed.

When he was fourteen Ketter became a member of the Hagannah. He was responsible for burying weapons beneath the earth in this very backyard, to deter British arms inspectors. Gardening and sharpshooting were taught to him at an early age, he says matter-of-factly. Ketter shows off a full-scale diagram he's made of a 1934 German Mauser, his personal favourite. He used it in the War of Independence and in the 1956 Suez War. Ketter holds his father's sawed-off shotgun, polishing it affectionately with a white towel. A 1953—or was it '54?—he can't remember exactly—machine gun from Czechoslovakia. He hands me empty shells and used grenades from the '67 war, and a grenade he is now working on: an exact replica of one from the 1950s. He recounts the bombing of the King David Hotel with pride. "The world called us terrorists, but we were fighting for our very survival."

His worst memory of the early days were the executions the Hagannah carried out on Jewish informers to the British. "We were Jews butchering Jews," he says, placing a dab of white glue to a piece of metal falling off the model grenade, and adds, "but we knew what had to be done. The same way Ben-Gurion knew he had to blow up Begin's arms cache in the Mediterranean, we had to kill the traitors. That's how it is when a country is born."

We return to the table in the garden where Ketter pores over the land-plot maps. He looks at me, flustered. As far as he's concerned, I must have misunderstood Rana. "This house you are searching for does not exist," invokes Ketter, dipping a sesame cookie into hot, sugary coffee. "We don't live together, do you understand? We simply cannot, have not, nor will we ever."

But perhaps there's an exception?

"Maybe in certain neighbourhoods, in Akko, or Yaffo," two old Arab cities, one neighbouring Haifa, the other Tel-Aviv. "But not in the same house. And not on my street!" What baffles Ketter most of all is the idea that there is an Arab landowner on Mekhor Chayim. He goes over the maps again and again.

"I don't understand how you can be so adamant there will never be peace," I say, licking the sesame seeds stuck in between my teeth.

"That's because you are an idiot," says Ketter, eyes still fixed on the maps.

"Thank you," I say graciously.

"No offence." Ketter looks straight at me. "You are Canadian. You have no idea what life is like here. There can never be peace. We must live here, and they want our land."

I don't know how to respond to this. Sixty years ago, Ketter and I would have been speaking Hebrew en route to the gas chambers. It is difficult, perhaps impossible, this argument between generations and geography. Ketter has known only bloodshed and anti-Semitism. He's defended his country and nearly died for it. I know nothing of war or anti-Semitism. Know only what I have read in newspapers, books, or gleaned from conversation. Know maps I have drawn over and over again, abstractions on the page that I am trying to understand in the flesh. I can't truly understand the situation because I have never lived in it.

"We offered them land, but they want all of it."

"And negotiation?"

"There is none. It is ours historically, and it is ours in this moment: we have won every single war there is to be won. They terrorize us, and now Europe waves its finger and calls *us* the terrorists. Europe—where all these problems began." Ketter pauses and looks at the map. "Hold on a second." I can see the wheels in his head turning. "This Arab you speak of must live in the neighbourhood Mekhor Chayim, not the street. But to find this, I will need another map."

The bicycle ride to Bethlehem is a tough climb through the hills of Judea. Minus the eighteen-wheel trucks whisking me into the shoulder, the jets screaming overhead, and the signs saying, Entry is Forbidden, I feel an extraordinary sense of freedom. The ritual of travel, the euphoria of curiosity. Like all good Jewish boys, I have a bit of a thing for Jesus. I want to visit his birthplace the way a rock 'n' roll pilgrim heads for Graceland. I also want to follow up on the effects of the forty-day siege in the Church of Nativity from spring 2002. Ketter said he would phone me when he gets any more clues for the house.

The desert opens its arms to travellers on both sides of the road, marking the miracle of growth—shrubs, cacti, and sun-hewn stone. I pass exit roads to Hebron, ancient city of the Patriarchs. In the distance, a hill rises glorious, and stone houses become silver coins in the sun. Beyond the village, a rainbow points nowhere.

There's a checkpoint farther up the road with no lineup. The Israeli official looks at the blue-and-white Israeli flag flapping off the end of the large green mountain bike I've borrowed from an Israeli friend. My friend—who'd recommended I see Bethlehem by bicycle—had never mentioned anything about the flag, so I assumed it wouldn't be an issue. The official shows a mixture of suspicion and surprise. He asks me where I'm going. I say to the Church of Nativity. I show him my passport, he lets me through and soon enough I discover why there are so few travellers on this road: there's a large concrete wall smack dab in the middle of the highway, where a large, blue-and-white Israeli flag hangs slightly ruffled. The security fence.

"You cannot enter here, brother," a man with prosthetic legs says to me in decent English. This legless man tries to walk towards me but the prosthetics are too large, they keep wanting to fall out of his hip sockets.

"Welcome to Bethlehem ghetto, Palestine," says his friend, who lifts the Legless Man by the waist so his fake legs dangle in the air. It looks like a cruel ventriloquist act.

"Thank you," I say.

"You are Israeli," says the Ventriloquist.

"I am Canadian," I reply.

"Why are you carrying this flag then?" asks the Legless Man.

"It's not my bike," I say.

The two men, Ventriloquist and Ventriliquee, have a heated debate not 6 inches away from my face. The debate is in Arabic but it's clearly about the Israeli flag on the bike. The Legless Man shakes the Ventriloquist while the Ventriloquist shouts at him. Suddenly the mood changes. They stop talking. And the silence now spells danger, the premonition of something terrible about to happen.

The Ventriloquist takes control of the bike, his hands pulling on the bars. The next moment I find myself on the ground tasting pebbles. I look up and they're gone, the Legless Man balanced precariously on the bicycle frame, hanging on to the Ventriloquist's neck for support while the two ride off, blue-and-white flag flapping in the wind. I'm dazed by the fall (did I fall or was I hit?), and before I can decide on a plan of action I find my legs leading the way, sprinting away from the wall, up the rough Bethlehem road. The two men turn right, up a side street, and I chase them, all the while screaming, "My bike, my bike!" The army officer, some 200 metres away, does nothing, his attention focused on a truck trying to enter Israel. I want the soldier to do something: shoot a flare, a warning shot, anything to help a tourist in distress.

The two men have turned onto a rather steep hill, which the Ventriloquist can't quite manage while doubling his friend. I catch up to them and pant, "Can I have my bike back?"

"I thought it wasn't your bike," says the Legless Man.

"It isn't. It's my friend's."

"An Israeli friend?"

"Yes."

"You can't have the bike back."

"Look, I'm sorry about the flag."

"You are in Palestine now, do you understand what this means?" asks the Legless Man.

"Sure," I say, and while instinct has carried me towards this hill, I wish I hadn't listened to it. After all, it's just a clunky bike. It wouldn't mean the end of the world if I let them have the damn thing. The Ventriloquist puts the Legless Man onto the edge of a rusted garbage can. Beside us is an apartment building with no occupants; blown-out windows, mattresses with bullet holes that may have once acted as shields against military fire. Bullet-ridden glass, rusted rebar, and dirty toilet paper litter the edges of the street.

Willing to forsake my friend's bicycle, I start to back away, quietly exiting the situation as best I can. The Ventriloquist mentions in Pictionary language that he has a knife with a large blade on the inside of his leg. I'm not sure if he's bluffing or not. Pulling out a fresh pack of cigarettes, I opt for the Jean-Paul Belmondo technique.

"You have cigarettes?" asks the Legless Man.

Fortunately I am carrying two unopened packs with me today. I pull the second out of my pocket and give one pack to each.

"Lucky Strike," says the Ventriloquist. "Now, *that* is a cigarette."

"They toast the tobacco, right?" says the Legless Man.

I tell them I've never watched them being made, but I had heard the same thing as well. I ask if I could have one of their cigarettes from the packs I just gave them. They comply, and the three of us smoke together, silently.

"You are idiotic to ride here with a flag like this," says the Legless Man. "You are asking for trouble."

I tell them I'm not looking for trouble, I was only borrowing the bike.

"If you're going to have a bicycle with an Israeli flag on it, you have to have a Palestinian flag on it as well," explains the Ventriloquist.

"This seems reasonable," I say.

"We are reasonable men," says the Legless Man, who lights a new cigarette off his old one.

"Where do I get this Palestinian flag?" I ask.

The Ventriloquist says, "We will sell you one."

"How much?"

"Fifty dollars."

"Fifty bucks? That's ridiculous."

"Of course it's expensive," says the Legless Man.

"We are in fact ripping you off," says the Ventriloquist.

"But you have to understand, we are in dire circumstances here," adds the Legless Man.

"There are absolutely no tourists visiting."

"Look," I say, not sure about the protocol of haggling in this situation. "I'm sympathetic to your predicament. But I don't have fifty dollars."

"How much do you have?" asks the Ventriloquist.

"Thirty."

"We'll take it."

"But that's all I've got."

"That's more than we have."

"We have nothing."

"We have twelve mouths to feed between the two of us. How many do you have?" asks the Legless Man. The point is well made. I give them my last thirty dollars. "We'll throw in a free tour of the Church of Nativity too," adds the Ventriloquist.

"From you?"

"No, no, my brother will take you," says the Legless Man.

"Your brother? Where is he?"

"He is at the store, drinking."

"I don't know if I need a tour."

"Isn't that why you came here? To see the tourist sights?"

"I suppose it is," I say.

"You may have this necklace too," the Ventriloquist adds, pulling out a wooden necklace from his shirt pocket.

"I don't want a necklace."

"Please, accept this as a gift."

"I won't wear it."

"Give it to your mother."

There's a giant wooden cross on the necklace, and somehow I know my mother won't appreciate it. I take it anyway. Today is a day to say yes.

The Ventriloquist and the Legless Man leave me in a Christian gift store not far from the Bethlehem refugee camp. They head off on a journey to find the Palestinian flag and promise to be back within the hour. I'm not sure if what has just occurred falls under the category of robbery, but the fact is I'm alive and they seem to be acting like friends on account of the cigarettes and paltry amount of cash I gave them. The gift store is completely empty of customers and full of Christian tchotchkes; notebooks with Mary painted in watercolour on the cover, iridescent Mary/baby Jesus postcards, whistle-me-Jesus key chains, God the Board Game, John the Deck of Cards, the three Wise Men engraved into a backgammon board. In the midst of this mess, two bearded men, Abdul and Ishmael, one drinking coffee, the other drinking white wine, sit and play backgammon. A glass of sweet Bethlehem wine is brought for me.

"I love *shesh besh*," I proclaim, using the Arabic name for the game.

"How can you love *shesh besh*?" asks Abdul, brother of the Legless Man.

"It's a fine game," I reply, "combining luck with strategy."

Abdul strokes his moustache, his focus completely on the game, and takes a sip of strong coffee. "For two years, we've been doing nothing but playing *shesh besh*. You win, you lose, it doesn't matter. *Shesh besh* is waiting. It's the game of the damned."

I watch them play one game after another while my glass continues to be filled with wine. Ishmael drinks with me. He wears dark tinted sunglasses and says nothing. Silence is broken by Abdul to discuss politics.

"This is what they have given us. This is their peace," says Abdul. "For two years, not a fucking tourist comes into this store. Because they're scared. Like any tourist should be. The army likes to shoot at us when they're in the mood to shoot. Terrorist threat. Like hell! You rolled a double six."

"Heh, heh, heh." I realize that Ishmael is blind. Abdul tells Ishmael the roll of the dice, and Ishmael tells Abdul where to move his pieces. This is impressive, for Ishmael has obviously memorized every possible backgammon move, not to mention the shifting positions of pieces on the board. This handicap, I think, would make the game much more interesting than Abdul lets on, but I restrain from voicing this observation. I ask Abdul if he lives in the refugee camp.

"Thank God no. They are the true unfortunates."

I ask him if he'd like to leave.

"Leave? This is my home." He lights a cigarette and looks at me for the first time. "Why? You want to help me get out?"

"How?"

"It doesn't matter. One way or another, there's no escape."

Another drink, another round of *shesh besh*. I'm starting to feel a little tipsy from the wine, talk, and absence of food. Just as I wonder if we're going to make it to the church at all, the Ventriloquist and Legless Man return with a Palestinian flag painted onto a piece of white cloth, the dimensions crude, the lines uneven. The red, white and black colours of Palestine hang off a broom handle. They lend me duct tape so I can stick this makeshift flag onto the back of the bike, and they nod their approval as it is larger than the Israeli one. Larger, but doomed to fall, break off, blow away at any second. I look outside at the darkening skies, and surmise that a rainstorm would likely wash out this feeble paint job.

Ishmael starts to laugh infectiously.

"Double sixes again," says Abdul, grimacing the end of his cigarette into the ashtray. "The blind have all the luck in this part of the world."

I give up on the idea of the church, choosing to bike south and west, deeper into the West Bank. Abdul has shown me a map of the road ahead: villages and olive groves, ancient desert palaces. Children run after me, laughing at the two flags flapping in the wind, one trim and taut, the other flailing and huge. Somehow the two flags stay on. The children continue to laugh and point. A man plows his field, two oxen pulling at the earth. He turns at the sight of me, wipes the sweat from his face.

I have spent the past few days searching the Jerusalem archives, exploring other neighbourhoods—to no avail. I wonder if I have simply willed the house, made Rana's story into something it isn't. Then I get a phone call from Ketter. "There is one street," says Ketter, pointing to a map from 1951 with the housing plots of the day, "completely unmarked, and a dead end. From what I can tell, they are houses of Arabic origin. Whether or not Arabs still live there now, I cannot be certain. But it's not far from here. You should go and look."

The route as outlined by Ketter involves crossing a dirt road, hiking through a field of yellowed grass up to the waist, and hopping over the Palestinian Railway tracks. A fence has been cut away allowing for a path to the other side, where a dirt trail cuts through grass fields that grow stones, stones, and more stones. Rana had described the rock-strewn landscape as stunning, but what affects me more is the silence, a commodity rarely experienced in this country. Barbed wire, broken fences, abandoned concrete structures punctuate the open space. Even the encroaching shopping malls and billboards seem restrained in their shouting.

I follow the dirt path to a narrow, unpaved road, turn right, and ask the first man I see, white shocked hair, stooped over and digging earth, if he knows where a man named Abu Dalo lives. He does not stand up, he barks at me and says, "The asshole is over there."

He has pointed to the other side of the street to a small stone bungalow. Its front lawn is littered with broken bricks, shattered windows, and burnt rubber tires. The sun bakes the stone of the house so it is hot to the touch. There are two doors on either side of the house—I assume separate entrances for each apartment. I choose the one on my right and knock. A woman opens the door slowly, peering out from behind the chained door. She is in her mid-thirties and covers her long black hair with a blue burka.

"What do you want?" she asks me suspiciously in Hebrew.

"I've come to see the house," I say in broken Hebrew.

"What house?" she asks.

"This one."

"There's no room to rent, if that's what you want."

"I don't want to rent a room. I want to see the house," I say, "that Rana lived in."

"Rana?" she asks. "Who's she?"

"She lived here eight years ago," I reply, and thinking up something quick I add, "And she's asked me to take a picture of where she lived."

"I don't know Rana."

"You don't?"

"What did she do wrong?"

"She did nothing. She moved to Canada. We're friends."

"You speak English?"

"Yes, of course."

She starts to talk in English. It's as though the neutrality of my native tongue has relieved her—she is calmer now, and she unchains the door. "Do you want to come inside?" asks the woman.

We do the cursory introductions. Her name is Mary, a Christian Palestinian. She has no idea who Rana is, but is willing to let me take pictures. I take shots of the uneven, sloped floors, of the crooked brick walls, of the glass that used to be a greenhouse now transformed into house windows. I try to imagine this place with an entire family, but it's too small to imagine more than one or two people living in it.

"Where is Abu Dalo?" I ask, assuming Mary is his daughter.

"Abu Dalo lives in the house behind this," she says. "He owns this house, and the house across the street."

"You mean—there's more than one house?"

"Yes, Abu Dalo owns three houses."

"Three houses?" So Abu Dalo is some kind of business tycoon?

Just then there's a knock on the front door. A man with white spiked hair wearing a navy blue polyester Adidas track suit speaks Arabic to Mary. She translates.

"This is Abu Dalo," she says. I am so excited I jump over to him and shake his hand. He is taken aback by my enthusiasm. "He wants to know what you want."

I give him the Rana story again, this time with a bit more precision. I mention she was studying at the Hebrew University. It doesn't register.

"Rana?" he says, shrugging his shoulders, and turning to Mary he adds, "Who is Rana?"

"She lived here for a year or two," I add.

Abu Dalo shrugs his shoulders again. *I don't know what this crazy foreigner is talking about,* say his eyes.

I say she shared a house with some other Palestinians, and a Jew named Shimon.

"Shimon?" says Mary. "He doesn't live here."

"Where does he live?" I ask.

"Across the street."

She points at the white-haired man who directed me to this place. Things are not making sense.

The "interview" with Abu Dalo goes nowhere. He's in a rush and has no idea why I'm here. Admittedly my story is suspicious, and in all the excitement of having found the house—or three houses—I had forgotten a very important angle: I don't really have a reason as to why I am here. The best I can do is come up with the Rana story, but that has no currency because he can't remember her. I manage to get his phone number after some finagling. He agrees to sit down for a few hours when he has more time on his hands. Business is very busy right now, Mary explains on his behalf. I try to ask him what he does for a living, but he rushes off to his silver Mercedes convertible and speeds down the dirt road. Hardly the impoverished Palestinian I had been imagining.

I explain to Mary that I am interested in Abu Dalo's relationship with Shimon. She starts to laugh.

"What's so funny?" I ask.

She says, "There is no relationship between the two of them."

"Haven't they lived together for years?"

"They used to. Now Abu Dalo lives across the street. And before, they never talked."

I have trouble believing this.

Mary laughs nervously. "What do you care?"

"I'm interested in learning how people live together."

"Shimon," she whispers to me, "he's worse than Hitler."

"Hitler?"

"He's a bad, bad man," Mary continues.

"Has he murdered someone?"

"I don't talk to him anymore," says Mary.

"Why not?"

She giggles nervously and says, "You must come back and talk to Abu Dalo. Friday night," adds Mary, "is his best night."

Upon leaving the house I feel woozy. I have not drunk any water since nine in the morning. The sun beats down on my head. I look at old Shimon bent over at work, wiping fluid from his left eye. I head towards the sun, hit the Palestinian Railway, grass growing between the track's abandoned feet. Somewhere between the end of Jerusalem and the beginning of Beit Tzafafa—you can see the mosque and barbed wire piercing the cumuli in the soft blue sky—I crawl into an abandoned caboose, graffitied and silent. I sleep there, sun-beaten, in between the Arabic and Hebrew slurs and slogans. I dream that the words of the caboose, the graffiti on the walls, start to mingle with each other. They become animated, sentient, sun-wobbled. The graffiti converses—a slander in Arabic is replied by a prayer in Hebrew, and vice versa. "Go fuck your mother," "God is 7," "2000 years hope," "Jew = Nazi." Prayers and curses, in brother-languages, sister-gestures. Soon the words are coming out of the mouths of two men, their faces clear in my head. Shimon holds an M-16 on his right shoulder and a Bible in his left hand. Abu Dalo laughs, rubs sticks of dynamite with his hands as though he were reading Shimon's fortune. Abu Dalo and Shimon. Shimon and Abu Dalo. The two become the words of the caboose, yelling at each other in graffiti-language. When I wake up, I see the words on the wall of an old house, spray-painted in black on a blue background, rainbow framing graffiti. "Blind," it says.

Shabbat eve in Jerusalem, and it's the only night I can get an appointment to see Abu Dalo. His house is behind Mary's, hidden by a thick tangle of trees. Abu Dalo warmly greets me at the gate and shakes my hand. He lives in a mansion.

He takes me through the narrow passageway of his house and we walk up three flights of stairs. There is barely enough room to stand in the main third-floor room, as it is crammed wall to wall with a bizarre array of tourist paraphernalia from around the world—paintings of belly dancers from Cairo, wooden dolls from Russia, chopsticks that light up "Beijing" when clicked together, cheap Mexican rugs that say "Cancun" and "Ixtapa." There are dragon statues from Indonesia inlaid with fake silver, imitation Degas and Velazquez paintings bought on the streets of Western Europe, African masks bought last minute at duty free. Amid this mess I am invited to sit on a rather thin and uncomfortable wooden rocking chair—"our best furniture," Abu Dalo assures me with a grand hand gesture. Abu Dalo introduces me to his wife, Fathiyah, who smiles meekly. She is dressed all in black—jeans and a sweater. Cookies and coffee are laid out on the table. Mary acts as translator and sits beside me.

Mary informs me that Abu Dalo remembered Rana not long after I left the other day. Abu Dalo nods, smiling, as though understanding everything Mary is saying. Mary goes on to explain that many people have lived in the house since the early 1990s, and he apologizes for his abruptness the other day. The apology seems odd, out of character.

"You are a writer," says Abu Dalo, smiling. He says this to me in English. I don't know if Mary taught him this phrase or not.

"Yes, I am a writer," I say.

"I am a writer too!" he exclaims.

"You mean publisher," says Mary.

"I am a writer," says Abu Dalo.

"He is a publisher," says Mary. Fathiyah asks if I want more coffee. I take her up on the offer. "He has a printing press downstairs," adds Mary.

"You will write big article for newspaper!" Abu Dalo exclaims.

"A play," I reply.

Abu Dalo looks at Mary and she provides the necessary translation. He turns to me and clasps his hands. "Theatre!"

"Yes," I say. Abu Dalo rubs his hands together like a little child.

"Richard Gere?" he asks.

"So-so," I say.

"Richard Gere?" he proclaims, pointing to himself.

"I'll try my best," I say, "but the play hasn't been written yet."

Mary tells him this. Abu Dalo is slightly perturbed. "When will the play be written?" she asks.

"I'm trying to find out the story," I say. "Tell Abu Dalo I need to find out the story of the house to write the play."

As soon as this is translated, Abu Dalo leaps to his feet and exits the room. He returns with a stack of photocopies: visas of him and his wife for their pilgrimage to Mecca, pictures of their apartment in Cairo (which Abu Dalo claims they cannot get to because the Israelis won't let them leave the country nor will the Egyptians let them enter theirs), and a bank statement for 1.5 million shekels. This, he claims, is what it cost to purchase his land from the state.

"He would like you to have these documents," says Mary. Abu Dalo is smiling profusely.

"For what?" I ask.

"Your research," Mary says.

Abu Dalo joins his hands together at the wrists, miming the universal hand signal for handcuffs. Mary explains, "Mail them to Canada. Don't take them out with you. The customs will arrest you."

While putting these items into my bag I notice a photocopied article in Arabic from a newspaper—the Arabic version of the *Jerusalem Post*—with a picture of Abu Dalo holding up a document. He's offered the camera a large, toothy smile, and I want to know what the article is about. Abu Dalo beams proudly. Mary explains, "He won his court case to own the house."

Abu Dalo launches, via Mary's assistance, into the details. "In 1908 my father built the house Shimon now lives in." At the mention of Shimon's name, Fathiyah spits on the floor. "In 1948, al Naqba (the catastrophe) occurred." Abu Dalo pauses, listening to Mary's simultaneous translation by staring at her intently, placing his hands firmly on his lap, and nodding in agreement with her every word. "The Jewish army told us we had to leave, so we fled to Beit Tzafafa. After one week, we decided to return, only to find that Shimon had moved in."

"How old were you?"

"Three."

"You remember this?"

"Of course. We slept right outside the house, on the earth, while Shimon slept inside laughing at us."

"He is worse than Hitler," adds Fathiyah.

"Meanwhile my father made plans. He fought back. He would not let the matter rest."

"He hid himself in the bathroom, right?" I ask.

This sends Abu Dalo, Fathiyah, and Mary into hysterics. They have a prolonged argument in Arabic, mixed with laughter and much knee-slapping. "This is a story," says Mary, "nobody knows if it's true or not."

"Abu Dalo doesn't remember?"

"Maybe his brothers remember but they don't talk to each other. He's suing them for the land."

"I see."

"All Abu Dalo remembers is after two weeks his father had built a hut right next to Shimon."

"Did he talk to Shimon?"

"There was a lot of shouting."

"Did they share any of the house?"

Abu Dalo scratches his head. He doesn't remember. He does remember his father taking the matter to court. In the intervening years, the Abudalo family built a new house directly across the street from Shimon's. It was a rushed job, and it's where Mary lives today. She explains, "After twelve years of fighting in the courts, the judge decided that Shimon could live in the original house."

Abu Dalo solemnly adds, "My father died because he couldn't get his house back. He died with a broken heart." He points his right index finger at the sky and adds, "But the judge said, when Shimon dies, the house is mine."

Mary continues, "The problem became worse when Azzulay moved in with Shimon."

"Who's Azzulay?"

"Azzulay was a Moroccan Jew. We lived across the street in our house and the Jews lived in theirs."

"Where's Azzulay now?"

"He died," says Fathiyah, pouring teaspoons of sugar into her coffee.

"He died," says Mary, "and then his estranged daughter from Tel Aviv moved in. Declared the house her rightful inheritance." Abu Dalo points to the picture in the *Jerusalem Post*. "When Azzulay's daughter moved in, Abu Dalo took her to court. The daughter claimed she'd lived there the past six months. If this could be proven, then the house would become the daughter's."

Abu Dalo adds, "But the truth is she don't talk to her father for fifteen years. So I say fuck you. I take her to court, and I win the case."

"That's when Rana and the other Palestinian moved in—"

"When was this?"

"1997."

"Are there any Arabs living with Shimon now?"

"No, the last one is in jail, I think," Mary says. "When this intifada began, Youssef put up a Palestinian flag. Shimon did not like this, so he called the police." Abu Dalo scratches his head. "There was a lot of fighting then."

"And so what about the house now?"

"Shimon pays Abu Dalo rent," says Mary.

"I wait for him to die," Abu Dalo adds for good measure.

He is impatient. Abu Dalo paces the room, restless.

"So what is your relationship like with Shimon?" I ask.

A pause for heated debate. Mary and Abu Dalo volley arguments back and forth. Abu Dalo looks at me with disgust. "We have no relationship," he says and starts to leave the room.

"No relationship at all?" I ask, following him.

"I own the land, I own the house, I own him! You wonder where I get the money, asshole?" asks Abu Dalo, dancing back towards me. "I get it myself, I get it from no one but me, me!" He prances to the end of the hallway. "Come with me, Mr. Writer, and I will show you how I make my money!!!"

The discussion with Abu Dalo about the history of the house is confusing. I try to do the numbers in my head—who lived where and when, what was built, how it was divided—but none of it matches what I was told. Rana never mentioned Azzulay in any of our discussions. She'd also said that Shimon's "occupation" began in 1967, not 1948 as Abu Dalo claims. Each time I try to ask Abu Dalo about the house or Shimon, he changes the subject to his printing press, where we are now standing.

"Postcards?" He holds out a stack of several hundred postcards of Palestinian women standing in traditional dress in front of the Al-Aqsa Mosque in Jerusalem. Abu Dalo pretends to kiss them, "Beautifullll," he says. On the back it says, "Jerusalem: everlasting capital of Palestine."

I notice a stack of science magazines in Norwegian. "What the hell are these?"

"Biology." He smiles proudly, indicating he has printed these journals.

It appears as though Abu Dalo prints magazines, books, posters, and postcards in a variety of languages. This particular Norwegian biology journal is about symbiosis. Abu Dalo presents me with a copy of an Argentinian porn magazine.

"Gift for you," Abu Dalo says, handing me the magazine ceremoniously.

On the afternoon of the first night of Passover, I return to interview Shimon. The house is more narrow than Mary's bungalow, and I have to pass under a canopy of jasmine to get onto the property. The design appears to be Arabic in style—several columns decorate the porch, supporting the flat roof. When I knock at the door, nobody answers, so I take the liberty to get a feel for the place, to take some photographs of the original house where this small history began. In the backyard, the normal signs of life: white laundry on the line dries innocent in the sun. A few toys—trucks, tanks, plastic tea sets—lie scattered about. When I wander through the back gate towards the front, there's Shimon, standing with an armful of groceries.

"What are you doing here?" he asks in Hebrew.

"Forgive me for intruding," I reply, careful to speak with a strong accent. "I wanted to ask you a few questions about this house."

"Who are you?" Shimon asks, putting down the groceries.

"I'm a writer, from Canada."

"Who do you work for?"

"Nobody."

"What the hell do you want?"

"I want to know the story of this house."

"Why?"

"Because I want to write about it."

"Go away."

"But Shimon—"

"How do you know my name?"

"Abu Dalo and Rana—"

"You see these two hands? They built this house. Every brick, column, and plank. Then that asshole came and stole it from me."

"Really?"

"Now, if you don't leave my property, these two hands will make you leave."

"But Shimon—"

"Leave now! Or I'll call the police."

My feet won't listen. They're saying *not yet, not yet, there is so much more to find out*. "Shimon," I want to say, "tell me *your* story." But the look in Shimon's eyes, the almost prophetic-like pointing of his finger to the canopied gate, to the road back to the old city, all tell me to leave. And so I do.

On the other side of the house I see Abu Dalo, who's watering Shimon's lawn. He's playing with his five-year-old grandson, spraying him with water and laughing.

"And what are you doing here, Mr. Writer?" asks Abu Dalo, smiling.

"I was asking Shimon some questions," I reply.

This response makes Abu Dalo suddenly angry. "Do not ever talk to that man about this house. Do you understand me?"

I tell Abu Dalo there's no need to get angry. That Shimon wouldn't talk anyway.

"Just by bringing it up you create problems for us," Abu Dalo says. His grandson hides behind Abu Dalo's right leg. Angrily he adds, "Leave us alone. Leave us in peace."

Dusk. I have spent the final hours of the day trying to interview neighbours about Abu Dalo and Shimon, but nobody wants to talk. In this never-ending debate over land ownership and rights, of I-was-here-first proclamations, curiosity is unwelcome, and questions about the past are best left unasked. But I want—need—to understand something of this country beyond the maps of my Zionist childhood.

It is likely the strangers I questioned in this maze that is Jerusalem, who laughed at me and shook their heads in disbelief, are right. *North American ignoramus*, said their faces. Perhaps I am still a child in Bialik, looking at everything as if it were a map. Palestinians and Israelis living together in peace? Only on the page.

The theatre director in Tel Aviv is expecting me to bring the beginnings of a play about the house. But there is no new story here, only the one we already know—conflict, hatred, and disputed histories. The idea that I could stumble upon a blueprint for peace now seems ridiculous and naïve. But in a country that has been at war with itself for over sixty years, and will likely be so for another sixty, a story of peace requires childlike innocence. I don't want to give in to pessimism. And so I make a promise to myself—to continue travelling through Palestine and Israel, to fill this divided house with a story, one that holds out at least the hope of some answer.

I walk past the house where Shimon and his family live, where candles flicker, and shadows climb faces, alive on the walls of the dining room. The night of the Passover Seder, celebration of the passage from slavery to freedom, has begun. I think I can see Shimon rocking back and forth on his chair, reading from his *Haggadah*. His wife is with him, I imagine, as are his children and grandchildren. What message of freedom are they retelling tonight?

Finding East

Deborah Ostrovsky

"*Pourrais-tu me passer les assiettes qui sont au bout de la table?*"

I start to panic. I am not sure if my husband's aunt is speaking to me, and if so, I don't know what she is asking me to do. I pick apart the words carefully, attempting to fit them back together like a jigsaw puzzle, hoping to form some comprehensible statement.

I am sitting at a picnic table in a sunny field on a farm just outside of Saint-Alfonse-de-Rodriguez, Quebec. My husband's relatives—thirteen uncles and aunts on his father's side alone—surround me on all sides. We are at a baby shower for one of his many cousins whose names I can't remember and can't pronounce very well. They are all similar in their distinctive looks, their thick, dark hair that some of the younger cousins have fashioned into dreadlocks and others have swooped up into ponytails to show off their piercings.

Although I am in my native country of Canada, I can no longer express myself. In a sense I have to start learning how to speak all over again. These are my first few consecutive weeks of living in the province, and I am meeting my husband's large extended family for the first time. I am the only native English speaker in the history of this family.

Although I took French in high school, I dropped it as quickly as I possibly could. Like so many Canadians of my generation, my knowledge of French is completely superficial and has left me unprepared for speech. Even the toddlers here speak more French than I do.

The sun, the crisp air, the sunflowers on the picnic tables, and the smell of roasting corn, *blé d'Inde*, is infused with an overwhelming, intolerable cheeriness. But I am absolutely miserable; I can barely communicate with anyone. The family is too numerous and chaotic for anyone to take note, and I try to mask my discomfort with an emphatic grin so wide that the corners of my mouth begin to ache.

I watch snapshots of conversations going on around me, sensing shifts in the intonation of voices. This family scene is so foreign, with its size and informality, its ease in a rural setting. My father-in-law points to the farmhouse behind us. He explains that twelve of his siblings were born in the bathtub with the help of a local farmer's wife. Number seven died at birth, and the fourteenth—my husband's youngest aunt sitting just to his right—was the only one born at the hospital.

The offspring are all here, and they reflect the whirlwind of change in Quebec society over the past forty years. The older uncles and aunts still go to mass, the younger among them support Castro's Cuba, credit unions, and have a long history of activism in socialist politics. Most of them would like to see a *Québec libre* before their final days. Their children wouldn't mind that either, except that they are growing impatient with ideologies. They are more interested in travelling the world than taking over the family farm.

This is a large French, Catholic family. Its size reflects the demographic legacy of *la revanche des berceaux*, the "revenge of the cradle," in which priests encouraged the *Québécois* after the French defeat on the Plains of Abraham to outnumber the English with large families. Here, roots are still important; people in Quebec speak of "*les aïeux*," their forefathers, or "*les vieilles souches*," being of old stock, with alarming regularity. This is a family proud of their ancestry.

"Having a good time?" one of my husband's teenage cousins asks me graciously in English. Because I desperately want to show I am trying to learn French, I answer back:

"*Oui, ça va, merci, et comment vas-tu?*"

Something about my accent is so stiff, so rigid, that she asks me again where I am from. What are you originally? German? Dutch? No, I was born in the suburbs of Toronto. Really? She looks rather alarmed, and I invent a thought bubble, placing it over her head in which she expresses her disbelief that I sound so foreign, although I am now part of the family.

An older uncle approaches to ask me about some of the things I like about Quebec. Is it difficult to *s'acclimater*, to acclimatize myself, to adjust to, you know, the language thing? This uncle has a kind face. He is also very educated, having studied at the Vatican before leaving the priesthood and spending years travelling throughout Europe. He has had little contact with the English world, which is a fairly normal aspect of the French-Canadian experience for a man his age from a rural part of the province.

This uncle knows I barely understand him, but he looks right at me when he speaks, which I recognize to be a genuine attempt at engagement across the language barrier. It is also the acknowledgement of a pact that I've made by becoming part of this family: to understand the language also means to forge a new grammar of relationships and knowledge of history. It means learning French. It might mean becoming a little more *Québécois*.

I try to answer but I need my husband to translate, and I give him a detailed, long-winded explanation of my idea of "cultural difference" while the uncle sits there with his hands clasped together on his lap, as if preparing himself for a long, arduous game of broken telephone. I notice that my husband is shortening my answers to simplify things. I feel annoyed, although I shouldn't be. You can only remember so much when you are constantly called upon to be the messenger. So I try to interject, add a few more details before this uncle thinks I am a shallow, inarticulate person, only prepared to give a pat answer, which is always the easiest thing to translate.

The Quebec poet Gaston Miron once said, "Speech and language are the whole of a man's presence in the world." There is nothing worse than to find you are suddenly mute, relying on others to communicate. It can make you feel like an overgrown baby who can only gurgle and coo, or a mime imprisoned by the limits of hand gestures and exaggerated smiles.

A few days later, I made up my mind to learn French. I was driven initially by fear and a series of images that floated through my head, depicting what life might be like without speaking the language.

Family gatherings in silence. My stories and opinions meted out in spoon-sized phrases translated by my husband. Films and plays I could not attend. I already had premonitory glimpses of what this might be like with some of our friends, mixed French-English couples, with one spouse never being able to hold their own. Some had built their relationship around the language barrier. Their social lives were shaped around language or its absence.

I spent an entire afternoon in front of our bookshelves, separating all my English books from the French ones. I picked through titles and removed all the English translations of French novels: Romain Gary, Victor Hugo, Georges Perec, Anne Hébert, Marie-Claire Blais, and Gabrielle Roy. I put them in a cardboard box labelled "English" and donated them to a library downtown. From this point on, everything would have to be read in the original. I began my own interior shift across the language line in the direction of French, distancing myself from English. I did not know yet what doing so would entail, and what it would mean to live in a new language.

In *Hunger of Memory*, Mexican-American writer Richard Rodriguez speaks about "intimate utterances." He believes that words hold communicative power, but not intrinsic intimacy. Words assist in passing along feelings of intimacy with their sounds and syllables, but there is something more powerful in human relationships that don't necessarily need language.

And yet, you first need language in order to come to that realization. My husband had made the decision to improve his English when we first met in Ontario, where he studied briefly. We both laughed at the way he measured his progress, telling me that when we conversed in English he understood about 70 per cent of me. What was lurking beyond the other 30? When we moved to Quebec, I understood less than 5 per cent of what he said in French, missing entire conversations and jokes he would make with friends or colleagues. I was also missing all the subtleties and nuances in his voice because I did not have basic knowledge of his mother tongue.

In the past in a city like Montreal, the language you spoke—English or French—meant having a specific and unbroken sectarian association. Growing up in the 1950s, academic Sherry Simon found the city as "divided as colonial Calcutta." The writer Mavis Gallant described the French and English populations as "two tribes who knew nothing whatever about each other."

So much has changed here. The city has become a Petri dish for linguists, a city where French is the official language of public life, but where English can be heard just about everywhere. This duality and criss-crossing between the two languages is exciting. It is not uncommon to hear people start a sentence in one language, finishing it in another. *C'est la fin de la journée so let's go get a drink. I bumped into my friend par hasard au métro. Anyways, c'est poche!* The historical tensions between languages have evolved into the same cultural dynamism found in large European capitals. Studies on friendship and language in Montreal have also shown that friction over language issues is gradually dissolving. A Missisquoi Institute study on Quebec anglophones revealed that half of English speakers surveyed support government efforts to defend the French language.

Still, to be the only anglophone in a large francophone family meant being faced with penetrating some of the historical differences that had kept the two communities apart. My in-laws had rarely met an English speaker who had tried to learn French fluently.

In my new life in Quebec, French was everywhere. I had been here for a few months and yet I did not have enough intimacy with the language to even pick out sounds of affection or sarcasm in the voices that surrounded me. I had no access to my own thoughts and feelings in the language that I desperately needed, and wanted, to speak.

In my own family, Canada was the place you came to shed language, and the concept of home was resolutely "English." My parents met while studying in Britain, my working-class mother having been brought up outside of London, and my father a *sabra*, a native-born Israeli who was a teen during the War of Independence in 1948. My parents decided to relocate entirely: to live in a "new" country far from both the prickly heat of the Levant and post-war British rations. The prerequisite was that it be "English enough" to have a similar school system to the one that they thought best for their children. But it also had to be a place where class did not exist and things would be too new to have yet caught up with Old World hierarchies.

We rarely talked about family history. If we did, it was always in third person, as if these stories belonged to somebody else. There were the occasional confusing utterances about distant Russian-Jewish relatives—my father's side of the family—who took a much earlier route to Ellis Island and ended up "becoming American." But who did they really become? We barely maintained contact with family south of the Canadian border, and I never learned whether their experiences of immigration mirrored our own.

My mother told me that she used to close her eyes and envision "Canada" while listening to Dvorak's *New World Symphony* on the BBC. The nation didn't even have its own flag. Canada was the empty page they wanted to fill with a collage of charming and innocuous images that included forests, tundra, and a woman homesteader wearing a calico dress.

Reinvention was the theme of my parents' times, guided by the need for security. Perhaps this is why they did not really have a chance to develop a more intimate language to describe personal and family history for the period before their arrival. The act of immigrating—when it is done because of hardship or desperation—is like learning a whole new language, and the personal reflections about the process are often expressed in vague platitudes. Any uncomfortable question could be pushed aside with comments made under the guise of moralistic stoicism. "Things had to be done." "Because it was like that for everyone." "We had fewer choices."

My parents started their new lives here on the West Coast, dipped down to the United States, and finally settled in southern Ontario. Other family members from all over the world followed suit, arriving in Montreal during Expo 67, excited by all the possibilities. Even today they seem to be only vaguely aware of the French fact or the "Quiet Revolution," the period of tremendous social change and modernization when the French in Quebec became radically anti-clerical, shedding their image of being "priest-ridden" and "backward-looking" and redefining their identity in secular terms.

Our Montreal relatives lived here entirely in English. This was not exceptional for immigrants in an era famously summed up by the writer Hugh MacLennan as the "two solitudes," describing the historical tensions between French and English communities in Quebec. For them, French implied an economically underprivileged religious and social class that most newcomers wanted to avoid.

The era dictated the destiny for those who may have been curious about life and relationships on different sides of the language barrier. In *Le Chat dans le sac*, a classic 1964 New Wave film by Gilles Groulx, cross-cultural exchanges in Quebec are explored between "French" and "English." A young woman of Jewish descent from English Montreal named Barbara has a covert relationship with Claude, the French protagonist. She cannot understand the changes going on in society that concern him, including the nascent political rumblings of French revolutionary nationalist circles that Claude, a journalist, wants to join. Barbara wants to see the world; Claude wants to stay rooted to the land and protect its language, French, from being washed away by an English-using industrial system.

Claude eventually leaves Montreal, returning to the countryside, spending time in pastoral landscapes, walking through wintry farmer's fields, contemplating his future. Claude's speech is infused with political idioms about class struggle and French identity that are not part of Barbara's vocabulary. She struggles with French and with her accent, disappearing before the final scene to let Claude move towards his destiny. "I am Québécois, so I must find my own way," he says, before he and Barbara part forever and return to their separate lives.

Times have certainly changed. But *Le Chat dans le sac*, a film hailed as part of the political and cinematic canon for its generation of young French Canadians, released less than a decade before my birth, is still eerie for me to watch. The narrative thread in the film drew its inspiration from an accepted social vernacular in Quebec that determined what relationships between "French" and "English" were possible. My family might have fit into the cinematic "Barbara" and "English" part of the film. My husband's family shares an uncanny resemblance to that of "Claude" and "French."

Four decades later, no one would have ever imagined that Barbara and Claude, my husband and I, would defy all plot devices set out for them, and that we would be sitting together, married and meeting in-laws, in a farmer's field. Despite decades of battles over language, the question of "finding one's way" would be answered with an alternative ending that *Le Chat dans le sac* did not predict.

There have been more absurd events in history than Barbara and Claude getting their happy ending. So there I was, sitting in a farmer's field outside of Saint-Alphonse-de-Rodriguez, Quebec, without any words.

Nestled uncomfortably between Generation X and Y, my childhood seemed to be split right down the middle of out country's bilingual hopes and dreams. Watching Catherine Annau's documentary *Just Watch Me* about youth culture and bilingualism before the 1995 Quebec referendum, I was amazed by how nostalgic her subjects become when they discuss learning both of Canada's official languages. They belong to a moment in our nation's history that belong to some other Canadian childhood, a place where learning French meant "being a good Canadian" and participating in a national project, rather than inspiring a love for a language or genuine curiosity about a culture undergoing social and political transformation. Language was simply flattened to its role as an occupational utility: to get ahead in the civil service, to enter politics, or to move up in the ranks of the military.

Sometime in the 1980s, and by the age of ten, I had the strong impression that French classes were simply a perfunctory tribute to the Canadian bilingual ideal and did not really matter much. Most kids at my school had this feeling; it had been passed down to us by the invisible hand of school administrators, to the teachers, and then to us. French was either taught like a foreign language, or as part of a larger, national and political obligation.

My early training in French bears a startling resemblance to writer Eva Hoffman's memories of growing up in communist Poland, where the much-dreaded study of Russian was compulsory, also starting in grade five. Besides a few lackadaisical Russian exercises, Hoffman's teachers would stop teaching and chat about other things—in Polish. Mine had done something similar by making us feel that some larger force had foisted the class upon us. We started the class by reciting the alphabet followed by a few vocabulary exercises, but spent the rest of the class telling jokes and stories in English.

We once watched a short film in our French class, *Twice Upon a Time*, a satirical political allegory produced by the National Film Board in 1979. In the film, English and French citizens of Stereoville are harnessed together, back-to-back with straps, living in a kind of linguistic, Dante-esque limbo where no one could speak both languages so they have to be joined together in pairs. They could not see each other's faces, but could only turn in clumsy movements to answer questions when strangers approached them. One day, a stranger comes to town and speaks both languages. He is bilingual. In Stereoville, this causes a fair bit of confusion.

Years later, I finally understood why we watched *Twice Upon a Time*, a film most likely shown at public schools across the country. In the classroom, the film's scenes of awkward *jumelage*, twinning, of English and French, was a way of making a case for bilingualism. We learned that speaking two languages was a clear advantage, but also a patriotic duty in the decades following the 1969 Official Languages Act, the era in which the film was made.

Somehow, all the awkwardly constructed messages we schoolchildren learned about language eluded me. *Twice Upon a Time* became the quintessential image of an antagonistic linguistic duality, leaving me with the impression that Canada's bilingual vision would materialize in our being strapped to one another, blundering about on the streets of Stereoville.

Before I dropped French in high school, I was assigned a *French for Fluency* textbook, a book that I have kept until this day. Its cover is as shiny as a red Corvette, and its opening pages are crammed with photos of artisan cheese makers from France, beret-clad truffle hunters with pigs on leashes, and smartly dressed Sorbonne students with angora scarves looped around their necks. Leafing through it now, I realize what a great guide it is for explaining many of the complicated intricacies of French grammar, including the subjunctive tense, *le subjonctif*. This is the verb form used to express possibility, will, desires, which is often baffling for non-native speakers because of its subtle uses to express volition or doubt that alter the emotional direction of a phrase. *Il faut que tu m'aimes. You must love me, it is necessary that you love me.* A command or plea to be loved. Perhaps both.

Despite solid grammar instruction, the relevance of learning French for English Canadians was nowhere apparent. Apart from a handful of small reprints of government tourist photos (*Prenez le tour du Québec/Take the tour of Quebec!*) or of Quebec City carnival scenes, it is replete with ads for Parisian brand names. *Hilton International Paris (Au Hilton: un étonnant art de vivre) Champagne Robert Dufour & Fils, Jules by Christian Dior and Yves Saint Laurent.*

The kind of French that I felt it was trying to teach me was inextricably linked to a culture inaccessible to the average child of immigrants at a public high school. For someone from a family where "travel" was associated with immigration, rather than a form of cultivating cultural experience, the French we were being asked to acquire was about as possible to obtain as the fancy Parisian *haute couture* advertised in my textbook.

French was a part of old Europe: difficult, slightly selective about the people worthy of using it, dogmatic, chronically secure. I had assumed that French was still the language of an elite class who "finished" their daughters at lycées and "polished" their sons off on a "Grand Tour" through Paris. Most of us teenagers at Oakwood Collegiate Institute in Toronto could recite the names of Juventus and Benfica soccer team players with greater ease than those of the Fathers of Confederation. French was a passionless idea and a cultural concept situated far beyond our borders, far away from anywhere.

Living in Quebec would start to correct all my linguistic baggage. After trying to study on my own, I had started to measure my progress by the amount of speaking I did at my husband's family gatherings, which was still very little. I eventually registered at a Montreal adult education centre in a *Programme en francisation*, an intensive "francization program" offered to adults who are Canadian citizens and permanent residents with more than nine years of schooling in their country of origin. These programs are free, and they provide intensive training, primarily to immigrants.

In English, "francization" means to "Gallicize" or to "Frenchify." However dramatic the term sounds when translated, I liked the sound of *francisization*. It conjured up images of a surgical procedure used to convert my original self into a "French" person, who speaks French and lives a "French life." I wanted what the writer and journalist Solange Chaput Rolland called "a French mind."

In late summer of 2001, I found myself in a large drafty classroom, sitting around a table with fourteen other students, immigrants from Venezuela, Russia, Romania, Mexico, Iraq, and Sudan. I was the only person in the room who had a Canadian passport. Over the next three months our time would be spent trying to figure out who we were in a new language, what parts of ourselves to translate into French, what experiences to leave behind.

Born in Algeria, our teacher, Madame Udama, spoke impeccable Parisian French. She had studied in Algeria and taught in Europe, but she never told us any chronological details about her arrival here. This is perhaps because we did not ask, or maybe because she seemed so at home, both as an Arab woman and a *Québécoise*, discussing North African *pop rai* music with the same ease as Quebec talk shows. She had formidable posture, and held herself so upright that she looked like she would shoot straight through the ceiling. We arrived in class at eight-thirty every morning, and Udama was already there, immaculately dressed in twin sets and colourful pantsuits, her hands crossed on the desk with the day's exercises photocopied and stapled in front of her in neat little piles.

"In my class we can call each other by first name, but we must always address fellow students with *vouvoyer* and never *tutoyer*," Udama explained in French. *Vous* is the formal way of addressing elders, authority, or strangers. *Tu* is used for addressing peers, friends, children, or a spouse.

Udama was unapologetic about her rigour and discipline with French, and her philosophy towards pedagogy was transposed into other aspects of her world view. Like others in the class, she was also an immigrant and she had a hard life, having lived under the reign of *les intégristes*, fundamentalists, until her family fled to Canada. Algeria, she explained, is a country so poor that in her village people could not afford toothpaste, scrubbing their teeth with salt and living without running water. Life is not easy; she knew this. But the French language is above all these social and political hardships, and her focus was to make us the best speakers possible in the months to come.

Udama's class became a surreal lens into the immigrant experience that pulses under the surface of "normal" life in every large Canadian city. Our lessons were geared towards competency in filling out health forms, job applications, and explaining a medical emergency over the telephone. None of us was comfortable enough in French, the only language we had in common. But the hardship that most of my classmates had been through became suddenly clear. During conversation periods, Madame Udama listened patiently to tragic stories of childhood under Ceaușescu in Romania, of kidnappings in Mexico, or Russian mafia corruption. Just as students described intimate, heart-wrenching details of loss, she corrected their speech.

Udama stopped a fellow student, a lawyer, who had only been in Canada for two months, in midsentence. He explained that he had come here from Latin America with his wife because of death threats after blowing the whistle on his government's maltreatment of an indigenous group. His future and ability to practise law in his own country was uncertain due to corruption. His wife had also received menacing phone calls. *If I had been killed, I would not be here in Canada.* Udama made sure that he used the proper past tense, the *plus-que-parfait* instead of *l'imparfait* in order to express the exactness of this statement. After all, you can only be killed once. *Si j'avais été tué, je ne serais pas ici au Canada.*

A Romanian couple explained that they had lived without heat, and sometimes hot water, for more than a year. It was too expensive during the period when national industries became privatized after Communism. They also needed to save money to have their immigration papers processed. *Il a fait froid en Roumanie.* Udama makes sure they use the imperfect tense in order to explain that being cold was not a one-time action, but a continuous, gruelling repetition, causing long periods of discomfort. Our home was always cold in Romania. *Il faisait toujours froid chez nous en Roumanie.*

The stories continued, and Udama corrected our grammar throughout tales of grandparents and uncles taken by the KGB, bribes, and jailings. These stories were only bearable because they were told in a second language that we were all struggling to speak, and our reactions were delayed the way they might be while watching a badly dubbed horror film, where the impact is diminished by clumsy attempts at lexical fidelity to the original.

A student from Latin America came to class one morning, desperate to tell us about a huge misunderstanding he had over the weekend. He and his wife visited the gay village in Montreal, and saw two men kissing in a café. The student stopped to watch their embrace because he could not believe that people are so free here, that they can express themselves like this in public. He had nothing against homosexuality, but in his country they might be beaten and jailed. So he stood there, frozen on the sidewalk, looking at them through the café window, incredulous at this new place, which was now his city, his home. The men noticed him and started yelling through the window, making obscene hand gestures. He wanted to apologize to them. *I'm sorry I stared but I am unused to such freedoms*, he wanted to say, but he did not yet have the words readily available in his arsenal of vocabulary for public encounters.

One morning, I explained proudly that my husband is *Québécois pure laine*, "pure wool," an expression used to describe descendants of the first French settlers who put down roots here between 1608 and 1763. The concept of "pure wool" was still discussed with relative frequency but is practically a falsehood; so many French Québécois have mixed backgrounds of Irish and Native Indian origin. But I thought saying *pure laine* would be funny; I had no idea that this term can also be perceived as racist and exclusive, implying that there is a "real" or "ideal" breed of Québécois.

Udama gave me a disgusted look. "If your husband is *pure wool*, then what does that make us? Nylon?," she asked me with her hands in the air, pointing to the rest of the students in the class.

There were so many other misunderstandings, and Udama made it her job to clear them up, explain how things are here, the difference between certain Quebec expressions and those from France, like *piastre*, the common expression used for dollar coin, or *char*, a car, which derive from older French words and are still used here. There were also struggles with the pronunciation of words and expressions that are clipped dramatically, unlike the "International French" spoken in the classroom. *Tsé* for *tu sais*, or *pantoute* for *pas du tout*. Udama was aware of all these local variations, and she taught us a little bit of both. That's how people speak here, she says. So that's how we should speak, too.

One day, an engineer explained he could not practise his work, his *métier*, here in Canada. *Je ne vaux pas rien*, I am worthless, he said. Udama made him repeat his feeling of worthlessness properly: *Je ne vaux rien.*

At first, Udama's corrections seemed ruthless and unrelenting. Later, I realize how relieved I was by the much-needed breaks she provided with her grammar nitpicking. Her corrections were well-meaning, an attempt at healing by taking a broken conversation and fusing it back together into something more resolute. She could not give my classmates new personal histories, but she tried to give them the dignity of speech, of proper grammatical form, to tell their stories.

It happened gradually or suddenly, I couldn't remember which. I slipped into French, perhaps out of volition or maybe as a way of escape. French—even the informal variety of expressions often used in everyday speech in Quebec—became the language in which the past could be expressed with mathematical precision, the exact point where the sides of an isosceles triangle folded towards each other with elegance.

I had witnessed some of the most intense moments of story-telling in Udama's classroom, in my own country, but in a new language. This was absolutely new to me; I had spent so much of my life in classrooms, and yet I had never experienced anything as powerful as this spoken in my mother tongue. My parents' experience of immigration, including the confusion and the hardship they faced as they struggled to establish themselves in a new country, had not been given any descriptive language. It had all been shut out. English had never been there to tell me anything about the "things that had to be done," "because it was that way." French was giving me something; it became the scaffolding used to describe the experiences of extraordinary lives from the ground up, starting with verbs and tenses, accents and new intonations, to full sentences woven intricately into stories and testimony.

Learning a new language can make you feel as vulnerable as a child. It was a strangely physical experience to get my mouth to move a new way, to relearn how to pronounce words I could hear in my head but could not repeat, even in slow rhythmic steps. It is hard to accept that your speech is less than perfectly pronounced, to acknowledge the necessity for brute repetition and imitation of accents and expressions. I learned to make humiliating mistakes, admit to things that I didn't understand, suddenly acknowledging my strangeness. We are all foreigners in one language or another, and it is the process of accepting this that forced me to communicate the things that matter most.

I had yet to complete my transition into fluency, which would take more years of reading and studying. But I was beginning to think in a new language, because I witnessed people doing so who had no other choice.

"That's Limoges porcelain. It looks *authentique*."

"*Pardon?*"

"It looks like Limoges; you should buy it. It's probably worth something."

An elderly woman moved up beside me at a local church bazaar in Montreal's east end. She nudged me excitedly with her hand, and proceeded to guide me by the elbow while we walked along a row of folding tables. She pointed to pieces of fine dishware and crockery being sold for the price of a cup of coffee, all guarded under the watchful eyes of Les Sœurs de Jerusalem, an order of nuns in grey robes.

We chatted about a transparent glass Pyrex pitcher that reminded her of childhood, and a gravy boat she had found in the shape of a duck. Circa 1950s or 1960s. "All worth something now," she said, still holding on to my arm with maternal affection. I told her that I admired her extensive knowledge of the past century's fine dishware, adding that she was a good person to shop with.

Her expression suddenly changed. She had noticed my accent. I prepared myself for a barrage of questions. Where are you from? How did you end up here? How did you learn your French?

I told her that I had lived here for a few years, that I married a francophone and that I have studied French for thousands of hours, that I once banned myself from English radio, newspapers, and TV in order to learn the language. I explained that where we live, the public library has a poor selection of English fiction, consisting of a handful of John Grisham novels, which happily forced me to read more French than English. I told her that I have grown used to speaking it as part of my "public" life. I even tried to make a bad joke, telling her that French is my "stepmother tongue," which is a rather clumsy play on words, also implying that it is the "language of my mother-in-law." She started to laugh. Like so many of my older working-class neighbours in this part of the city, she was incredulous that an English speaker would go to such effort to enter her linguistic world. We are in North America, English is capitalism after all, she said.

She was part of an older generation living here who still remembers the staunch historical divisions between east and west, French and English. St-Laurent Street, "The Main" is at the heart of this division between the two cardinal points. Moving farther east—past St. Denis Street, past Papineau and beyond—continues to reveal deeper gradients in this bisectional nature of city life.

In Montreal, "crossing to the east" has historically been a political act. At one point it was considered a form of rebellion against Anglo-conformity, a way of lashing out against the bourgeois element in North American culture. People came here to join the ranks of the working classes fighting to assert their identity and to make French the language of public life. Now the east end is slowly being forced to absorb the bourgeois they once felt alienated by, as the housing shortage edges outward from the city's core like a circular wave.

But there was a time when "turning east" meant taking distance from one's relationship to "English." In 1966, a young Canadian journalist named Malcolm Reid decided to never return home to the same "English life" in Montreal. Reid descended from his room in the centre of downtown and turned east. "To the west," Reid explains, "is the part of town you would direct a tourist to: the shops are best, the buildings tallest, and the clerks speak English. But I walk eastward, following the boulevards that thread the city east and west."

The Shouting Signpainters: A Literary and Political Account of Quebec Revolutionary Nationalism is the story of Reid's journey into an utterly different world just beyond his front door. He walked east, and farther east, turning up any street: it did not matter which one. *Rue de la Visitation*, *Beaudry*, or *Amherst*. His story is part travelogue and part social investigation, one in a series of crosstown adventures into the "other" Montreal.

For an anglophone in Montreal forty years ago, the east was unexplored terrain. Its dingy record shops and diners, with their chintzy Arborite counters, belied the fact that a journey into this part of Montreal was like turning towards the political future. The east was the territory of social change, a place of discontent against the English establishment, and home to a group of young French writers known by the same name as the journal in which they wrote, *Parti pris*. Reid, an English speaker, met and interviewed them, attended their meetings, and translated what they said.

I return to Reid's journey east again and again, like an amateur historian examining the many French words and *joual*, the argot of Quebec French he tried to define for an English audience. These translations mark a turning point, a time when French Canada was redefining its relationship with language. He even provides a glossary of terms used by young French "revolutionaries" at the time: *aliénation*, *ambiguïté*, *assumer*, *authentique*, *canadian*, *clérico-bourgeois*, and *colonisé*. He reproduces the Québécois accent and mixture of English with French words common in *joual* expressions: *Kessay j'ai fait?* (What'd I do?), *Watch out! Tu vas vwere!* (Watch out! You'll see!).

Before the 1960s, French had been frayed and whittled down by a combination of weak education under the infamous reign of Premier Maurice Duplessis and the proximity of English, the language of capitalism. The French-English mix gave birth to a new but frustrated way of expression, with English intruding into every phrase and mucking about with standard French syntax. Being so heavily salted with English, *joual* expressions could not be understood by the French from France.

But English Canadians could not understand it, either. As Reid explains, "In Quebec the poor are here, on Visitation Street; the English words and forms that enter their language are no graceful borrowings, but the imprints of an English-language using industrial system, owned partly by English-speaking Canadian entrepreneurs to the west, partly by United States holders and managed by English Canadians."

Published in 1962, Augustin Turenne's *Petit Dictionnaire du 'Joual' au Français* entreats *joual* speakers to clean up their act, wipe the language clean of English once and for all. The back cover promises this: "Of COURSE you can speak better French . . . This modest dictionary will be your handy companion. After having ridiculed those who speak good French, soon YOU will be laughing at those who speak *joual*!!" Turenne's dictionary runs over ninety pages, highlighting expressions in need of correction: *C'est féké* (it's fake), *l'avion a crashé* (the plane crashed), *c'est funny*, *c'est free*, *c'est cute!* French had always been an imperialist's language. But in Quebec, it was French that had been colonized, its narrative possibilities violated by close contact with English surrounding it from all sides.

Reid's east end streets have changed so much since the 1960s. The demarcations between east and west—French and English— have become impossibly blurred. The linguistic fault lines have shifted, but the paths they have carved out cannot be completely stamped out by collective memory.

The absorption of English words into Quebec French continues, but the borrowings have become ironic, funny and clever. Languages borrow from each other constantly. A large percentage of the English language relies on the influence of French from centuries of contact dating back to the Norman Conquest.

For me, this has meant relearning many English words in the original, getting to know *faux amis* or "false friends" between the languages that mean different things. *Eventuel, fabrique, accidenté*. I have often found myself rewinding songs and films in French from Quebec because of missed lyrics or dialogue, only to realize that the words I did not understand in a phrase were anglicisms or words that

I should have recognized, because they are used in a similar way to English. *Trippé. Scoré. C'est twisté.*

In some ways I have renewed my relationship with my mother tongue. I appreciate the complexity of these "graceful borrowings," the way French and English try to resist each other, but are endlessly tied together here, across history, time, and place. Amid the linguistic tensions and resistance, perhaps "turning east" is just another way of finding a new route back home.

Sometime in Montreal in the early 1970s, during another period of political change in Quebec and as debates about language continued to rage, a young student in sixth grade named Paule G. wrote her geography notes on *La Carte*, "The Map," with the following two headings:

> *La carte est la représentation simplifiée d'un pays.*
> (The map is a simplified representation of a country.)
>
> *La légende d'une carte explique les signes employés par le dessinateur.*
> (The legend of a map explains the signs and symbols used by the draughtsman.)

On the other side of her notes, Paule had jotted down misspelled English lyrics by John Lennon:

> Imagine no possessions/
> I wander if you can/
> No need for greed or hunger/
> a brothohood of man.
>
> I didn't wont to hurt you/
> I'm just a jealus guy.

I found Paule's notes tucked into an old French dictionary I had bought from a used bookstore. On one side of the paper, Paule was a French schoolgirl copying class notes with studied precision and excellent penmanship. On the other, she was trying to be an English child, with wilder handwriting and lousy spelling, surreptitiously flipping the pages over to write out song lyrics while her teacher wasn't looking. Nothing about them, including their dictums praising the uses of geography, was particularly special.

This was not until I realized that they embodied all that goes on in the mind of someone trying to learn another language. Paule was doing so much more than flipping over the pages. She was entering a different world, exploring the larger geography of English popular culture; perhaps this was done in a moment of boredom or escape from her own.

"Learning languages," writes Alice Kaplan, "can show up people's craziness in dramatic ways." Perhaps this is because we think we need to adopt a culture when we learn a new language. I have attended so many French courses in which some eager Canadian student thinks they can absolve themselves of an alienating middle-class upbringing by finding a francophone girlfriend and getting involved in Quebec politics. When I eventually studied at university, there were always a handful of politically socialist Americans in my classes who felt that learning French was an act of attenuation from their own culture, as there was something in it that they found offensive and sterile.

In general, romance languages are ineluctably attractive to English speakers. They are intrinsically passionate. French music, for the most part, is plaintively and unapologetically lyrical, sometimes to the bafflement of anglophones who find its storytelling quality shockingly earnest or old-fashioned.

Once you get past the received cultural associations with language, you move into new territory. I am more relaxed in French. Although it is a language I have learned recently, I know that I am allowed to make mistakes. I am perfectly comfortable asking for help with my speech. Somehow this has made me a more patient and understanding individual. It also means understanding the limits of speech, as there are so many places that translation can't reach.

I have often revisited my first few months here in Quebec and the many family gatherings I attended in complete silence. Sometimes I have tried to reach back to fill in the gaps of conversation that I was not capable of having. I am a different person now than I was then: I can ask questions, get into an argument, or make jokes in French. I can also sit quietly, comfortable with the knowledge that my silence is not an indication of words and feelings unexpressed, but a sign of ease with soaking up bits of conversation and the emotional textures of the voices around me.

Among my own circle of friends, the indicator of fluency is not perfect grammar or sophistication of vocabulary; it is whether you dream in your second language. I have been dreaming in both for a few years. In French, my dreams are often complex, with huge amounts of dialogue that I never remember by morning. In English, my dreams are short and simple. I suppose this means that one language is always a counterpoint to the other. One will always be stronger; the other is more colourful and expressive.

My feeling is that much of Montreal lives with this tension and counterpoint between the two languages. "From now on," the writer Régine Robin explains, the city is "the time of between. Between two cities, between two languages . . . two cities in one city."

Why be one person, one city, when you can be two?

Hotel Leeward

Jaspreet Singh

We shall meet again in Srinagar
— AGHA SHAHID ALI (1949–2001)

IN MY STUDY the walls are covered with old black-and-white photos of Kashmir by Henri Cartier-Bresson. Bresson visited the valley in 1948, shooting pictures with his new way of seeing, the "decisive moment." He captured locals outside a mosque, Bhand Pathers, performance troupes, a solitary man in Shalimar gardens. My favourite is one in which five or six women in Islamic garments are standing on a sheer cliff. Only their backs are visible. Two or three are praying; one looking at the immense Kashmiri sky, another surveying the valley below—the poplars, the willows, the plane trees, the lake, the timber-framed houses. Another stands barefooted, her arms uplifted, palms open in prayer. A ribbon of a cloud is passing by and it is unclear if the cloud is touching her palm or the folds of the mountain. At the bottom left corner, a lonely shoe. One small push and it would fall into the valley.

In 1975, when I was only six, my mother, sister and I moved to Kashmir with my father, who had received his "posting" orders from the general's office in Delhi. At the paramilitary camp in the high Himalayas, our arrival was celebrated by the regiment bagpipers and snare drummers. Like many other army children who lived in the camps, I didn't understand why we were there. We had limited contact with the Kashmiri people; they lived on the other side of the barbed wire. For us children, a visit to see MiG-21 fighter planes or battle tanks was as exciting as playing in the pastoral landscape or an evening spent in seventeenth-century gardens designed by the Mughal queens. We could not comprehend the awe-inspired gestures and words of the tourists, both Indian and foreign: "So beautiful, without any flaws; this place must be paradise, or at least its shadow."

I left Kashmir for Delhi in 1983. Later I moved to Canada to do my graduate work on the physics and chemistry of surfaces. But the surfaces of Kashmir never left me. They have emerged several times, directly or indirectly, in my scientific and non-scientific work. Increasingly tense confrontations between India and Pakistan have turned the area into the world's most dangerous dispute. Kashmir has the highest ratio of soldiers to civilians in the entire world.

In 2002 the strong words between the Hindu nationalist leaders of India and the Pakistani dictator General Perez Musharraf escalated beyond comprehension. Both nuclear powers threatened "total" war. Quickly the two armies marched to the border: a million men in combat-ready positions; anti-personnel and anti-tank mines planted along its entire length of 1800 kilometres.

A year later, I returned to Kashmir for the first time in twenty years. I had just finished my first book, a collection of stories. My father had retired in Delhi after serving thirty years in the Indian army and paramilitary. He had read two or three stories from the collection. He looked very worried as he dropped me at the airport, and asked, Why write when the world is about to end? There will be no one left to read your work.

From the air the Himalayan foothills, the Shivaliks, give way to mightier mountains. The snow on the Pir Panjal Range holds no traces of the movements of invading armies, nor the white bones of the elephants that carried the Mughal emperors to Kashmir. Even clouds have a different consistency. The ravines still belong to Hindu gods. This is where Shiva, the lord of destruction, chased his consort

Parvati after a tense quarrel. A mighty river filled Shiva's giant foot-prints, which knew no rest until peace was established with Parvati.

Moments after the high Banihal pass, the valley emerges out of a purple haze. The suddenness of its arrival gives the impression of a vast mathematical discontinuity. The mountains, 15,000 feet above sea level, form a natural border. Just when one gets used to them, we start descending.

Srinagar airport is a vast army base on high alert, ringed by four or five concentric circles of combat-ready soldiers. A few red and yellow flowers sway mildly around the tarmac. I am the last one to leave the plane. Later in the lounge I spend a long time waiting for someone from my past to appear and accept me as whatever I had become. But no one showed up and embraced me. I waited until the conveyor belts all stopped and the guards grew suspicious.

Departing the airport, we passed 139 check posts. I was still overwhelmed by the fact that the flight from Dehli to Srinagar had lasted a little over an hour. With my father, we used to drive twelve or thirteen hours on the narrow, dangerous road, a marvel of moun-tain engineering. The journey taught me words like "avalanche," "landslide," "nullah," "khad," "convoy," "migraine," "vertigo." The most thrilling bit was the last leg. The convoy drivers would cruise through the 3 kilometre-long Banihal tunnel, the tunnel that fasci-nated David Lean, who featured it in his film, *A Passage to India*. The same tunnel reappeared in Salman Rushdie's book for children, *Haroun and the Sea of Stories*.

Our jeep passed by the martyrs' graveyard, then the Zero bridge and the silk factory. Waves of *namaz*, Islamic prayer, wafted out of the mosques and Sufi shrines downtown. Big-lettered slogans, in Hindi, served as reminders to the locals that they were under occu-pation. They were everywhere: on windowless armoured cars, mili-tary bunkers, bridges, and government buildings. *Desh Bhakti, Desh Seva, Mera Bharat Mahan.* (Patriotism. Selfless work for the sake of the country. My India, the greatest.)

Then it happened: a grenade hit us. Our jeep had slowed down to negotiate a speed-breaker. Out of nowhere a boy appeared, and hurled the thing so fast we didn't have time to leap out. So we closed our eyes and froze. There was a loud sound of a stone hitting rubber, then metal, and when I looked over my shoulder, the boy was running towards a line of mulberry trees. He stopped, grabbed another stone, and hurled it with incredible force, this time in the direction of the lake.

June 1, 2003. Srinagar. No water in the Hotel Athena. It is a four-storey, yellow stucco building with a blue gate, the only Mediterranean connection other than the name. The Indian paramilitary occupied the hotel in 1996. Overnight they beautified the building with red bunkers, piles of sandbags, watchtowers, and barbed wire spirals.

My room is cheap and mouldy. It is getting dark. Outside on the street, soldiers in full battledress stand 10 feet apart, forming a necklace, or as a physicist might put it—a long polymeric chain with branches. Strange fears penetrate my bones, and by not stepping out of the room, the fears only worsen. The solitary 40-watt bulb does not encourage reading. Now and then sounds from a distant mosque penetrate my room. As the evening progresses, the prayers grow more and more amplified. I remain on the bed in fetal position observing the beige wall. Close to the ceiling huge military boot prints stamp the wall. Someone tried walking the wrong way—from the ceiling, down to the floor—or perhaps attempted a sudden war on an entire battalion of mosquitoes.

In the morning I stand on the balcony with a cup of tea. The splendour of the old Hotel Athena can still be found in a little garden, not far from the gate. The roses there are taller than the soldiers, their pink flowers the size of soccer balls. Walking from the lobby to the gate I notice a lattice fence on both sides—Mughal style, not more than 2 feet tall.

"Sir," the captain tells me, "the hotel penthouse is Tiger's office-cum-residence."

"Tiger?"

"Our commanding officer, sir."

Close to the garden is a badminton court, which today is going to serve as the site for Tiger's court, or rather, Tiger's press briefing. A *shamiana* (tent) is being erected. Sleep-starved *jawans* (soldiers) unroll two long carpets. The captain (who has an MBA degree) is fussing about the display, "terrorist catch," which is kept on an oblong table. Close by a portable blackboard rests on an easel. On the left side of the *shamiana* is a high brick wall where roosters crow majestically.

Twenty-five kilos of high-density RDX in gunny sacks are on display. From a distance, RDX ($C_3H_6N_6O_6$) resembles a pile of black cardamom in the bazaar. In addition to the explosive there are three other items on the table: timers, flame carriers, and detonators.

Tiger climbs down the stairs. He shakes hands with the journalists, then stands next to the blackboard with a pointer.

Tiger has noticed me. He beckons the captain. The captain and I move very close to him.

"Do you know how much is 25 kilos?" he asks his audience, like a professor. "This is no plutonium but twenty-five kilos of high-density RDX is enough to destroy ten big hotels."

Location of the raid?

"Confidential."

How many men nabbed?

"Confidential."

Night- or daytime raid?

"Confidential."

How did they get the leads to the explosives?

"Confidential."

Did the soldiers kick down wrong doors searching for insurgents?

"Con . . ."

We can no longer hear Tiger. He has moved away. Crowing and beating their wings, the roosters have taken over.

I first read *An Area of Darkness* in an army officers' mess. It was a green, bound volume, with a crumbling spine. An erudite major had tick-marked the chapter headings on the contents page (*"A Doll's House on the Dal Lake," "Medieval City," "Pilgrimage"*), and he had underlined all the passages connected to Srinagar and its surroundings. Words kept exploding across the page as I read them. "Stay away," said the major. "That writer chap is deadly."

Tiger drinks tea with me in the Kipling lounge.

"What is that book in your hand?"

"*An Area of Darkness.*"

"Who by?"

"V.S. Naipaul."

"The Nobel wallah?"

"Yes," I say. "He wrote this book here. He set three chapters in Kashmir."

"When?" he asks.

"Sixty-two or '63. Naipaul spent four months in Srinagar in 1962."

"Where did he stay?"

"Hotel Liward," I say.

"Liw-ward or Leeward?"

I consult the book.

"Liward."

"Same thing," he says. "The Kashmiris don't know how to spell properly."

"I would like to visit the hotel."

"Really," he says. "Dr. Naipaul stayed at the Liw-ward? We will put a notice outside, and inside too in the VIP room."

"Who owns the hotel?" I ask.

"Don't worry, Dr. Singh! Liw-ward is under our control!"

"When did you occupy?"

"Nineteen ninety-six."

"Same hotel?"

"Yes, it is under our control."

"What do you use it for?"

"The hotel is what it is," he said. "Would you like to visit? My company commander will show you around."

"Of course I would like to visit."

"But promise me, Dr. Singh . . . I need something from you as well. One page on Dr. Naipaul's stay at Hotel Liw-ward."

Tiger dispatches me to the hotel in his *shikara*, the Kashmiri gondola. He orders four armed men to escort me. I refuse the escorts. "You are with us now," he explains. "For militants you are a *target* now."

My escorts, who moved to Kashmir from the distant Bengal or Bihar or Karnataka regions two and a half months ago, are still acclimatizing. They have little contact with the locals. No one knows the Kashmiri language. But they speak frankly about the occupation (in Hindi), and their analysis is far superior to the one on TV.

"How do you deal with fear?" I ask.

"We want this to end, sir," they say. They do not brag like their commander. "I killed men," Tiger had said. "Thirty-seven men I killed. Militants know me well. They are after me . . . But fear never comes near me. Every evening the boatman paddles me on the *shikara* to the *exact* middle, where the lake is the deepest. There I pour myself a drink and admire the shimmering stars."

"Sir, we are in Tiger sahib's personal *shikara* sir," my escorts tell me. "Militants might use a silent gun this evening."

What am I doing here? Do I really care about Hotel Liward or Leeward? It is too late to turn back. I take a deep breath and recline on the "full spring" seats of the *shikara*. The springs are fatigued and noisy, encouraging an ambush from a militant's gun.

In the lake the dark green leaves of water lilies fold in the wind. Blue dragonflies negotiate new laws of surface tension with tiny waves of water.

"Sir, this is the first time I go to the lake. We benefit from militancy, sir. We get to patrol the beautiful Dal lake for free. Also, when we nab the militants we use their weapons and ammunition."

I tap a finger on my escort's chest, and ask if it is made of Kevlar. He grabs my finger, guides it around the sponge, the first layer of the camouflaged bulletproof vest. I dig deeper. My finger feels the cold metal. Liward. How far is Liward?

Dark clouds descend, threatening rain. We make an emergency stop at the Isle of Chenars. The guards use a walkie-talkie and request a motorboat; it arrives with the company commander aboard. He is an enthusiastic, duty-bound performer, reminding me of the

"10-gallon hat" Texan in *Dr. Strangelove*. Close to retirement, he still possesses the feverish enthusiasm of a new recruit. "What our force needs is good PR," says the company commander. "Our Tiger has coined a new slogan. WE ARE HERE FOR YOU KASHMIRI PEOPLE." He waves and smiles at the locals on the boats in the lake as the motorboat darts through the weed-infested waters. The Kashmiris wave back nervously, but they do not smile.

Leeward Hotel. The area is dark and smells of dead fish and ammonia. There is no power. Old men smoke hookahs in C-class *shikaras*, waiting for the rain. A loud Kashmiri quarrel is brewing not far from the landing. A shaft of light forces its way through the low clouds, the way it does in Hindu calendars, depicting divine intervention.

I inquire about the "real owners" of the hotel. "That can be arranged," says the company commander. He dispatches two *jawans* in the motorboat to fetch the owners. The *jawans* return with two old men. Gulam Qadir was twenty-five years old when Naipaul stayed in the hotel in 1962. Gulam Mohammed was only ten.

Both speak at the same time. They tell me that Naipaul liked to sit in the garden; that when he objected to the clothesline there, they removed it; that when a party from India started cooking in the garden, he grew angry and ordered them to stop. They show me where he smoked his water pipe; tell me of his aversion to loudness, that he allowed only a mild tap on his door.

"Last year a man from New York visited us. He asked about Naipaul's marriage. We said he came here on honeymoon with his new lady."

They walk with us to Naipaul's room. The paramilitary has transformed the writer's honeymoon suite into a signal centre, where Pakistani messages are intercepted. Lists of local mosques, dangerous neighbourhoods, and released militants cover the walls.

Gulam Qadir and Gulam Mohammed invite me to their house, and offer to arrange a meeting with some of Naipaul's characters: Mr. Butt, who is now a hundred years old, and Mr. Aziz, who is eighty. Mr. Ahmir Darz the cook, though, was taken away twenty-five years ago by the Khuda (God).

"Before Naipaul sahib arrived in Kashmir the name of our hotel was Hotel Iqbal. Then in 1962 we changed it to Leeward. Beautiful rooms then, beautiful furniture in Leeward. Beautiful people coming and going. Dal lake was so pure then, sahib, the tourists drank its waters. It was in 1996 during the militancy the Border Security Force occupy the Leeward. Twenty-fifth of July 1996. But Leeward has kept the same phone number, despite everything. It has not changed since 1962. Tell Naipaul sahib to call at 247-4040."

Most of the barrack-like houses where we lived in Kashmir meant nothing to me. The one house that really stayed with me was Mr. Khan's, in Srinagar, the only place where we lived beyond the barbed-wire fence. Mr. and Mrs. Khan lived upstairs, we lived downstairs. At the upper-storey windows, the corrugated-tin roof gabled and curved, then ran parallel to the ground on both sides, forming wings. Behind the house was an almond orchard. In spring the trees would blossom, suffocating the place with a sharp white and purple scent. During summers I would climb my favourite tree with my favourite book and sometimes from that swaying tree the house resembled a giant Dakota on tarmac, ready to lift itself, along with its tail and the entire orchard. . . .

Two days before my flight to Delhi I finally gathered the courage to visit. I found the house near ruin. The watchman, who had the keys, was nowhere to be found, so I stood by the living room window and peeked inside. It was not easy to see through the window. In addition to the usual barriers—glass, scrim, and wrought-iron grille—there was twenty years of thick dust. I saw piles of old suitcases, shoes, fractured wooden planks, cigarette butts, and dead animals. The only thing intact, like old times, was the wooden false ceiling (*khatumbund*).

The view through my parents' bedroom window was the most devastating. Here, not even the ceiling remained intact. It appeared as if a large diameter bomb had just hit, creating a colossal cavity. The floor was a sea of rubble. The walls were slowly shedding their paint and plaster and long-forgotten smells. Years ago in this room we used to watch a little battery operated TV, our sole connection to the world. We watched the Olympic Games, the nonaligned summit, Fidel Castro hugging Mrs. Gandhi, the funeral procession of the great Sheikh Abdullah, Lady Di's wedding at St. Paul's.

I sat down on the veranda and examined the cracks in the ceiling. Leonardo da Vinci used to encourage his students to look at cracks in old walls. Cracks always inspire, he used to say. Inside them, you will find an entire cosmos waiting for you, a cosmos you have yet to witness. I waited for a long time on the veranda, but nothing emerged from the cracks.

The guard posted outside the house next door stood like Precambrian rock. He was very reluctant to let us in, so I jotted down a quick note. *Hello: We used to live here . . . Perhaps you remember? I have come all the way from Canada.*

A little boy appeared at the gate and guided me to the living room of Mr. Naser Khan, the retired inspector general of police.

"I am Mr. Khan's younger brother," said the old man. "The elder Mr. and Mrs. Khan do not live in your house anymore."

Inspector General sahib wore a blue shirt with a long tail, baggy trousers, white skullcap, black sandals, and a grey beard. His wife looked exhausted and sleep starved, but spoke in clear Punjabi, my mother tongue, to make me feel at home.

"You were a major when you rented the house from the elder Mr. Khan?" she asked.

"His father rented the house," corrected IG sahib.

Madam IG apologized. "You look exactly like your father," she said,

"Exactly like his father twenty years ago," interjected IG sahib.

I confessed that I could not recall ever meeting them. "Your house was always vacant," I said.

"Now *your house* is vacant!"

"Of course you don't remember," said Madam IG. "We never met."

"I was posted in Jammu those days," said IG sahib.

"Son," she recalled, "we used to hear about your family from Mrs. Khan. Once your beautiful sister stopped growing vertically, which greatly alarmed your parents. So they made her stretch from a tall pole for hours and hours. True? And you were a funny boy. You would follow my sister (Mrs. Khan) everywhere she went. You did not like your mother's cooking, but you loved to eat my sister's roganjosh."

"His father was a colonel then," said IG sahib.

"No," she disagreed, "a major."

"Colonel."

"Major."

I did not interject.

"A Pandit (Kashmiri Hindu)," they said, "bought the house from the elder Mr. Khan."

"Pandit who?" I asked.

They did not know. All they knew was that "Pandit" never moved into the house. His timing was wrong. Pandit bought the house fourteen years ago just when the uprising began in Kashmir. Pandit is now a small-time film producer in Bombay. His watchman takes care of the house, or rather he does not take care. "The bugger!" said IG sahib.

The little boy brought us more tea and bakerkhani pastry on an unsteady tray. The shaking stopped only when he planted the tray on the table.

"People want *azadi* (freedom), but are fed up with militancy," said IG sahib.

I asked about the strawberry plants and the almond orchard.

"Dead. Long ago. We are happy you shifted. Our daughter, too, is flying to Canada soon to study literature. Everyone in our family seems to be fleeing."

They told me that the elder Mr. Khan's son was so fed up with his police job, he turned in his resignation letter, and "shifted" to Ontario.

"And where are Mr. and Mrs. Khan?"

"Brampton, Ontario."

He gave me their new address.

"Son," asked Madam IG. "You managed to stay away from drink in Canada?"

"Once in a while, Auntie."

"Once in while," winked IG sahib as he walked me to the door, and then to the street. It occurred to me then that we never used to receive letters in our mailbox when we lived in Srinagar. The letters always arrived at my father's office (and he brought them home in his briefcase), and I had a hard time explaining our strange address to my friends and pen pals scattered all over the world.

Master Singh
s/o Commandant Singh
c/o 56 APO
INDIA

IG sahib told me that the street had finally got a name, Lal Ded street, named after the fourteenth-century Kashmiri Sufi poet Lal Ded, who was loved by Hindus, Muslims, and Sikhs.

"But," said IG sahib by way of parting, "*Lal* in Kashmiri language means an unnatural growth."

Salam-a-laikum, I said.

Val-e-kum-salam, he said. "Say my hello to your father."

I wanted to tell IG sahib more about Father, but changed my mind at the last minute, and responded to his lifted hand with a military salute.

In his retirement my father has discovered a new career. He studies alternative medicine, and sometimes prescribes Ayurvedic remedies to his neighbours. Most of them are retired colonels, majors, and brigadiers, and they spend long hours in my father's living room in Delhi, learning from him the medicinal properties of a rare mushroom extract.

This mushroom extract comes in 200-ml bottles. Sometimes the label resembles the ominous 1945 black-and-white photograph of the Hiroshima cloud. (My father closed his tired eyes when I first pointed at the nuclear association, and remained silent for a long time.)

"Contrary to what you think," he told me outside Delhi airport, "your mother and I are pleased you visited Kashmir."

Then he added faintly, "I, too, am planning to visit the house where I was born." He was born in a small town, now in Pakistan, long before the bloody partition and *azadi* of India in August 1947. For my father to say what he said outside the airport was not easy. All his life, he guarded the borders. He rarely speaks about our family's forced migration.

"In August," he said, "the bus service between India and Pakistan is going to reopen. Your mother and I want you to accompany us. *Our* house is only an hour from the border."

There was a long pause.

"You okay?" he asked. "Why are you silent?"

"I am fine," I said. "I got this little gift for you."

I showed him a paisley scarf I'd bought at the silk emporium in Srinagar. My father loves paisley patterns.

"At the emporium the salesgirl gave me a silk cocoon to look at; and, when I held that hollow white ball, I could feel the worm inside, stirring."

"Was it alive?"

"I can still feel the vibration."

My father held my hand.

Driving Lessons

Megan K. Williams

"IF YOU WANT a hope in hell of passing the exam, forget everything you see happening out there."

Like a warning out of Dante, these words are delivered in the poorly lit, sparsely furnished backroom of my neighbourhood driving school in Rome. Wearing a tight T-shirt and an expression so jaded it would make your average cop appear credulous, our instructor Leo points his finger to the front door, out towards the circus of illegality that is Roman traffic. Do not, he exhorts, assume there is any overlap between driving theory and driving reality.

After years of participating in that circus without the legally required Italian licence, I take his point.

If a society makes breaking rules easy, you can be sure of one thing: it will make following them hard. There was a reason, I soon learned, that stationery shops in Rome have sections devoted to cards that read, "Congratulations! You Got your Licence!"

First, you have to pay. I'd been warned: driving schools are a racket. Shell out the hefty fee and you had a good chance of getting your licence within a few months. (Shell out a heftier bribe and you could forgo the whole ordeal completely.) This was especially the case for foreigners, who had the choice of taking an oral exam and whose examiners had discretion to pass or fail you. Signing up at a school also took care of paperwork and scheduling of exams, bureaucratic hassles that could take hours out of a day. If, on the other hand, you chose not to go through a school, you had to be prepared to fail.

I paid. Two hundred and twenty euros, almost $400, that covered the cost of driving theory lessons, an eye test by a medical doctor, and an all-important slip of paper called *il foglio rosa*—the pink sheet— which gives you the chance to do three exams within six months. The cost of the exams, about $100 each, was extra.

I chose to ignore a few things. Like the fact there was no eye doctor. The receptionist, a plump young woman named Rosa with long dark hair, French-manicured nails, and an evasive look, tested me herself, slapping the classic eye chart with shrinking rows of letters up against the wall.

"OK, you can see well enough to drive," she said after I had read out a few rows. "When the doctor is in next, he'll sign the test. He does it all the time."

For the next several months, one or two evenings a week, I sit in the gloomy *scuolaguida* classroom, sandwiched between pampered Italian teens and foreign domestic workers. Our instructor Leo is somewhere in his early forties and emanates all the moral authority of a regular at a racetrack. I'm not sure what the qualifications are to teach driving in Italy, but I am pretty certain Leo hasn't been exposed to much pedagogical methodology.

"*Noooo*," he rolls his eyes when one of us gets a question wrong. "What are you, dumb? *Retarded?*"

"But my mother always triple-parks for a few minutes when she picks me up at tennis. . . ." one of the teens invariably argues.

"How many times do I have to tell you? *Forget* about what your mother does!" Leo barks back. "Just answer what I tell you to."

In a world-weary drone, Leo assails us with driving theory so all-encompassing it touches upon everything from thermodynamics to the moral imperatives of road signage and the Ten Commandments. "'To be law-abiding people,'" he reads from page two of our driving handbook, "'respecting the legal norms is not enough; one must adjust one's behaviour to the fundamental principles of human co-habitation that forbid one to do unto others that which one does not want done unto oneself. In other words, even on the road, one must adjust one's acts towards collaboration with others, avoiding abuse, rivalry, bravado, risk-taking, and retaliation.'"

The questions he reads out from a quiz book aren't designed so much to test our road knowledge as to confuse us with complicated language and nuance.

"True or false?" Leo reads. "To avoid causing danger or being a hindrance to circulation, it's necessary to:

a) unite a strong civic sense with the application of the fundamental norms of circulation.
b) always drive at a moderate speed.
c) give, no matter what, right-of-way to all vehicles at intersections."

I'm not sure about "a" because I'm not sure you're supposed to stop to help drivers pulled over on the side of the road, which could be an action deriving from a strong civic sense. . . . Nor am I sure about "b": moderate could mean in relation to the speed limit or it could mean some undefined, average speed. . . . "C" I'm pretty sure is false, but then again . . .

"*Ma regà, avete capito?*"—*You guys taking this in?* Leo says in Roman slang and with a heavy air of skepticism.

The theory questions are a piece of cake compared to the set of wildly theoretical rules to determine the correct order of vehicles through five- and six-way intersections: streetcars, buses, trucks, fire engines, or cars with no traffic to their right. I spend hours figuring out who has the right-of-way. And yet, have I ever once come across a five- or six-way intersection without a traffic light? What makes it all the more frustrating is that the real-life answer to each and every right-of-way is simply the bastard who pushes on the gas pedal first.

But not everyone struggles. A svelte Ukrainian beauty in the front row who flirts with Leo seems to possess a steel-trap memory. When we do our practice quizzes, she inevitably scores the highest. If I get half right, I'm on a roll.

It would be nice to think that sensible cultural traits transfer with people as they move from one place to another, but the truth is, they often don't. We adapt. When I moved with my Italian husband and young kids from Toronto to Rome six years earlier to work as a foreign correspondent, I was struck by the different forms adaptation could take. It could involve appreciating new foods. How on earth did I survive three decades without fresh figs wrapped in prosciutto? Or it could mean a new passion for world sporting tournaments. Who knew men could look *that* good chasing a ball? Or it could lead to engaging in regular, unapologetic and, at times, ecstatically up-your-ass law-breaking.

Take traffic lights. When I lived in Toronto, I'd think twice about biking through a red light on a deserted side street at five in the morning. That's because a friend had been slapped with a fat ticket from a hiding cop for doing just that. But it was also because, like all young Canadians, I'd been brought up to follow the rules. I still recall the annual police visits to my suburban-Toronto primary school. In a pitiable display of authority pleasing, my scrawny arm strained upward and my heart thumped in hopes of being picked to make my own contribution to the class discussion of why jaywalking was just *so* wrong. And Elmer the Safety Elephant was so cuddly and fun. Above all, he was right.

As I grew older, the lessons stuck. It's not that I never broke laws. I got up to all the hackneyed bored-teenager antics: underage drinking, dabbling in drugs, skipping a lot of school. My parents, if they were even aware of it, never displayed any alarm. But these were acts that rarely inconvenienced or harmed other people—acts that didn't infringe on the collective civic sense that so strongly permeates Canadian culture. I may have ended up most Saturday nights at age fifteen and sixteen passed out in a puddle of my own vomit, but I wouldn't have been caught dead trying to butt in a lineup at the subway. Like the vast majority of my fellow citizens, I considered the civic code of conduct sacrosanct. I heeded the Please Stay off the Grass signs. I "gave a hoot!" and didn't pollute.

Yet barely a week into my new life in Rome that code felt about as relevant as yesterday's losing lottery ticket. The world out there was chaotic, charged and bursting with interpretive possibility. Traffic lights started striking me as bossy impositions. Stop signs began to carry the same weight as warnings from some Bible-thumping literalist. Soon I was cruising through red lights, with visiting friends clinging to the back of my Vespa *motorino*, quipping, "What's red but a darker shade of yellow!" Taking my cue from those around me, I broadened my repertoire: I revved the wrong way down one-way streets. I overtook traffic in the oncoming lane. Sidewalks began presenting themselves as perfectly sensible—no, as the only *smart*— alternatives to waiting out traffic jams.

The transformation might have been alarming had I stopped to think about it, but I didn't. I was having too much fun. The thrill of the illicit never came so cheap. I recall a particularly giddy *motorino* ride to interview the new head of the RCMP at the Canadian embassy—running five reds, zipping the wrong way down one-way streets, and ditching my vehicle smack dab in front of the No Parking sign beside the embassy gate. Off I trotted to discuss Italian-Canadian law enforcement co-operation.

I'd discovered a whole new realm of self-expression and no matter how many regulations I violated, people rarely objected. When they did, there was always the wonderfully expressive range of rude Italian hand gestures and verbal insults to tap into. I took full advantage. (At times, *too* full. One day, after a car had honked at me for descending the wrong way down a one-way street with my two daughters on the back of my *motorino*, I swung my lower arm up and shot off a favoured epithet. Later, when I picked the kids up at school, a teacher came up to me and said, "I tooted hello to you this morning and you told me to fuck off!")

On the one hand, breaking rules is part of a long Italian tradition of resisting authority; on the other hand, it's a way of belonging. Cheating is *solidale*. Community building. And the more brazen and outlandish, the more you're in. This became clear to me the morning my husband made an illegal left turn through a red light at an intersection with our two small children on the back of his *motorino*. It actually won him a nod of approval from a cop in a passing cruiser— making an illegal left of his own in the opposite direction.

I began to take more seriously what my husband and Roman friends said about driving. That Italians drive better than anyone in the world. That in goody-two-shoes, safety-crazed nations like Canada or Australia, the major cause of accidents isn't alcohol or cellphone distractions, but hopelessly nervous Nellies whose entire toolbox of emergency responses consists of either shoving a foot on the brake or shoving a foot on the gas—or more likely, *both*, in jerky, panicked succession.

"You know what's so irritating about Canadian drivers?" my husband once grumbled after a Toronto driver honked at him for making a swift left turn ahead of oncoming traffic. "They're not only incompetent, but they're *sanctimonious* about their incompetence."

Later, he added, "They're driving nerds and proud of it."

What really bugged him about Canadian drivers was that he suspected driving envy lurked behind all the cowed complying to rules and the tsk-tsking at those who didn't. If only they weren't so uptight and reined-in, they, too, would love nothing more than to let loose on the road.

In Rome, I finally got what he meant. Driving became an everyday chance for creative improvisation. For Italians, it was clearly an extension of their bodies—a kind of rubber-and-steel appendage to their identity. It reflected the ease with which they occupied their bodies and the comfort with which they showed off their best assets and moves.

I shuddered to think there had been a time in Canada when, sitting beside my husband as he wove through traffic, I'd say, "For Christ's sake, just pick a lane and stick with it!"

In Rome, it was all slip, bump and grind. A boisterous thrusting of your body in space.

A sensual, vehicular cha-cha-cha.

Then somewhere along the way the thrill began to dim. I found myself slowing at yellows, grinding to a halt at reds. I began to note a righteous swell in my chest when, at late-night intersections, car after car ran the red while *I waited*.

I was getting older, too, and it began to dawn on me that cheating is a young person's game. The beating heart as I cruised without a licence past a cop made me feel alive in my mid-thirties. As I slid closer to forty, each little scare felt like a year or two coming off my life. It was also getting tougher to ignore those daily accident scenes on my way to work: the crumpled *motorino* splayed across the intersection; the bored *carabiniere* officer filling out forms; the sticky little pools of blood.

A recent British study placed Italy (after Spain) as the most dangerous country for pedestrians among ten European countries surveyed. In Rome alone, sixty or so pedestrians are killed a year and a hundred twenty more on *motorini* or in cars. About half as many pedestrians are killed in Toronto, which has about the same population. But reliable comparisons are difficult to make; for one, far more people walk in Rome than in Toronto.

More than anything I witnessed on the road, though, it was the *off*-road Rome that began to wear on me. Nothing worked. It took me six visits to get my Italian passport renewed, *with* the correct documents. My daughters' public school was in such a state of decay that only duct tape kept the stair rails attached to the walls. Dog shit transformed sidewalks into fetid minefields. And if I ever managed to get through on the phone to the electric or gas or water company, the best service I could expect was a surly voice at the other end saying, "*Ma Signora*, what do you want me to do about it? Try calling next week." That's if the line didn't go dead while being transferred to another department.

The city was driving me nuts. Nobody was accountable. There was no bottom line. And yet, there I was, driving without a licence.

It was time to get legal.

After several months of lessons and quizzes, Rosa informs our class that the date has been set for the written exam. Leo is twitchy with anxiety during our last lesson, which he devotes to cheating techniques. After verbally batting us all into silence, he launches into a pre-exam pep talk. We can expect to encounter two types of examiners, he warns, "*cattivo e buono*." Bad and good. By bad examiners, Leo means not incompetent ones, but sticklers—people who actually enforce rules. By good ones, he means weasels.

"If you get a bad instructor," Leo says, "sorry, guys, not much I can do."

If we get a good one, there are options. He trots out the grade-school golden oldies: we can scribble the speed limits on our forearms; we can roll our pencil down the exam page to the question that stumps us and wait for him to casually pass by and mumble the answer. We can raise our hand to ask the examiner a question and wait for Leo to dart behind him and hand-signal the answer.

"Don't worry about how moronic you sound," he coaches, "just put up your hand and ask a question."

As it turns out, Leo needn't have bothered with the final tutorial. A few days later, I find myself across town at a driving school with speed limits, road signs, and driving dos and don'ts all displayed on posters on the wall. We need only to glance up and half the answers were laid out for us.

This, however, is not enough help for my quiz-challenged mind. I fail. Four mistakes are permitted to pass; I make seven. I wrongly mark as "false" that the colour of the little light to indicate your seat belt is undone is red. I answer "true" to a statement that we should stop to help drivers with car trouble pulled over on the emergency laneway. I screw up the right-of-way order at a four-way intersection.

My teenage classmates pretty much all make the grade; for most of them it's their second or third round. On her first attempt, Ms. Ukraine passes with flying colours.

Over the past several years, Italy has produced an unprecedented spate of books exposing the corruption, abuse of privilege and greed of those in power. They mostly take aim at the country's gerontocracy, the older men who have recycled themselves through a lifetime of public roles, and who despite public discontent, show no sign of going home. Some have been enormous best-sellers, such as *The Caste: How Italian Politicians Became Untouchable*, selling almost two million copies in a country where 20,000 is a best-seller. *The Caste* lays out a laundry list of excesses: The budget for the president's palace? Four times that of Buckingham Palace. The salary of a typical Member of Parliament: $23,000 a month—tax free. The book's central observation is that in Italy, politicians treat public money as if it's *nobody's* money, and therefore, up for grabs. (The same point can be made about public space; with its rampant graffiti, garbage, and doggy-do, public space in Italy is literally a no man's land.) Another hit has been Roberto Saviano's *Gomorra*, an investigation into the state's collusion with organized crime, which was made into a film that won a top prize at Cannes in 2009.

A recent entry into the considerable stack of exposés is a slim, unassuming volume simply entitled *Sulle Regole—On Rules* by former Italian deputy government prosecutor Gherardo Colombo. In it, Colombo argues that universally shared, applied, and respected rules form the basis of democratic, or what he calls "horizontal," society.

While the premise is something of a no-brainer for citizens of most western democracies, in Italy it's a direct attack on the way most people operate. The opening chapter reads like a fairy tale turned on its head:

> This is an imaginary country. At the corner of the street is a deli. An urban police officer enters the store to verify the scale is accurate. After a few hints, vague allusions and winks, the officer leaves with a couple of bags full of groceries. He received them free in exchange for verifying nothing. The shop owner can continue cheating clients. Two floors up, a woman is paying a plumber who just finished fixing the sink. "If you want a receipt, it's 120 Euros; with no receipt it's 90 Euros, a little discount." "I don't need the receipt, thanks." Just down the street is the government tax office. A distinguished gentleman is discussing with a bureaucrat some taxes he failed to pay. After a while, he understands that if he slides an envelope full of money into the bureaucrat's hands, he'll take it. After a couple of shared jokes, they shake hands and say goodbye: the taxes owed are wiped clean off his record. . . .

And so on, for another four pages.

What's striking about Colombo's imaginary country is the utter familiarity of the language and scenes, the mundane and reassuring web of relations throughout, the jokes and bonding, the little shortcuts that bring people together. Cheating framed as mutual helpfulness. Only the passing mention later in the chapter of another "distinguished gentleman," one who purchases the favours of a young woman "imported" from a poor country and reduced to slavelike conditions, does the sharp, metallic flash of violence rise up off the page. Just like the real-life country this chapter is describing, most of what is illicit is swathed in the warm reassurance of belonging; only when you talk about groups whose entire code of conduct is illicit, such as organized crime, does overt force make an appearance.

Sulle Regole (which has not been translated into English) came out in early 2008, a year after Colombo left a formidable career as government prosecutor. He had headed up some of Italy's highest-profile corruption cases, from investigating politicians in the secretive Masonic P2 Lodge, to the Clean Hands bribery scandal in the early 1990s that wiped out the long-dominant Christian Democrat party. More recently, he's conducted inquests into Silvio Berlusconi, earning the ever-returning prime minister's vitriolic disdain. Then, at the age of sixty, after more than three decades at the top levels of the justice system, he did something virtually unheard of in Italy: he retired early. Even more remarkable is that he did so in order to devote himself full-time to talking to school kids about "*il perchè delle regole*"—the *why* of rules.

As Colombo writes in his introduction, a profound sense of futility spurred his decision: "I quit because inquest after inquest, case after case, verdict after verdict I became ever more convinced that it would be impossible for me to make the justice system any less bad off than it is." (Note: not *improve*—Colombo is a realist—but make *less* bad off.)

Colombo is a gentle man with a receding mop of greying hair. He has a warm chuckle and the trademark French-like pronunciation of the letter "R" of the Milanese. We spoke at length on the phone one day before he was headed to talk to yet another school group about rules.

"It's impossible for justice to work if people don't even understand why there are rules, which is the case of Italy," Colombo said. Or as he writes in *On Rules*, "Justice can't work if the connection between citizens and rules is floundering, strained, ill, damaged, marred by incommunicability."

Italians, Colombo told me, have just this connection. "When I travel in the rest of Europe, I don't see the things I see in Italy, this total disrespect for the most basic rules. Cars double-parked, cars ignoring people crossing at pedestrian crossings, this sort of thing. Or the person who comes along in a taxi lineup and says, 'Excuse me, I have an emergency and I need to take the next taxi,' when there's no emergency at all. I'm sure you've encountered this sort of thing, no?"

At the other end of the spectrum is the more serious act of deception for which Italians are so renowned: tax evasion. "In other countries, average people don't even ask themselves whether they should pay taxes. They pay them and that's that. But here, given the chance, many people—and I mean *many, many* people—don't pay," Colombo said, before adding what should have been implicit. "And by not paying, they break the law."

But he says when there is a serious, concerted effort, Italians can follow rules just as effortlessly as other cultures with a more developed civic sense. He cites the success of the nationwide ban on smoking in 2005 as an example. While smoking stopped overnight, the ban was pre-announced a long time in advance and backed by a critical mass of non-smokers, who had no vested interest in allowing smokers to continue. Fines were posted alongside No Smoking signs, a visual aid to help bar and restaurant proprietors enforce the law. "People started to feel ashamed about smoking," Colombo added. "They were regarded badly. And there was a strong propaganda. All these things came together."

Colombo says cheating, though, has long been a way of understanding life and relationships in Italy. He points to several historical factors that have shaped the culture. Italy is a young country, unified only in 1870, and therefore still lacking a sense of nationhood or shared values that countries such as France, Germany, England, or Spain have had centuries to develop. More important, it's a land that has been long the object of foreign domination; government has more often than not been imposed from the outside. From the Barbarians and Moors to the Spanish and French, almost all of Europe and environs has had a crack at controlling parts of Italy for the last 1600 years. As a result, rules and laws haven't been perceived as something created and shared so much as something inflicted—and thus, something to be resisted and undermined. Also never to be discounted is the presence of a second state-within-a-state: the Vatican. It wasn't so long ago that the Vatican was a separate power inside Italy. The fact that it continues to hand down its own voluminous edicts that are often in conflict with those of the Italian state certainly does little to help matters.

I wonder aloud to Colombo if it isn't also post-war Italy's embracing of the *furbo*—the rogue, the weasel, the entertaining con artist—so present in pop culture and *commedia all'italiana* movies made during the boom years that's also helped legitimize everyday cheating. In neo-realist films, most of which were shot throughout or right after the Second World War, the hero was the victim, the honest guy screwed by the *furbo*. Instead, in *commedia all'italiana* films that came later, the hero was what director Dino Risi called "*il mascalzone dolce*"—the sweet scoundrel—often played by beloved actors (and comic geniuses) such as Vittorio Gassman and Alberto Sordi. The figure quickly became a celebrated archetype in an Italy buoyed by fresh wealth—a figure emblematic of consequence-free fun: breaking hearts, cheating and corrupting without ever having to pay the price.

"Yes, in Italy, the arrogant, brass *furbo* is a very popular figure," agreed Colombo. "But there is a danger of too much laughter. If we laugh at all the transgressions, this figure starts to be seen as acceptable."

Those in Italy who follow the formal laws (it being understood that a whole set of *informal* laws is what really governs things), Colombo observes, are overtaken each day by those who don't. Privilege, cunning—*furbizia*—and force come to form the three pillars of what he refers to as a vertical society.

Given how all-pervasive the use of privilege and cunning is in everyday Italian life, Colombo has no difficulty coming up with examples in his talks to kids. One of his favourites targets the double standard teachers rely on when they're late.

"When kids arrive late for school, they have to go to the principal's office and get a permission slip, then they get a lecture from the teacher and a form parents have to sign," he said. "If teachers are late, they come in and say, 'The traffic was terrible today,' and that's the end of it. But kids perceive the disparity of this situation. Just as kids perceive the difference in the way teachers treat their older siblings and their younger siblings, and how these differences bring us closer to a horizontal or vertical society."

With his school talks, Colombo is reaching a tiny percentage of Italian kids. His hope, though, is that the kids he does reach will demand more coherent behaviour from their teachers and parents, but especially from themselves. That they'll "enter into the world of rules," as he puts it, and take personal responsibility for their own behaviour.

"In general, Italians see the defects of others very easily and are happy to point out when other people behave badly," he said, "but they don't see their own bad conduct."

This in part explains why books such as *The Caste* or even the political movement led by comedian-turned-activist Beppe Grillo have been hugely popular, yet so far have failed to bring about political change. Grillo is one of Europe's most read bloggers and organizer of the non-partisan, nationwide "V-Days"—*Vaffunculo* or Fuck-off-to-Politicians Days. In hilarious tirades, he rants to crowds of thousands against the high number of convicted criminals in Italian parliament (twenty-four) and the shameless self-interest of the country's leaders. Neither Grillo's movement nor the books, however, require much private questioning and soul-searching; instead, they keep fingers pointed at the parliamentarians, senators, and judges.

"It's funny," Colombo told me towards the end of our conversation. "At the beginning of the Clean Hands investigations, everyone was happy when we went after the bigwig politicians, who most people couldn't identify with. We had terrific public support. But as soon as we started going after the smaller fish, with whom people *could* identify, then the public no longer supported the investigation. As soon as it became clear that if things were going to change in Italy, then *everyone* had to start following rules and adjust their behaviour, Italians abandoned us."

"*Questo è un paese di merda,*" Leo says. *This is a shitty country.*

No one has trouble condemning things when they don't go as they should. Not even Leo, who by the nature of his job, deals every day with obstacles and gridlocks.

We're standing in the Motorizzazione Civile, Rome's motor vehicle centre, on a relentlessly sunny Friday morning in late July. I've waited the one month and one day required by Italian law before I can retake my driving theory exam. During that month, a small technical revolution has occurred at the motor vehicle department. Computers. Foreigners now have the option of sitting in front of a monitor and punching in their true or falses to questions posed in one of five European languages.

The Motorizzazione Civile is located on the northern outskirts of Rome on Via Salaria, the ancient route used to carry salt from the Mediterranean to empire headquarters. (People were often paid in precious salt, hence the derivative "salary.") For the past half century or more, though, the main commercial purpose of the road has been sex. In post-war years, Italian prostitutes would sprawl in beach chairs, fires burning in oil barrels to keep them warm. These days, young women, trafficked from Eastern Europe, stand day and night in stiletto boots, a thong and bikini top.

Leo and I arrive at the centre by 8:30 a.m. when the exam is scheduled to begin. A crowd of immigrant men, mostly Chinese and South American, is already waiting near the entrance. Through large glass windows we can see several grey-haired men turn on the computers, one by one, literally scratching their head as they go. An hour later, we're still waiting. Leo gripes about the incompetence and laziness of Italian public workers. "It's always the same story: be here by eight-thirty, then make us wait hours."

Outside the classroom, one-on-one, Leo seems slightly reduced and less sure of himself, as if he'd been poked with a pin and deflated. He tells me he's from a small town in Calabria, that he started out teaching driving there, then got a job through someone he knew in Rome and moved here. What he'd really like to do is get out of Italy altogether. "Canada must be nice. . . ." he says, half-heartedly, his eyes drifting down at his watch.

At 11 a.m., an examiner finally invites in the first batch of students, which doesn't include me. Leo tells me he has an appointment and gives me his cellphone number. I get a coffee, then sit in the hallway doing practice tests, passing a few. Thirty minutes later, the first group emerges from the exam room, looking like they've just been lined up and spanked. They mill nervously about the hallway until an examiner steps out carrying a stack of tests. One by one, he reads out the names and results, sighing in exasperation at all the four-part Hispanic names. . . . *José Maria Garcia Lopez* . . . The men blush and laugh apologetically. "In our country," one explains, "people have very long names."

Out of the group of thirty, three pass. Most have more than twenty answers wrong. What driving school in its right mind, I wonder, has sent such an unprepared bunch to do the test?

At noon, my group is finally let in and we take our seats at the computers. An examiner in the far corner stands smoking. I'm already irritated at having waited three and a half hours, but this pisses me off. Since smoking was banned, I have yet to see anyone light up in public, even at an after-hours club. What bothers me most about the guy smoking is that I sense the only reason he thinks he can get away with it is because, with the exception of me, the group is all immigrants.

I catch the attention of the closest examiner, a tall light-haired man in his mid-forties. "Excuse me," I say, pointing to the smoker, "there's no smoking here."

He glances over at his colleague and makes a smoking gesture.

The smoker moves closer to the exit, but keeps puffing.

"Excuse me," I say again, a few minutes later, "this is a *public* place."

"*Basta*," he snaps. "Don't push it."

Before things heat up, another examiner begins explaining how the computerized test works. He takes us through the explanation on the screen, then a mock exam so we can figure out how the program works, then the real exam of ten pages with three true-or-false questions each.

I tap past the explanation, past the mock exam and on to the first set of true and falses. With the questions written in simple English syntax, there's no more linguistic trickery. I get what they're asking. First batch done: on to the next.

Suddenly, all the screens go blank: the electricity has gone out. In a flustery panic, the examiners flip the light switches on and off and jab at the power buttons on a couple of computers. Nothing. One of them hurries off to locate the circuit box.

Fifteen minutes later, the computers surge back on. The initial page of instructions appears and then the page of mock questions. I *tap-tap-tap* my way to the end of the mock exam, press send, and start the real exam again.

Except the real exam doesn't appear. I raise my hand. An examiner comes over. I explain what happened. He presses the back button, and then says, "Did you press return?"

"At the end of the mock exam I did."

"There is no option to press return at the end of the mock exam. That was the real exam."

"But I only answered the first question. How can I get back in to finish them?"

"You can't. Once you press return, that's it."

"What do you mean, 'that's it'?"

We begin to argue quietly. Then less quietly. The tall, light-haired examiner comes over and tells me to leave. "You're bothering the others trying to finish their exam."

"I'm not leaving until I can finish my exam. It's not my fault the electricity went out."

We move to the side of the room where another examiner sits and I try my luck with him. The light-haired examiner follows us over. "Just come back in a month and do it."

I pull out my cellphone and punch in Leo's number. As succinctly as I can, I explain what happened. "You have to come and do something," I say.

"What are they saying?"

"They're saying there's nothing I can do. That I have to do it all again."

"Well then I guess that's what you'll have to do. . . ."

"Leo, there's no way I'm spending another month studying and then paying for a third test. Come here and do something. Please."

His answer transmits through my cellphone as a high, thin whimper. "You don't understand. There's nothing I can do. *I have no power.*"

And then the reality sinks in. Leo may be the know-it-all *furbo* who steers his little charges of innocents through a maze of make-believe traffic regulations, but in the end, he's just some schmuck from the south who managed to get a job as a driving instructor in the capital. Power isn't localized in rules and roles, it's in relationships and connections. Privilege and status. And above street level, literally, Leo is nobody.

But I'm not. I'm a journalist, which, in a country where people with a B.A. are still addressed as "*Dottore*," where professional associations rule like castes and come with state-subsidized restaurants and private clubs and ridiculously inflated social prestige, counts.

I phone a friend who works for a news wire and has press-office numbers at his fingertips. In a loud, self-important voice, I say, "Could you give me the press-office number for the Ministry of Transportation?"

The examiners look up at me. "*Sono giornalista,*" I tell them.

The men refuse to betray any reaction, but soon after, one of them quietly leaves the room. I scribble down the numbers my friend gives me. Before I'm even off the phone, another older man approaches me.

"Just tell me what it is you want," he says.

"I want to write the theory test."

He motions for me to come with him, and I trail him to an elevator, which we take in grim silence up several floors, and then along several wide, dim corridors. He knocks at doors, has quick, tense exchanges with people behind them, and emerges from behind the last door with a test, in Italian, in hand. I'll take anything at this point.

We go back down to the main floor. He knocks on another door and it opens. Inside is a small, elderly man with glasses and a short-sleeve shirt who's testing a trio of aspiring young truckers. My escort asks him if he'll oversee a written test. He agrees to. He pulls out a chair for me, looks at his watch, and tells me to begin.

In twenty minutes, I'm through. The man takes the test sheet, slides the old-fashioned marking grid on top of it, and tells me I got one wrong. "Congratulations," he says.

It's 2:30 p.m. when I exit the building and phone Leo to come get me. "Stay where you are, I'm coming," he tells me.

For forty minutes I stand in the Via Salaria parking lot, feeling not at all triumphant, but drained and slightly sullied. Across the street, a couple of hookers wiggle their asses at passing traffic.

Finally, the *scuolaguida* car swerves into the parking lot and wrenches to a stop in front of me. It's not Leo behind the wheel, but the flashy Ukrainian from my driving theory class, the one who aced the written test on the first go. She and Leo are in the midst of a driving lesson and have a case of the giggles. Still chuckling, he gets out of the passenger seat and motions for me to hop in the back.

"How many lessons has she had?" I ask.

"Don't worry."

"Are you even insured for passengers?"

His smile fades. "I told you, don't worry. Get in."

"Leo, I'm worried."

But he stands there, door open, jaw open, until I slide in. I fish around for a seat belt. There are none. This is illegal. I point this out to Leo, who ignores me. He's focused on coaxing the Ukrainian back into traffic. His fingers play upon her hand on the gearshift. He murmurs supple words of encouragement. We lurch forward into the stream of cars heading back towards downtown. She hasn't yet tackled lane changing and accelerates, then breaks, then swerves. I want the hell out.

After ten minutes of a white-knuckle ride—hers and mine—Leo tells her to pull over so he can initiate her into parallel parking. We're about a kilometre from where I live.

"Leo, let me out," I say from the back seat, in an odd croak.

He turns around, looking truly surprised I hadn't evaporated on the way home.

"Oh, right. The school's not far," he mumbles, getting out to let me out. "You don't mind walking the rest of the way, do you?"

I don't.

Summer passes and in the fall, I *motorino* down to the *Villaggio Olimpico*, the neighbourhood in northern Rome that was built to house the athletes for the 1960 Summer Olympics. The streets are laid out in a flat grid and lined with four-storey apartments squatting on pillars to allow parking beneath. At first the neighbourhood met the fate of so many housing projects, proving to be a magnet for prostitutes and heroin addicts. Then the driving schools moved in, drawn by the right angles, level terrain, and almost complete absence of human beings. (A guy I know who lives there says he longs for the days he got mugged coming home, when at least he didn't feel like he was living in a theme-park bumper-car ride.)

Following Rosa's instructions, I go to meet my examiner under a bridge. I wait a while and when no one shows up, I hop back on my *motorino* and cruise the neighbourhood. Nobody. I go back to the bridge and sit on a scrap of cardboard. Finally a car pulls up and a short, middle-aged man waves me over.

Things go surprising smoothly. He compliments me on my driving and observes I must have some experience. Twenty-five years! I tell him. He asks me to speed up and veer right up onto the road that follows the Tiber River. Along we cruise. Right again, then a full halt at the stop sign. I'm careful to look both ways before pressing back on the gas, then away we go again.

"Drive back to where we started," I hear him say from the back seat. "You didn't stop fully at the stop sign."

"Yes I did," I stutter. I was sure I had. At least, I was sure I'd stopped the longest I've ever stopped at a stop sign in Rome.

"*Signora*, the exam's over."

"But I stopped!"

He orders me to pull over. I do, and turn around to see him filling in forms.

"This is crazy. I stopped longer than anyone ever stops in Rome. I even looked both ways."

He keeps writing.

"I don't believe this," I go on, my voice rising. "I know people who've forgotten to put their seat belts on for the whole exam and passed. I know people who only had to drive once around the parking lot and passed. You don't have to fail me. You know I'm experienced. Twenty-five years and not one accident!"

"*Calma, signora.*"

But I'm on a roll and I let him have it. On what a racket the whole driving school system is; on how arbitrary the decisions to pass or fail are; on how foreigners are always the ones to get screwed; on just how *typically fucking Italian* the whole thing is.

I shove open the car door to get out.

"You would have failed on that alone!" he suddenly erupts. "It's the right hand you open the car door with, not the left! And you didn't look into the side-view mirror for approaching cars!"

"What difference does it make? You've failed me already!"

"What difference does it make?" he screams, trumping my outrage with his. "What difference does it make?! *You could have killed someone!*"

A few months later, I learn from reading the papers that the driving examiners have gone on strike. Over what, I'm not the tiniest bit interested. Strikes are about as newsworthy as a train pulling in late. Everyone strikes, even artists' nude models. And frankly, I'm relieved. The exam process has been one big downer. I'm even beginning to resign myself to never getting a licence. I know lots of expats in Rome who drive without one.

Months go by. Then, one day out of the blue, Rosa from the *scuolaguida* calls me at work. "The strike's over now and your chance to renew your pink slip is almost up. I'd advise you to do so and book another driving exam."

Rosa tells me for another 140 euros, $200 or so, I can get a new pink slip and redo my medical eye exam. With the cost of my next exam added in, I've spent almost $1,000 on the exam process.

"Will there at least be a doctor at this one?"

"There's always a doctor."

"Rosa, come on. You gave me the eye test last time."

"I think you're confused," she lies sweetly into the phone. "It's always a doctor who does it."

I don't even bother to argue. When I show up later for the test, a doctor is there.

Rosa calls again a few weeks later to give me the date and time of my driving test. When I arrive at the Villaggio Olimpico on the appointed day, I notice I'm shaking. I call my husband. "This whole ordeal is making me regress. I haven't quaked in years."

"Relax and remember it's luck either way," he says.

An examiner flags me over to his car and I slide into the driver's seat and put my seat belt on. Slowly, slowly, I release the brake and press on the gas, shift from first gear to second. Except for basic instructions—turn left up ahead, veer right after that bridge—the examiner is silent in the back seat. For ten minutes, I stop at the stop signs, look left and right, and signal before each turn. Then the examiner has me pull over. Once I've placed the stick shift back into neutral and pulled up the parking brake, he says, "Turn around." I twist my head.

"No, turn all the way around so you can see me."

I rotate sideways in my seat, and crane awkwardly around, waiting to be chastised. But he just gazes back. "You don't recognize me, do you?"

"No." I don't. I haven't a clue who he is.

"I oversaw your last exam."

Shit. I feel the sudden tug of gravity in my gut. How was it possible I didn't recognize him? He seemed smaller, and older, last time. I have no choice but to launch into the grovelly apologia of the cornered. "Listen, I admit I may have lost it a bit when you failed me, but I did honestly feel that I stopped at that stop sign. . . ."

The guy looks confused, then says, "No, I'm not talking about your driving exam. I was at your written exam at the motor vehicle centre. Where you kicked up such a fuss after the computers crashed."

Then it clicks who he is: the tall, fair-haired examiner who got testy with me when I asked his colleague to stop smoking and who then tried to kick me out when I insisted on finishing the exam.

"You're a journalist, right?"

"Yes."

"Well, I want you to know something. Those computers haven't crashed since. That day you took your exam was *un'eccenzione*, a fluke," he says. "So I wouldn't want you to write bad things about the motor vehicle examination centre because of that one incident. Especially with everything we've been through. You heard about the strike?"

"Yes, I heard." How couldn't I have? I was held up from taking my driver's test for months because of it.

"We're owed months of back pay," he explains. This I didn't know.

He then reaches into an envelope and pulls out a laminated card. Was it possible that in a country where it takes seven years to recoup back taxes, you can take a driver's exam and receive, instantly, the actual licence? I almost weep.

"But that's not why I remember you," he says, holding the card between his thumb and forefinger. "I would have remembered you even if you hadn't caused all that trouble."

"Really."

"Yes. I never forget a lovely face." Without skipping a beat, he hands me the licence. "I'm passing you."

There it is, I think: the sweet, sticky corrosion of the straightforward transaction. "You're passing me because you like my face?" I can't help asking.

"No, and not even because you're a journalist. You deserve to pass. You drive very well. You've obviously had a lot of experience."

"Twenty-five years," I say in private self-parody.

I reach to open the car door—with my right hand, tilting my chin to look into the side rear-view mirror—and get out.

"Please don't write badly about us," he calls, before the door swings shut.

In her essential collection of essays called *The Little Virtues*, post-war writer Natalia Ginzburg explores what it means to live in a world where the link between doing the right thing and rewards such as respect, acceptance, and money does not exist.

Ginzburg knew a thing or two about the arbitrary nature of this relationship. During the Second World War, she, her husband and small children (who had some Jewish heritage) were forced from their home in Turin into exile in the mountainous, backwater region of Abruzzo and then into hiding in Rome. While in Rome, her husband was captured, tortured and died alone in prison.

In her essays, first published in 1962, Ginzburg isn't so much interested in denouncing the unfair ways of the world as deciphering moral ways to navigate it. She's especially interested in how to pass on values and truth to children.

"As far as educating children goes," she writes in the final essay, from which the book title is taken, "we teach our children 'the little virtues' instead of great ones: thrift, instead of generosity; caution instead of courage; shrewdness, not frankness; tact rather than love; desire for success instead of a desire to be and to know."

Ginzburg writes that it's the great virtues that should guide our lives and the greatest disservice we can do to our children is to teach them that if they are good, and work hard, they should expect reward.

"Because," she writes, "life is rarely fair in how it distributes prizes and punishments: sacrifices usually bring no recompense and bad behaviour is most often not censured—on the contrary, it's often lavishly rewarded with success and money. It's thus better that children know from a young age that good behaviour won't get rewarded and bad behaviour will not be punished. And that all the same, they must love goodness and hate bad actions. And that it's not possible for this to be explained in any logical way."

It's advice that after almost a decade living in Rome, I find radical in its lucidity. It's also advice that strikes me as coming straight out of the Italian experience, but not only. After all, in how many places in the world today is good behaviour rewarded, greed punished, lying exposed? Even in those privileged places where, relatively speaking, consequences are fair, how fair is life itself?

I drive our car in Rome as little as possible these days and have given up entirely on the *motorino*. The summer before I signed up at the *scuolaguida*, an arsonist roamed the city at night setting fire to rows of *motorini*. Mine went in the first batch. I'd just paid $500 to get it repaired after it had been stolen and trashed and then held by the police in bureaucratic limbo for five months. I'm not superstitious, but I chose to take its charred remains as a sign.

I'm back on my bicycle. Rome is hilly, but it's got some decent bike paths and lots of parks and wide enough sidewalks to steer clear of pedestrians. (Lots of people cycle in the flat cities and towns of northern Italy, but very few people do in the capital.)

I'd never given much thought to biking in Rome until one night I was pedalling back from a movie with my husband. We were stopped at a vast, semi-deserted piazza near our home, waiting for the lights to change. Out of nowhere it seemed, a car shot across the intersection. As it passed us, it slowed. Just enough for us to take in four young guys as they stuck their heads out of the car windows and bellowed in unison, "*Vaffunculo, coglioni sulle biciclette!*"—"*Fuck off, you big losers on the bikes!*" We stood there stunned, suddenly feeling, well, like a couple of big losers on bikes, until we laughed at the absurdity of it.

When I later told an Italian poet friend about the incident, he said, "Of course, in the context of Italy today, even going by bike is perceived as a reproach to common values. As if you're making a big, alternative statement."

There are times, of course, when because of time constraints and distance, going by car is unavoidable. On a Friday night in the early summer, some Roman friends and I went to see *Gomorra*, the movie version of the book about the Neapolitan mafia. While the book had opened my eyes to what an integral part of the world economy the Naples mafia is, the movie had a more immediate and powerful effect. It left me and my friends agitated, awash in a sense of powerlessness, and full of anguish about the future of Italy.

Francesca, a fairly new friend who works as a school social worker, drove us from the theatre to the restaurant. As she drove, she launched into the usual tirade about Italy: how there's no civic sense; how no one is ever accountable for anything; how there's never a bottom line. Then she asked the question I get more and more often these days: Why, as a foreigner who can leave, do I choose to stay?

It's a question that gets more complicated to justify with time. The easy answer is that my children have been raised here and are by now more Roman than anything else. They could adapt if we left, but it would mean cutting them—and me—off from the resilient web of family and neighbour relations that makes life in Rome so rich and surprising and alive with human contact. As we drove along, I looked out up at the giant sycamores that stretched their branches across the *viale*: even the physical beauty of the city would be tough to give up. I was not sure how willing I'd be anymore to exchange baroque fountains in cobblestoned piazzas for the bleak concrete and oversized flashing screens of the Dundas Squares.

But it's more than all that. It also has to do with coming up against my own hypocrisy and shortcomings. With being reminded, day after day, of the effort it takes to live an honest and thoughtful life, a virtuous life, when the society you're in is not set up to help you live that way. It has to do with seeing how much I compromise and fail without that setup. And how, as a Canadian with a typical penchant towards self-righteousness, this hasn't been such a bad thing to see.

"Italy's past the point of no return," Francesca went on. "It's too much for individuals to take on. It's too overwhelming."

I thought of Gherardo Colombo. Change from the bottom up, personal responsibility and so on. "It may feel like too much," I said, "but the only way to start creating a civic sense is to start with yourself. Act like a decent citizen, follow the rules, even if you feel like you're the only one doing it." I sounded so wishful and naive, like someone who's just been turned on to a new self-help book and is gushing about the power of inner transformation.

I willed myself to shut up.

We were almost at the restaurant. It was a bad night to take a car; the school year had wrapped up that day and everyone was out letting loose. Knots of teenagers bulged at street corners, *motorinos* spilled out into the streets, and cars and *macchinette*—the 10-horse-power, tin-can vehicles teens can drive—clogged the piazzas. A week earlier, Rome's administrative court had ruled that all the paid street parking in the city, demarcated by blue lines, had been painted in contradiction to city regulations. By law, for each stretch of paid spots, there had to be a certain number of free spots, indicated with white lines. The former city administration had ignored the ratio and went to town, so to speak, with blue lines, slapping them down every which way, in some neighbourhoods even painting blue lines in the middle of traffic lanes. It was a quick way to fill the city coffers. But then someone sued, and won. Until the new administration repainted all the parking lines in accordance with the law—and who knew how long *that* would take—it was literally a parking free-for-all in Rome.

As we rolled along, the sustained wail of a car horn filled the evening air. Up ahead, a woman sat in the driver's seat of her Renault family minivan, her hands pressed to the horn, her two young children peering out from the back seat. Someone had left their car in front of her garage. Diners on the sidewalk clasped their hands together, imploring her to stop honking. *Yes, it's a terrible inconvenience that your garage is blocked,* they called, *but honking like that is making everyone suffer the consequences!* The woman, ghostlike with rage and hysteria, hissed back that she wasn't budging until the car moved. She pushed her hands back on the horn.

We inched forward, looking for a parking spot of our own. Up ahead, a gap appeared. When we got closer, we realized it was a pedestrian crossing. We all looked at each other: Should we? It was already past 10 p.m., we were hungry, and if we insisted on finding a legal spot, it could take half the night. It could take forever.

I stuck my head out the window. "If you squeeze to the right, I think there's enough space for a stroller or wheelchair to get by."

Francesca swung the car onto the crosswalk lines and flicked off the engine.

"Anyway," she said, casting a glance back at the car as we walked away, "it's not like they'll ticket me, will they?"

No, no, we all assured her. That's the last thing you have to worry about.

Painted Red:
Growing up in an
age of witch hunts

Penney
Kome

MOLL WATCHED HIS WIFE reading out loud, her hair spread out over her pillow, in the glow of the bedside light. He closed his eyes and rode on the rhythms of her voice, rising with mirth, sinking with sympathy, as she poured out the news from their friends' letter. She finished the letter, folded it, and said, in their intimate Quaker speech, "Thy turn."

So Moll picked up a book he had left on his night table and turned to where they had left off the night before. Adjusting his reading glasses, he leaned into his reading, giving her the same full expression that she had put into the letter. She listened appreciatively, blinking as she dozed and woke again.

When he finished, she picked up a magazine and started to read an article to him. After twenty years of this nightly ritual, the pattern was set. They traded off smoothly. He read last, watching her head nod, and droop, until he heard a soft snore. He reached across and snapped off her light, then he lay beside her in the semidarkness reviewing his plans.

When he was sure she was fully asleep, he sat up and stuck his feet into his slippers. Padding across the dim apartment to his study, he picked up a stack of stuffed envelopes and clicked on the lamp to make sure all five were there. He slid them around in his hands, one for each child, Peter, Ellen, Jane, Steven, and one marked "To my beloved wife, Sally." As an afterthought, he picked up the cheque-book and added it to the pile.

There was another envelope on his desk, addressed to him. He picked it up for a moment and weighed it in his hand. Without his glasses, he could just make out the university's name in the top left corner. His finger ducked into the open slit on the top and he almost drew out the sheet, but then he stopped. Rereading it wouldn't help, wouldn't make the news any different. He opened a side drawer and dropped the envelope in among a dozen other envelopes.

Then he opened the secret drawer in his massive rolltop desk and took out a bottle of pills. He stopped in the kitchen for a glass, and he almost filled it with water, but then he thought better. Instead, he carried it through to the dining room, and pulled a bottle of whisky from the liquor cabinet. He poured some whisky into the glass and washed down a pill with it, shuddering as the alcohol burned his throat. He sat at the dining table, tapping out pills and swallowing them with the whisky. When the pill bottle was empty, he picked up the envelopes and chequebook and carried them to the bedroom.

Sally stirred slightly as he climbed back into bed, leaving his paper pile on his night table. He leaned over and kissed her. "I do love thee," he groaned, "but I can't live with this." He lay down in the darkness, offered a silent prayer to God, and waited to drift into his final sleep.

That's how I reconstruct a night that was a turning point in many lives, including mine, although I was only nine years old. Behind the whispers that echoed through the following weeks and years swirled issues that the grown-ups judged too large for children to under-stand, issues of national security and loyalty hearings, of personal commitment and betrayal. We all woke the next morning to drama and confusion—confusion that reverberates in our lives to this day.

As a child, as a teen, and intermittently as an adult, I was caught up in the legend of Moll and Sally, and how Moll's work on the Man-hattan Project and their friendship with Alger Hiss affected their lives. But there was no agreement about what the legend meant.

"He was a brilliant, principled man," said Mother, who still dis-played a picture of Moll and Sally in her home decades later.

Dad, in his home, had a different view. "Moll was a wimp," he said, using his favourite tough guy's phrase: "a real pussy."

"He was trapped," said family friend Nick Rosenmeier succinctly, when I caught up with him in Copenhagen in 1981. "In a way, we all were." As a Danish exchange student in the 1950s, Nick had been bemused by American loyalty hearings. But all he had to do to escape was to return home.

For the rest of us, escaping was not so easy. Worse, for years, all my questions about what happened to Moll and Sally met with stony, embarrassed silence. The topic was taboo, mentioned rarely, and then in whispers. Over the years, I gently peeled away layer upon layer of excuses, such as: there was a stigma to suicide; Moll and Sally had broken the conditions of his security clearance; the memory was simply too painful. But I always sensed that there was some other unspeakable reason involved. The mystery remained a huge cloud of anxiety that still hung over all our heads.

Even now that I am well into middle age, the cloud has not dissipated. In fact, it's spread. My disillusionment with the American government, which began with the Flanders case, was exacerbated by the Vietnam war—to the point where I moved to Canada. (In fact, the majority of Americans who moved to Canada at that time were women, but that's another story.) Good luck and determination won me a journalism career, writing books and periodical articles. And yet, and yet . . . on regular visits home and through the news, I see the very elements that destroyed my dear friends, on the rise once again.

I was born in Chicago on November 2, 1948, the night that Harry Truman was elected president of the United States. As Mother lay in the recovery room after the delivery, an orderly handed her a bulldog edition of the next day's *Chicago Tribune*, with the wrongest headline in newspaper history: DEWEY DEFEATS TRUMAN! The family joke is that I've been trying to set the record straight ever since.

After my birth, family life quickly grew complicated. Friends and casual acquaintances sometimes ask why I don't talk about my family much. Then, when I do try to describe how I grew up, they look bewildered. "Everybody seems to have been married at least twice," one friend remarked. Four parents, six siblings, seven grandparents.

Before our wedding, my husband-to-be asked me to create a chart that showed how my family branches all over the place. Every fork, every branch, started traumatically.

Still, of all the catastrophes that beset my childhood, only one branch abruptly ended with two sudden deaths. I blamed myself for most of the turmoil around me, as children often do. We create our own worlds, and the world I thought I had created was full of adultery, abandonment, angst, anxiety and unfocused rage. Somehow, in the midst of all the upheavals, two of my favourite people disappeared, and I never understood why.

The question haunted me way into adulthood. On visits home, it would pop into my head unbidden: What happened to Moll and Sally? As a writer, as a journalist, I keep trying to make sense of their fate. Mother still doesn't want to talk about it much. On occasion, I'll hazard a guess, and she will either agree or correct me. So I've gone searching elsewhere. But interviews, books, and oral histories have revealed only a Rashomon-like complex of conflicting explanations.

Their real names, I learned recently, were Sarah and Donald. I knew them simply as Sally and Moll. I thought that they were Quakers, because they used "thee" and "thou" with family and close friends. It turns out that Sally was a Quaker, and Moll was raised in the Massachusetts Congregationalist tradition—which traced a direct lineage to the Puritans of the Massachusetts Bay Colony. But Moll adopted some aspects of Quakerism. As he explained at an Atomic Energy Commission inquiry: "The Friends use among themselves the so-called 'Friendly' speech which has degenerated by this time into using 'Thee' as the nominative case in addressing a Friend. My wife and I, when we became engaged, adopted this as a form of *tutoyer*, and have kept it ever since. In that sense we use it among the family."

"Is thee hungry?" Sally would ask, when I clumped up the stairs to their apartment, across the street from my school. "How is thy mother feeling today?"

"Better, thanks," I'd say some days. On others: "Not so well. She called the doctor and he told her to stay in bed." And as Sally headed towards her kitchen, I would call out, "I'm not hungry, thanks. I've just eaten," with my fingers crossed behind my back.

If I wasn't quick enough, she would duck into the kitchen and return with a plate bearing crackers covered with grown-up goodies—pickled herring, maybe, or blue cheese. I'd hop from foot to foot, trying not to wrinkle my nose, insisting that I really wasn't hungry. One time I darted into the kitchen with her and grabbed a plain cracker, before she covered it. What a breakthrough! "She likes *crackers!*" the adults cried. "The child likes *crackers*."

Their apartment was different from ours. We had a typical Chicago railroad flat. Room followed room like railroad cars in a row, all parallel to and opening onto one long hall. Windows overlooked air shafts which got sunlight only at high noon, or faced into canyons formed by apartment buildings next door. In contrast, their apartment seemed to sprawl out in all directions from the central entrance. We mostly visited in the living room. I never saw the bedrooms.

Of their four children, only Steve still lived at home when I knew them. Peter and Ellen lived elsewhere. Jane was married to Morty Ziff, and they lived in the neighbourhood. Jane Flanders and my mother were also close friends. Two or three times a week, Jane would walk down Fifty-seventh Street from her apartment to ours, carrying her cup of coffee. Then, every week or two, she would phone my mother, who would send me running down the street with the mugs she'd left at our house. A journalist, Morty rose through the ranks at the *Chicago Daily News*. I knew him best from community theatre. I remember a great big man with a bushy beard. When our theatre company presented the Passion play, I was an angel in the choir. Morty, his black curly beard and hair spray-painted gold, played God.

Sally and Moll Flanders's apartment was as dishevelled as ours, and decorated in similar spartan Early Intellectual: floor-to-ceiling bookshelves, dim lighting, and a few sticks of furniture. Take my bedroom: I had a complete forty-year-old set of the *Book of Knowledge* in my room, but no top sheet on my bed. The thick brown embossed leather volumes served as toys until I grew old enough to read them. Sometimes I stacked them like building blocks; other times, I strewed them around the floor and imagined they were stepping stones across a raging river filled with alligators. When I could, at first I read only the fiction in each volume. Later, I read the natural science articles as well, which muddled my understanding until high school. I thought there were eighty elements in the periodic table and was baffled to learn they'd discovered twenty more.

Sally, like Mother, always had a book in one hand. They read while they talked on the phone, while they walked around their apartments, while they stirred soup or coffee, while they bathed. One time, while she was putting laundry in the washer, Mother accidentally threw her book in as well. Her bare left hand looked almost indecently naked. She stared at it in shock.

Reading and literature were huge topics of conversation for them and for most of the people we knew. Reading was also Mother's escape, of course, from the constant pain in her knees, and her sense of failure at being divorced. After he moved out, Dad finished his master's in American literature, as she had pushed him to do, but Mother never returned to school to finish her own English degree. Nor did she look for a full-time job. She believed that a mother of two children should stay home and look after them—no matter what the cost, or to whom.

Housework was not a top priority for either woman. To be fair, Mother's mobility was limited. However, Sally and Moll always had food in the house. Our food supply was erratic. When Mother had a cheque, and her legs were feeling all right, she hiked from our house on Fifty-seventh Street over to the A&P on Fifty-third Street near the lake. Sometimes she went with a friend. Often, she took me. We sang and talked as we walked block after block past apartment buildings and townhouses, under the boughs of the elms and oaks planted on the boulevards between the sidewalk and the street.

Mother stocked up with as much as she could pull in our little red wagon, which also held my little brother, Dylan. She bought staples, fresh produce, meat for freezing, cigarettes and Scotch, and sometimes a spice cake. Then she (or usually we) hauled it home and made many trips from the sidewalk to the second floor, getting the bags up the stairs to our kitchen.

Dad sometimes picked us up on Sunday afternoons. He usually took us on long walks. Sometimes weeks went by when we didn't see him. I have vague recollections of Nick Rosenmeier acting as go-between, taking us kids back and forth, during the times that my parents couldn't stand to be in the same room together. Dad's new girlfriend (who became my first stepmother) prepared grown-up food like veal shoulder stuffed with sorrel, or boeuf bourguignon. I stuck to the buttered egg noodles.

At home, there were also long stretches when Dad's cheques were late, or Mother couldn't walk. Then we lived on peanut butter sandwiches and chocolate milk, which was all I knew how to prepare. The child who sat behind me at William H. Ray School used to complain and kick my chair furiously because my stomach growled so loudly.

As freethinkers, Moll and especially Sally overlooked some of the factors that made other families shy away from us. Never mind that we weren't scientists of any kind. They didn't care that my parents had a "mixed" marriage—Methodist and Jewish—or that both parents had renounced their religions. They didn't even care that my folks were divorced. Other parents did. One classmate's mother shooed me out of her big two-storey house and told her daughter loudly, "Don't bring that girl home again. Her parents are divorced."

We, in turn, overlooked some drawbacks in the Flanderses' lives: the whispers about their loyalty, the strange car that sat outside their apartment sometimes, Moll's deepening silence and sadness. Even when the other atomic scientists started keeping their distance, Mother's affection for the couple remained strong. In the self-consciously liberal and nonconformist neighbourhood of Hyde Park, surrounding the brilliant but eccentric post-war University of Chicago, the Flanderses were Mother's surrogate parents and Dylan's and my surrogate grandparents.

One afternoon, Sally buzzed me in at the front entrance, and I came upstairs to find her and my mother in her living room. Mother was red-faced and breathless with laughter. "Well, what did you expect?" she sputtered.

Sally would have cocked her hat if she'd had one. "All I said was . . ." she started, and Mother howled with laughter. "All I said was that I think we should all vote for Len Després." She shrugged. "We're supposed to say what's in our hearts, at meetings."

"Did the Spirit move you to talk politics?" teased Mother. "Has anybody else ever talked about politics at a Friends' meeting?" Sally retorted quickly, "It's about time that someone did!" She turned to me and offered a plate. "Cracker?"

I took a cracker and sat down in a corner. Dylan, still a toddler, was sleeping on a pillow in a cardboard box nearby. Mother and Sally returned to their conversation while I pulled a book out of my book-bag and settled in to read. As I sank into the story, sounds around me became muted. I heard ice cubes tinkling in glasses, chattering and chuckling, as the two women relaxed in the warmth of their friend-ship.

Sudden silence made me look up. Mother and Sally were staring up at the doorway to a section of the apartment where I'd never been. A shadow shambled and shuffled in the doorway, a figure in a bathrobe with his whiskers all awry. Moll stood there silently. He opened his mouth, but no words came.

"Does thee want something?" Sally asked, rising. She stepped around the coffee table and hurried to his side. "Moll, does thee need something?" I couldn't hear his muttered reply. Mother was gather-ing up her purse, putting glasses and saucers on a tray. I closed my book and stuffed it back in my bookbag. Mother picked up Dylan and jerked her head towards the door.

Sobbing came from the doorway. Moll started to slump inside his bathrobe, shrinking against Sally's shoulder. She glanced over at us and asked, "Could thee knock next door, and ask the neighbour to come over?" Mother nodded. I took the tray to the kitchen and we left.

As we started down the stairs, after alerting the neighbour, I couldn't help asking, "What's wrong with Mr. Flanders?" Mother's mouth grew grim. "He's very sad," she answered. I didn't understand.

"Why is he sad?" I asked.

"About something he did. He helped build a weapon." We reached the bottom landing and the big, heavy glass door to the outside. "It was wartime, for Christ's sake!" Mother snapped at no one in particular.

We turned at the corner of Fifty-seventh Street, to walk three blocks east and south under the trees to our own apartment. Two blocks west of the Flanderses' building was Stagg Field, which was still a sports stadium then. The University of Chicago stuck to its pledge never to have a football team, but field hockey, lacrosse, and track-and-field teams used the sports field daily.

In winter, when the weather was much too cold for track and field, the university flooded the area underneath the stands for skating. I skated there a few times. I guess there was some admission fee, or maybe the area was for U of C gym members only, because usually I skated on the Midway, which was much colder, and farther away, but didn't cost anything.

Under the stands was a plaque half hidden by ivy that proclaimed:

ON DECEMBER 2, 1942
MAN ACHIEVED HERE
THE FIRST SELF-SUSTAINING CHAIN REACTION
AND THEREBY INITIATED THE
CONTROLLED RELEASE OF NUCLEAR ENERGY

It was there that Enrico Fermi and his crew conducted the first controlled nuclear reaction in the world. In a time when most people would not have recognized the term "atomic scientist," we lived in a neighbourhood full of them. The Fermi family were important friends to my mother. The Flanderses, of course, were too. Moll's work at Argonne Labs had segued to working on the very first computers, but he and Sally maintained their ties to the scientists he'd worked with at Los Alamos, on the Manhattan Project. Sally often talked about "Oppie"—Robert J. Oppenheimer, who headed up the team that built the first atomic bombs.

Although I don't recall ever having seen him, Albert Einstein roamed the Hyde Park neighbourhood as well as the U of C campus. Our family was inclined to pay more attention to the neighbourhood novelists, such as Philip Roth (whose back porch adjoined ours),

Saul Bellow, and J. P. Donahue. But we mingled with the scientists too. Years later, when I visited the *Bulletin of the Atomic Scientists* office for research on a book, I already knew where the nearest water fountain was. I must have been there before.

Even as a schoolgirl, I knew in a general way what had happened under the stands. Our teachers warned us about the atomic bomb. We had "Duck and Cover" drills where we had to grab our jackets and dive under our desks with our jackets over our heads to protect us from fallout. We were reminded every Tuesday evening by the blare of the city testing its air raid sirens. When I cycled up Fifty-seventh Street to splash in Botany Pond under the gingko tree, I shuddered as I passed the Stagg Field gate. Something extraordinary happened there, something that changed the world, and something that directly affected many of our family friends.

Mother was always so graceful when she fainted. All her concerns about looking ungainly because of her height vanished as she crumpled gently to the ground or (if I was lucky) the floor. She would wrench one of her fragile knees, cry out softly, and down she'd go. I was a tiny child, thin and frail looking, although precocious. No way in the world could I pick her up. So I just stood beside her and howled.

I entered the world as my parents' first-born—and as the only baby in married students' housing, a factor that attracted adoration even for a wretchedly colicky newborn. Although, as Dad said to Mother in the taxi taking me home, "The hospital should be sued for malpractice, turning over an infant to rank amateurs such as we." He was partly right. They knew more about grammar than about infants.

My status was rather more like a pet than a person. Mother and Dad loved playing with their peer group, who happened to include actors at Compass Theatre and (subsequently) Second City: Mike Nichols and Elaine May, Paul Sills, Shelley Berman. Mother always swore that Mike Nichols dandled me on his knee and sang, to a tune from *HMS Pinafore*, "I'm called little Penney Kome, dear little Penney Kome, though I shall never know why. I scream and I holler, I ain't worth a dollar, but still, little Penney Kome, I . . ."

By the time Dylan came along, everything had changed. Mother always said that she eagerly wanted the baby who emerged as Dylan. As soon became clear, Dad felt differently. When she finally got pregnant the second time, everything went wrong, not just with her marriage, but with the world around her. My parents had advance tickets to see Dylan Thomas read his poetry. "We saw him before, and oh! he was riveting," she said. Thomas was due in Chicago after the holidays, but he died on November 9, 1953, in New York. Mother resolved to name the baby Dylan. Then, midwinter, Dad's father, Sam Kome, died. Mother broached the idea of naming the baby Sam, but the marriage was already in serious trouble, and Dad reacted badly. So Mother named him Stephen. Stephen Dylan. We always called him Dylan at home.

Dylan didn't talk to an adult until he was six. Nor did he show much interest in walking. He was a big, passive baby. An early photo shows us side by side on the sofa when he was six months and I was six years old. He looks almost as large as me. Yet I carried him everywhere. Mother was afraid to pick him up, in case her legs failed. She didn't really want him to be mobile. She used to leave him in his crib for hours at a time. Once, I left a chair next to his crib and he climbed out. She was furious.

There's an old joke about a boy who never talked until he was six. Then he spoke up at dinner to complain that the soup was too salty. When asked why he'd never said anything before that, he replied, "Everything was all right until now."

Dylan's story was similar. Day after day, Mother would sit him on her lap and ask, "Dylan, can you say 'clock'?" And he would just suck his thumb. She didn't send him to nursery school or kindergarten until he was five and a half. He was a March baby, so there was no hurry. The summer he was five, she walked into her bedroom and found him cuddled around our marmalade tabby cat. "Tawny," he was asking, "can you say 'clock'?"

If Dylan enjoyed (endured?) a prolonged babyhood, my childhood ended abruptly about the time he was born. Dad and Mother were divorced. Dylan was an infant, and Mother was on crutches awaiting knee surgery. I learned how to prepare the peanut butter sandwiches and chocolate milk, and carry them in to Mother's bedroom on a tray. She cried a lot. She cried for two or three years.

She stopped crying on special occasions, such as a visit with Sally or Jane Flanders. I thought of the Flanderses as lifesavers. If Mother had a problem, Sally told her what to do. Sally always knew what to do.

In retrospect, I have come to believe that surgery ruined Mother's knees—that if she had had physiotherapy at the very beginning, she could have avoided a lifetime of grief. But surgery was all that medicine had to offer in the 1940s and '50s. And as Mother's knees grew more and more painful, the orthopaedist recommended more surgery. This time, he simply removed both her kneecaps. Afterwards, she was in a wheelchair for a while, and then on crutches again. The surgery alleviated some of the constant aching, but did little to strengthen or stabilize her knees. Only elastic bandages supported them. One twist, one wrench, and she would faint from the pain.

In the midst of all this confusion, or shortly afterwards, Dad finally earned his M.A. in American literature. After Dad died in 1996, I asked Mother what his thesis was about. "Sin and redemption," she laughed ironically, "in Nathaniel Hawthorne's writing." *The Scarlet Letter*? At his memorial service, his second family swore up and down that his thesis was about Dylan Thomas. "'Do not go gentle into that good night,'" they recited. "'Rage, rage, against the dying of the light. . . .'"

Well, Dad showed plenty of rage when he left Mother, pregnant and on crutches, and moved into Brenda's apartment. But his thesis was about sin.

Like many American families, we got our very first television set in 1954, in order to watch the Senate Permanent Subcommittee on Investigations, headed by Senator Joe McCarthy. I remember people calling it HUAC, the House Un-American Activities Committee, which was the predecessor committee that investigated the loyalty of people who were accused of sympathizing with Communism.

Looking over the history of Senate committees, I was struck by the continuous efforts to investigate American citizens. Inventing enemies seems to generate a lot of political capital. HUAC was the first committee, the one that pursued unionists and accused-

Communists in Hollywood, resulting in the blacklisting of the Hollywood Ten. HUAC was where playwright Lillian Hellman famously snapped that "I cannot cut my conscience to suit the fashion of the times." Although HUAC's style of asking loaded questions that people refused to answer, and then charging them with contempt of Congress, came to be known as McCarthyism, McCarthy actually arrived on the scene later, to head up the Senate Subcommittee on Investigations.

As far as we knew then, the Flanderses' political problems began when their friend and Sally's sort-of cousin-in-law, Alger Hiss, voluntarily appeared before HUAC to answer accusations brought by Whittaker Chambers, editor of *Time* magazine. Among other duties in a long and distinguished career, Hiss had served as Secretary-General of the United Nations Charter Conference, which laid the groundwork for the UN we know today. At HUAC, Senator Richard Nixon charged Hiss with being a Communist and a spy for the Soviet Union.

The hearings were hugely controversial, and Hiss's subsequent two trials for perjury (which happened in 1949 and 1950) dragged the debate on and on for months. It was a *cause célèbre*. Every thinking person had an opinion on the Hiss case. As Senator Daniel Patrick Moynihan said in his 1998 book, *Secrecy: The American Experience*, "Belief in the guilt or innocence of Alger Hiss became a defining issue in American intellectual life." In the end, the second jury did convict Hiss on two counts of perjury, and sentenced him to five years in prison, of which he served forty-four months.

My folks were independent small-l liberals, intellectuals and existentialists, not Communists, but they cheered for witnesses like folksinger Pete Seeger, playwright Arthur Miller, jazz vocalist Lena Horne, and journalist Ring Lardner Jr. They spat at names like Senators Joe McCarthy and Richard Nixon. I was already in Canada when Nixon became president. My folks stopped urging me to return to the States—at least, while Nixon was in the White House.

Until recently, I'd always thought that Donald Flanders (1900–1958) testified before HUAC. I remember Mother coming home from a doctor's appointment upset because she was delayed so long she missed Moll's appearance. But when I went searching (as an adult), I couldn't find any records under HUAC. Since the topic was still taboo in her house—although I eventually won her over to the idea of me writing about it—I had to search for information in other ways.

Finding the information was both harder and easier than I expected. The hard part was figuring out that Moll's real name was Donald, not Malcolm. My earliest searches for "Moll Flanders" were confounded by references to Daniel Dafoe's 1722 moralistic novel about a lower-class girl who wants to better herself. "Malcolm Flanders" netted nothing relevant. Searching on "Moll and Sally," I finally found a cross-reference to Donald and Sara Flanders. A search on those names brought me to a Web site signed by someone named Jon Flanders, titled "The Ernest Flanders Family History Project." Although (as he told me in an e-mail) Jon Flanders regards the story as tangential to the family history that interests him most, he has posted both Moll's and Sally's testimony before the Atomic Energy Commission—yet another set of investigative hearings.

In 1946, Congress created a civilian Atomic Energy Commission that was intended to replace laboratories run by private industry—under military control—with a national network of university laboratories under civilian control. Argonne Labs, where Moll worked, was one of the first labs authorized under the new National Laboratory system. (After the war, he dropped the task of calculating fission, and moved on with building the first computers.) The military fought back, by impugning the loyalty of the AEC board members and university scientists. AEC management instigated a particularly heavy-handed investigation of about 400,000 personnel. They cast a very wide net, running routine checks on everybody who might be privy to atomic secrets. But in Moll and Sally's case, the investigation was personal, as shown by this AEC letter dated September 15, 1952.

Dear Mr. Flanders:

In accordance with Section 10 of the Atomic Energy Act, an investigation was conducted concerning your character, associations, and loyalty. Additional information reported subsequent to this investigation, when considered along with information obtained during the course of it, has created a question concerning your eligibility for continued security clearance and employment in Atomic Commission work.

Donald Flanders

It was reported that you and your wife have been close personal friends of Alger and Priscilla Hiss for many years, and that Hiss and his wife have visited in your house many times. It was also reported that your wife solicited funds for Alger Hiss. Alger Hiss was convicted in 1950 on charges of perjury, and was reported to have been involved in Communist and espionage activities in behalf of Soviet Russia.

It was reported that you received announcements of meetings of the Socialist Youth League weekly "Labor Action." Both organizations are cited by the Attorney General.

It was reported that you and your daughter, Ellen, have associated with Fred Meyer, reported to have been President of the Socialist Youth League.

On your Personnel Security Questionnaire, you listed membership in the Progressive Citizens of America, which is reportedly supported by the Communist Party.

It was reported that in 1948, your daughter, Ellen, was a member of the Young Progressives of America, the Youth division of the Progressive Party, and that the Progressive Party was Communist controlled.

It was reported that your daughter Ellen, attended night classes conducted by Peggy Kraft. It was also reported that Peggy Kraft was a member of the Executive Committee of the Communist Party, and had other Communist associations.

It was reported that in 1947 your wife wrote a letter to a government official in which she referred to the government's loyalty program as a Communist witch hunt.

You are requested to make a written response to the above.

That last attack illustrates the tenor of the times, insinuating that Sally transgressed by complaining to her congressional representatives about government activities. I can hear echoes of the same complaint in modern responses to complaints about the Patriot Act and other surveillance legislation: "If you have nothing to hide, you have nothing to fear." Apart from Sally's temerity in questioning government authority, every charge on that list amounts to guilt by association.

Moll handled the "witch hunt" question well, I thought, in his testimony. He dryly observed that,

> The phrase she used was rather a current one at that time, as illustrated by the fact that in 1947 Mr. Sumner Pike wrote an article in the Atlantic Monthly entitled "Witch Hunting Then and Now." That referred specifically to this sort of thing. It seems to me that no inferences should be drawn from the use of this particular phrase. What the origin of it was, neither of us has any clear idea. I am sure that an examination of current newspapers, and so on, will establish the fact that it was a current phrase, not the property of any one organization.

Moll also testified that he was much less politically active than Sally. Although he was a person of conscience, Moll's passions were pure math and music. Mother said he was the kind of person who could do calculations in his head while carrying on regular conversations—in the same way that most of us may hear a tune running through our minds while we talk.

Richard Courant, head of the New York University Mathematics Institute, testified at the AEC that he had recommended Moll to the Manhattan Project. He did so, he said, because Moll was too conscientious to function well as a professor. "Flanders is a prototype of a Puritan," he said.

"He is upstanding, Puritanical." By that, Courant meant that if Moll made a commitment, he exerted every effort to fulfill it. When Moll committed to grading student papers, he applied himself fully to the task. "It took him seventeen minutes for each miserable little paper," Courant said. "He thought it was his duty." And he was falling further and further behind in his grading. He began to feel he should stick to research and give up teaching. So in an effort to help this gentle soul find a job with limited, defined, manageable moral and ethical obligations, his friend Richard Courant recommended Moll to the Manhattan Project.

Dad moved in with Brenda Handforth, who was barely twenty-two at the time, as soon as he left our home. They lived together until Dad and Mother's divorce was final. One day—one of Mother's good days—an envelope arrived in the mail with a stiff ivory-coloured card formally announcing the marriage of Hal Kome and Brenda Handforth. Mother put the card on the mantel, where it stayed for several months. She then flung herself across her bed and burst into tears.

When I was twelve, Mother married George Victor Mather, a direct descendant of the Massachusetts Bay Colony "Mather Dynasty" that included Richard and Cotton Mather. They were clergy, not judiciary, but they oversaw the witch trials at Salem, where some women were hanged. "Hanged, not burned at the stake," as George emphasized whenever the subject arose.

I was thirteen before the two couples who were my parents (and stepparents) started having more children. Dad and Brenda had four: Jessie, Sonia, Hunter and Sam Kome. Mother and George produced one daughter, Christine Mather, when I was fifteen. I left home at eighteen and moved to Canada at nineteen, but I tried to maintain ties with all my parents and siblings.

Every time I travelled home as a young adult, I visited both sets of parents. At Dad's house, the routine was always the same. My stepmother, Brenda, would sit up drinking and talking with me late into the night. Eventually, she would work herself into tears.

"The first time Hal brought you to our apartment, you were friendly," she would say. "You let me hug you. The following week, when Hal brought you over, I reached out to touch you, and you flinched away from me. You flinched from me! You'd told your mother about me, and after that you didn't want me to hug you at all."

Little did she realize that I flinched from everything then. Walking between school and home, I imagined swirling vortexes rising from the sidewalk at every step, trapping me, keeping me from reaching either uncomfortable destination. Most days I tried to trick those whirlpools, by twirling myself, travelling in a long series of turns, opening and closing my arms as if I was fastening the turns together like a paper chain. I spun down the street whirling like a dervish, trying to escape other people's demons.

My school career began inauspiciously. The first time Mother tried to register me for kindergarten, the school staff said, "She's too small." Pointing to my November birthday, they declined to enrol me. Mother trembled and wept. All my excitement dissolved into tears. On the way home, I deliberately dropped my shiny new pencil case in the middle of the street and ran back for it as a car was coming, hoping it would hit me, but someone stopped me. She finally did manage to register me that year, by reminding the school that the cut-off was November 30, not November 1.

After the first two weeks in kindergarten, I asked Mother to braid my hair. She said I'd have to grow it, so I did. Only decades later, looking at the kindergarten photo, did the reason for my request jump out at me. Most of the other little girls were African-American, and wore tiny braids all over their heads, signalling that their families aspired to "good hair" and middle-class status. Even when my hair grew long enough for braids, I didn't look like them. Nobody invited me home. But I wore my hair in braids for the rest of my childhood.

At school, I spent days under my desk, or covering my face with my hair, or even hiding in the cupboards. A classmate named Arthur, a tall excitable boy with a high-pitched voice, shrieked and nearly fainted when he opened a cupboard door and reached in for a textbook, and I slid out from the shelf. I was so little, I could hide anywhere. And there was a lot to hide from.

By 2005, Mother was finally starting to come around to the idea that I might have the skill, the integrity, and the right to delve into the mystery surrounding the Flanderses' deaths. Her assent gave me permission to contact neighbours and long-lost friends. Clues were scattered all over her apartment, from Helen Bevington's *A Book and a Love Story* on the bookshelves (with a chapter about the Bevingtons' lengthy friendship with the Flanderses), to Leon Després' phone number in her address book, to a thank-you note from

Morty and Jane (Flanders) Ziff on her mantelpiece, asking, "Do you think Penney and her family could come visit us?"

I lost track of Jane and Morty sometime in the 1960s. I moved away, and Jane no longer walked up Fifty-seventh Street with her coffee mug. Morty landed a job with the University of Illinois in 1968, and then they moved back East, to Massachusetts, where Morty lost weight and gained gravitas as Professor Howard M. Ziff of the University of Massachusetts journalism program. (It suits him, but I still think he looked better as God.) More to the point, Mother lost contact with them too, for more than twenty years. Then suddenly, in the early 1990s, Jane made contact again, and they've been visiting Chicago occasionally ever since. For me to visit *them*, however, involved a journey of 2500 miles.

Finally, a Writers' Union meeting took me to Montreal. On a rainy May Tuesday, I rented a car and drove five hours through a torrential downpour to Amherst, Massachusetts, making regular cell-phone calls to Jane to keep her apprised of my progress. Morty met me at an abandoned gas station and guided me the last few miles to their home, surrounded by riotous gardens, in a small rural-looking subdivision tucked away very close to the U Mass campus. We spent four days catching up before I dared raise my request to write about Jane's parents.

By then, we had shifted locale to the Ziffs' country home, near Springfield, New York. Jane walked me through the lush green countryside where her parents (Sally and Moll Flanders) had been most at home, along the hard-packed dirt road that connects family summer homes sprawled across what was once a rye farm. She pointed to the tall trees swaying in the wind and talked about how her parents organized their friends to plant one thousand seedlings in one weekend. We visited the stream where she and her siblings and cousins spent countless hours in a futile effort to build a fieldstone dam and create a swimming pool. Then we turned left, uphill, and climbed to the house that was Aunt Bobby's. Aunt Bobby was Sally's sister, Roberta, who married Tommy Fansler. Tommy Fansler's sister was Priscilla (Fansler) Hiss.

This was Sally and Moll's real family, the extended family that gave their lives meaning. Every summer that they possibly could, her parents returned to that land. And most summers—before, during, and after her marriage to Alger Hiss—so did Priscilla Hiss, who was an integral part of the Flanders-Fansler clan.

Moll explained in his written response to the AEC charges that,

> My wife and I have always been very fond of Priscilla, and we liked Alger from the start. We had always felt at complete ease with them, and have discussed a wide range of topics with the complete freedom. In particular we discussed many social problems. All of us—Thomas and Roberta Fansler, Alger and Priscilla Hiss, Donald and Sara Flanders would properly be described as liberals. . . .
>
> The six of us found our companionship mutually very sympathetic and we discussed things with great freedom[.] This does not mean that we agreed on all topics, political or otherwise. There were certainly sharp disagreements and hot arguments. Under those circumstances, I think it would have been pretty difficult for Alger to obscure a passionate devotion to Marxist principles if he had one, (he displayed none), particularly if that devotion were so passionate that it would cause a man to behave in a manner completely contradictory to his everyday character as revealed rather intimately in the circumstances in which I have had opportunity to observe him. As I have known him, Alger showed himself to be morally and intellectually honest, highly intelligent, and a man of goodwill. Take the matter of intellectual honesty; for example. In all of our discussions I cannot remember that he ever intentionally used a specious argument, a fault of which I think I can fairly accuse every other one of the six of us. . . .

Our friend and neighbour Helen Bevington (who died in 1995) wrote about this place that "The two farms and their families [the Flanderses and the Fanslers] made a company that in good time I loved more than any other I have known. They became my family, closer than blood kin, the friends of a lifetime . . . [for twelve magic summers] it was a time of immense pleasure among life-loving, life-enhancing people, and then it was over. None of us could have guessed in those days the horror that lay ahead."

I was ten when I heard my first sonic boom. We were visiting my grandfather Mac, who was chaplain at an airforce base outside Amarillo, Texas. I was walking down the street with Mac, when the most horrendous KA-BLAM blasted the sky and lifted me off my feet. I knew exactly what to do. I threw myself under the nearest parked car and waited for the mushroom cloud. It was almost an hour before my embarrassed grandfather could coax me out. I was sure that the atom bomb and the Cold War, which had overshadowed my entire life, were finally eclipsing us all.

But, despite what I'd learned as a child, the Cold War wasn't an eternal concept. It came to a sudden end in 1991. Although it had always been part of my world, the generation before me remembers a sudden precipitous beginning.

"I was totally confused about Russia, growing up," said Peggy Bevington, Helen Bevington's daughter-in-law. A contemporary of Moll and Sally's children, she still lives up the street from Mother. Like others of her generation, she had thought the Russian Revolution exhilarating at first. And throughout the Second World War, said Peggy, "We'd all been contributing to the Russian war relief. There was all this pro-Russian propaganda. Then, to have the Cold War reverse the propaganda so quickly—it was stunning."

Sally Flanders said something similar at the AEC. "At the time of the original Russian Revolution, I read the new constitution, and thought it was probably the most superb document that I had ever read, ever been written," she said. "And then as time went on, it seemed to me that they were, that it was a pretty piece of paper, and for a long time, I guess probably to the time of the purges, I felt they had demonstrated and done great things in Russia. At the time of the purges, I could not see how they could be justified, and from that time on, I lost more and more sympathy with them."

All the same, she noted, after the 1929 stock-market crash, she did volunteer time with a socialist league. "I would say that it was in the winter of 1930 or 1931 that people were starving in New York

City," she recalled, "and the socialists were definitely doing something about it. I think it was Priscilla that came and asked me if I wouldn't help collect old clothes in my building, and help serve refreshments in the socialist headquarters. . . ."

Who, facing the Great Depression, could be unmoved by the plight of so many destitute people? Not Sally. As a person of conscience, she sought volunteer opportunities and political campaigns that would improve life for the people who were suffering. And that was another bond with the Hisses. "I felt that the Hisses were always very much concerned about the general welfare," Sally said. "Priscilla and I, being somewhat more sentimental than our husbands, thought the small amount we could do was sufficiently valuable to put an awful lot of work in it."

Jane Flanders Ziff thought that her mother had only the best motives. "These were people who were concerned with world peace," she said, "and who wanted to have good relations with the Russians."

Leon Després acted as Moll's advocate at the AEC hearings. Després is a Chicago legend, for twenty years the only alderman to stand up to Mayor Richard J. Daley. In 2005, at the age of ninety-six, Després published *Challenging the Daley Machine: A Chicago Alderman's Memoir*. The city now officially recognizes the importance of Després' work. When I walked a few short blocks from Mother's apartment to interview him in the spring of 2006, there were two authorized street signs on the corner lamppost outside his apartment building. The top one says, "Stony Island Blvd." Underneath that, an identical green rectangle says Leon M. Després Way.

Després was a lawyer and managed to maintain his law practice in addition to his civic duties. "There were so many people that had loyalty cases against them, it hardly attracted attention," he recalled. "I handled a dozen cases. Alex Ellson must have handled a hundred.

"It wasn't difficult to defend the scientists," he said. "[Although] an ordinary lawyer might not be willing or able to do it effectively. In one case, one of the charges against my client was knowing *me* . . ."

Després and his wife Marion lived near the Flanderses' home, and often saw Moll debark from the Argonne Labs bus on his way home from work. "He was a small man with a big black bushy beard," he recalled. "My son called him, 'the mad scientist'."

For Moll's defence, Després took the high road. "We had wonderful witnesses," he was proud to say. "They gave the impression of a man with a supremely fine character. The agency [AEC] recognized that if he said he wouldn't see Alger Hiss again, he would keep his word." The problem was, as Després acknowledged, that Moll "thought that [condition] was unacceptable." Moll—straitlaced Moll, widely regarded as "a living saint," to use Helen Bevington's term—could hardly bear to imagine that anyone would lie, much less someone whom he regarded as a close friend.

By 1952, Després was "no longer an admirer of Alger Hiss," who remains a controversial figure to this day. Amazon.com lists more than 1700 books with "Alger Hiss" in the title. Declassified files in the United States and former USSR seem to confirm that Hiss *was* a Soviet agent, although the cryptographic evidence is murky. Hiss himself proclaimed his innocence and fought to clear his name until his death in 1996. His son, Tony Hiss, carries on.

Even if he was guilty, huge questions remain about the political ends which Senators Richard Nixon and Joe McCarthy pursued by making a circus of Hiss's prosecution. "The Hiss case helped launch the 1950s McCarthy period, a decade of fear and distrust," states "The Alger Hiss Story" Web site. "Senator Joseph R. McCarthy's anti-communist crusade, during which 10,000 Americans lost their jobs, began less than three weeks after Alger Hiss's conviction in 1950." Hundreds of thousands more Americans were forced to sign loyalty oaths or face loyalty hearings. Wild accusations abounded, to the extent that "McCarthyism" entered the language as a pejorative. The *American Heritage Dictionary* defines it as:

1. The practice of publicizing accusations of political disloyalty or subversion with insufficient regard to evidence.
2. The use of unfair investigatory or accusatory methods in order to suppress opposition.

When I was a child, FBI agents in trench coats and fedoras stood in my schoolyard in order to watch Moll and Sally's apartment, across the street. If Leon Després were alive today (he died on May 6, 2009), he would probably be advising clients facing similar hearings today.

Some of them would be the same clients—the American Civil Liberties Union and the American Friends Service Committee are both suing the federal government for surreptitious surveillance—while others might include people charged with illegal immigration, refugees from Iraq and Afghanistan, or the families of detainees at Guantanamo Bay.

Out of curiosity, I sent Tony Hiss an e-mail asking, "Do you hear any echoes of the 1950s in what is happening in the U.S. today?" He replied, "My basic sense is not that current events echo what happened then but are a continuation of the same event which, back then, was visible only to a few and now can be sensed by many."

Settled around the kitchen table on our last morning together, I finally worked up the courage to ask Jane and Morty for their perspective on her parents' deaths. They laid out for me some of the reasons that Moll was depressed. He felt terrible guilt about the Manhattan Project; the tragedy of the Hiss case touched him deeply; he was dragged down by Sally's depression at being displaced from her beloved community in New York State when they moved to Chicago in 1946; his work on the earliest computers was not going well.

"He wasn't a big glorious success, which was a burden to him," said Howard (Morty). "But he always did solid work."

"The terrible blow about the AEC hearings was that Len's [Leon Després'] case depended on the argument that Moll didn't know Hiss very well," said Jane. "My father, being so honest and transparent, couldn't believe that anyone else could be dishonest." Sally "was always a person who could handle everything," Jane recalled, "while Moll just had to be intellectual and mysterious." But the move to Chicago undermined Sally's role. "She liked to be in the community. In the summer, she was always organizing people, telling people what to do, running square dances in Bobby's [Roberta Fansler's] barn. When we moved to Chicago, she had a lot of trouble recreating that community, and fell into a depression." And then Jane said something that floored me, as it reversed all my childhood perceptions. She said, "Your mother was very helpful to my mother. She was extremely important to her." Here I had thought that Sally's intervention was Mother's mainstay in recovering from her own depression.

Did Sally maintain contact with Priscilla despite the AEC tribunal decision that Moll could keep his security clearance on condition that he never have contact with the Hisses again? "Of course she did," said Jane with a warm laugh. It was simply inconceivable not to.

Also, I may have another piece of the puzzle that Moll didn't share with his children. In 1981, I talked with a go-between. Nick Rosenmeier, an American literature professor at the University of Copenhagen, was an exchange student at the University of Chicago in the 1950s. He took me and my brother to Dad for Sunday visits during those dark times when my parents couldn't stand to be in the same room together. And, he told me, he took messages between Sally and Priscilla, in order to evade the FBI surveillance.

Nick said that Moll repeatedly tried to find another job so that he could leave Argonne Labs, where he felt stymied by security issues. He said that Moll applied for university-faculty jobs all over the United States. Usually the university's first response was enthusiastic, he said. There were even interviews and job offers. But then, a few weeks later, the universities would send embarrassed letters saying that they had decided to hire someone younger, or someone cheaper, or not to hire anyone at all. "He was blacklisted." Nick was sure. "He was at a dead end at Argonne Labs, and the government wasn't going to let him work anywhere else. He was trapped."

When I told Jane and Morty what Nick said, they just shook their heads. They had never heard anything about job applications before.

My parents were divorced in 1954. Mother had almost recovered her physical and emotional health when Moll's death sent her into shock. She managed to rally, and supported Sally and her family through the funeral and the subsequent public curiosity.

One month later, Sally was moving furniture in her station wagon. She was always the "get-it-done" type, more interested in results than process. She loaded the car in slapdash fashion and was racing along the country road when she took a wrong turn. A mail truck slammed into her car. The furniture behind shot forward and crushed her to death against the steering wheel and the dashboard.

When Mother heard what had happened, she dissolved into tears and went back to bed.

Dylan was four years old at the time. He still hadn't spoken a word in front of adults. Two or three years later, we were all in the living room after school. Dylan and I were watching the first *Superman* TV series, with George Reeves. In this episode, Superman rescued a small child by throwing himself in front of and stopping a truck that was about to run over her. Dylan looked up from the screen. "If I was Superman," he said, "I could have stopped that mail truck."

One Glass and You're Dead

Taras
Grescoe

CREATURES OF MYTH, by their nature, disappear before they can be grasped. Wood sprites, leprechauns, fairies—they lead a merry chase, and then, after alighting on a stump in some idyllic glade, evanesce, leaving the covetous with the echo of a laugh, alone in the middle of a darkening pine forest, to be tracked and slaughtered by more malign ogres. These are not the talking animals of pastoral fable—the grasshopper who, watching schoolchildren net a magnificently meretricious butterfly, concludes: "*Pour vivre heureux, vivons cachés.*" (To live happily, we must live in hiding.) These are the creatures of Celtic forest panic, and they issue from deep in the collective psyche. In the Jura, the mountainous forested region that straddles the French and Swiss border, the reigning numen is the *vouivre*, a snake with a seductress's head that haunts secluded torrents. The *vouivre*, according to Jurassien legend, appears in a cloud of mist, tempts unwary hikers to the riverbanks with a bejewelled ring, and then sucks them to their deaths in the icy waters. As a creature of myth, rather than fable, the *vouivre* illustrates no clear moral point: rather, it is an incarnation of deep-seated fears, unavowed desires, and wisdom that must not be forgotten. Like any myth that is authentic—and I use the term advisedly—the myth of the *vouivre* is beyond possession.

This is the story of those who would seek to grasp a myth: collectors of spoons, eBay auctioneers, competing distillers of essences, and (not to exclude myself from the list of the covetous) territorial writers. The myth in question is liquid, and its pursuers are chasing a magic vial that, depending on the play of light, veers between iridescent blue, milky yellow, jaundiced green, and an opaque opaline. The names attached to the legend are suitably ominous: *Grabkraut*, wormwood, hogsmack, α-thujone, *chernobyl*. Only one term, *absinthe*—French for both the liqueur and the flowering herb from which it is distilled—is sonorous enough to seduce one to the river's edge to drink.

I've wanted to try absinthe ever since I first saw its name in print.

It must have been in one of those stories of expatriate life that I devoured as a teenager. Was it an allusion, already nostalgic, to pre-war life in one of Henry Miller's Parisian confessionals? A sensuous mention of a Green Fairy in a volume of Anaïs Nin's diaries? Probably neither. By the time the Lost Generation made it to Paris and started their serious drinking, the *belle époque* idyll of *poètes maudits* and decadents had already been ravaged by mustard gas and shell shock, and absinthe had been banned in France for almost a decade. In 1920, the resourceful Ernest Hemingway discovered it was still available in Spain, a country known for its devil-may-care attitude to public health. "One cup of it," the hero of *For Whom the Bell Tolls* recalled, "took the place of the evening papers, of all the old evenings in cafés, of all the chestnut trees that would be in bloom now this month." But a terse entry in one of Hemingway's journals was more suggestive of debauched youth-hostel antics: "Got tight last night on absinthe and did knife tricks. Great success shooting the knife underhand into the piano."

Absinthe, then, was a symbol of waking dreams and excessive behaviour, of a lost era of Bohemian community and clandestinity. When I was in my thirties and could afford to travel, I learned they'd never stopped drinking absinthe in Barcelona. Mary, a Scottish artist who'd been living in Spain for years, agreed to be my guide to the Barrio Chino, the infamous warren of narrow streets where Jean Genet set *A Thief's Journal* and Salvador Dalí went slumming.

"Absinthe?" She whistled. "That's brain-damage stuff!"

Which didn't stop her, I noticed, from drinking it. We went on a late-night pub-crawl, which involved jostling for counter space with prostitutes and taxi drivers at a bar called Kentucky, listening to Edith Piaf on the jukebox at the Bar Pastis—a refuge for home-sick Parisians—and watching aging transvestites at a cabaret called El Cangrejo, "The Crab." At each stop, we knocked back a glass of absinthe, which in Spain seemed to be a licorice-flavoured aperitif that turned cloudy green when mixed with water. At the last bar, the agreeably dilapidated Marsella, an elaborate ritual was involved. After soaking sugar cubes in the transparent, oily-looking liquid, poising them on a three-tined fork, and lighting them on fire until the alcohol burned off, we dissolved the caramelized sugar in the pure absinthe. Topped up with cold water, our brandy glasses became the crucible for the now-familiar alchemy of opacity, and the burnt sugar leavened the bitter herbal bite. As Mary and I chatted, a Catalan drummer with a sleeveless Slayer T-shirt sat down at our table. He started shouting out the name of obscure grindcore bands, and when I tired of responding with the appropriate upraised index-finger-and-pinky devil gesture, he made a clumsy feint at my forehead with his absinthe fork. Then he fell backwards off his chair. Then he fell asleep.

I leaned back, well pleased with myself: I was not only drunk on the legendary Green Fairy, I was having a real experience of gritty Spanish Bohemia. Mary, who knew the Barrio Chino well, was quick to disillusion me. "Most of the people in here are tourists, you know." I looked around: the other tables were indeed occupied by hipsters in their twenties, most of them shouting at each other in English. The surly barman was a big redhead with an Australian accent. It was the kind of ersatz expat scene you could find in Prague, Antwerp, Reykjavik, or whatever other European city happened to be hip that year. Fortunately, I was drunk enough not to quibble about authenticity. I'd tracked down my absinthe; a teenage dream had been fulfilled.

I wrote an article about the experience, which appeared in *Salon.com* and *The Face*. One of the editors asked the inevitable question: "Are you sure you had *authentic* absinthe? I mean, the same kind that got Verlaine and Rimbaud off their tits?" I launched into a spirited defense of my intoxication: I'd had five glasses, and the experience was neither the sloppy, belly-bloating blottitude of beer nor the full body blow of bourbon: I'd felt quick-witted yet tranquilized, an alert mind observing a plastered body with amused detachment. Even the hangover was remarkable: I'd slept till noon and then taken the metro to the beach, where I lay prone in the sun, oozing toxins, until the jackals stopped chewing out my belly and the larvae had finished tunnelling through my brain.

"Authentic absinthe—definitely," I affirmed, with full journalistic authority. The piece ran, and was later anthologized. My claim to absinthe had been copyrighted. I felt, in a small way, as though I'd become a possessor of the myth.

That was in 1997. Over the next few years, I watched with a jaundiced eye as a full-blown absinthe fad developed. A group called Green Bohemia, made up of musicians and writers from the magazine *The Idler*, started importing a Czech brand named Hill's to England, a nation where the drink had never been popular enough to be banned. (I bought a bottle of Hill's in Vienna, and drank it one night with my girlfriend. It looked like Windex, tasted like Listerine, and came on like agricultural rum. Overproof vodka, we agreed, spiked with food colouring.) In the French Quarter and the West End, absinthe was promoted as the cocktail of the new millennium. Nicole Kidman swilled it between acts in the *belle époque* musical *Moulin Rouge*. Johnny Depp, playing a psychic detective, debauched himself on emerald absinthe and jet-black opium as he tracked Jack the Ripper in the movie *From Hell*. New brands—Absente, Versinthe, and the Hill's I'd found in Austria—started showing up on North American liquor-store shelves. Even Martha Stewart got in on the act, showing off her collection of absinthe-related memorabilia in *Vanity Fair*. I snickered at all the hype: Hill's and the brands being imported were nothing like the absinthe I'd had in Spain, still less like the drink of nineteenth-century boulevardiers and *flâneurs*. Robbed of their essential herbs, they were just high-test booze with curlicued labels; trendy and overpriced tipples for a passing novelty market.

Inevitably, though, questions assailed me. Had there been anything authentic about my pub-crawl in Barcelona? I started googling around the Internet. In the past few years, it turned out, an international absinthe underground had sprouted—stretching from Uruguay to New Zealand, by way of New Orleans and Manchester, and largely dominated by Goths. On louchelounge.com, makers of "hogsmack"—from the German *Hausgemacht*, or homebrew—traded tips, but even the most enthusiastic partisans wouldn't claim hallucinations or waking dreams. Reading their exchanges, which often degenerated into exchanges of porn, was like being in a rec room full of thirteen-year-olds, gagging on their first joint of loosely rolled homegrown, unable to agree whether they were stoned or not. Meanwhile, mediocre Spanish absinthe—which retails for €16 at the Madrid airport's duty-free shop—was being auctioned off for $75 a bottle on eBay.

One
Glass
and
You're
Dead

141

Here is one definition of authenticity: in a world of mass-produced and prefabricated experiences, it is the search for something original, issued from uninterrupted tradition, whose sacred and cult value—its aura—remains intact. Interestingly, though the Greek word αύθεντικός means "of first-hand authority, original," it was derived from the substantive αύθέντηδ, "one who does a thing himself, a principal, a master, an autocrat." Thus, authenticity can also imply a sense of elitism, prerogative, ownership. (When collectors speak of authenticity, they're usually talking about genuineness: a Wedgwood plate, say, with the verifiable imprimatur of the artisan.) Thanks to globalized tourism, where whole infrastructures have been established to sell simulacra of traditional experience—Swiss-folklore nights, ayahuasca trips in the Amazon, chaperoned hill-tribe treks to the border of Myanmar—it is now a suspect commodity. Inevitably, quotation marks descend on "authenticity," like mosquitoes on exposed shoulders.

With absinthe, authenticity seems to lie in the presence of a single herb: wormwood (from the German *wermut*, or man-root, a reference to unsubstantiated aphrodisiac qualities. Ukrainians call it *chernobyl*, a fact that gave some chiliasts pause, as the Apocalypse

According to St. John predicted a star named Wormwood would fall from the skies and poison a third of the earth's rivers). I started to research the science and history of its active ingredient, α-thujone, a constituent of chartreuse, Vick's VapoRub, vermouth, and Absorbine Jr. Some anecdotes suggested that in high doses it was a hallucinogen; medical studies, dating from the 1970s, that it acted on the brain's cannibinoid receptors—implying that the decadents of the *fin de siècle* demimonde were merely tripping on a groovy THC-like high. I found a book by a Parisian author who forcefully argued that the banning of absinthe, invented by a French doctor exiled in Switzerland, was a conspiracy of scientists of dubious merit and vintners determined to find an alternative scapegoat for the alcoholism then plaguing society. Finally, I downloaded an article from a journal called *Current Drug Discovery*, in which several types of absinthe had been subjected to a gas chromatography analysis. According to the author, the products being passed off as authentic in Prague and Barcelona contained virtually no α-thujone. Surprisingly, even a duly sampled and volatilized bottle of 1900-vintage Pernod Absinthe contained only trace amounts of the substance. The highest levels were found in a bottle of moonshine absinthe, purchased in a little valley in Switzerland; the paper referred to this high-octane brand as "La Bleue." Other Web sites described it as the "holy grail" of absinthe, adding, on the subject of its availability: "Bootlegged—Good luck!"

A miracle. I had localized authenticity—a quality whose chief attribute, in my experience, is that it always lies elsewhere. A little more probing revealed that an absinthe festival was scheduled in a village in western Switzerland on June 14. I bought a plane ticket, reserved a car, booked my hotel rooms. I would hunt down an authentic bottle of La Bleue, and re-establish my claim to the myth.

The journey, I knew, would have to start in France. Not only was a plane ticket to Paris cheaper, but absinthe, once France's national drink, was suddenly experiencing a revival—which was a distinct change from a few years ago. Whenever I'd asked about absinthe in the late 1990s, I got the same spitfire reaction from barmen and liquoristes: "*Absinthe? Non non non. C'est la boisson qui rend fou!*"—

"The drink that drives you mad"—the exact phrasing the anti-alcohol slogan temperance campaigners used in the 1890s. In his *Dictionary of Received Ideas*, Gustave Flaubert had neatly summed up the bourgeois consensus: "Absinthe: A super-potent poison: one glass and you're dead. Journalists drink it while they're writing their articles. Will surely be the end of the French army. Has killed off more soldiers than the Bedouins." Not to mention the legions of artists and poets decimated by the drink. In the collective memory, absinthe turned Paul Verlaine from Parnassian genius to Latin Quarter bum, sent Henri de Toulouse-Lautrec to the sanatorium, and drove Vincent van Gogh to make a lover's present of his own earlobe.

One
Glass
and
You're
Dead

143

Van Gogh ended his life in Auvers-sur-Oise, a riverside village that now lies within the orbit of Paris's northern suburbs. In the same lane he followed to carry his palette and easel to paint in the upper pastures, I park my car, and walk towards a modest building of buff-hued fieldstones and green shutters. An oversized spoon, shaped like the Eiffel Tower and bolted to the house's upper floor, announces that I've found the Absinthe Museum.

As I inspect the exhibits—sheet music celebrations and condemnations of the Green Fairy; tapering glasses with boll-shaped protuberances on their stems; a framed letter ordering 60 litres of absinthe for the famed Montmartre cabaret Le Chat Noir; metal trowels as sinister as superannuated gynecological instruments—I listen to the comments of older couples, all of them wearing straw boaters with black bands, part of a group on a steam-train outing from Versailles:

"It was a drug, *non*?" asks a white-haired woman.

"My grandfather used to drink it . . ." says another. "They banned it because it was too strong. Seventy per cent alcohol, that's dangerous!"

"Everything's dangerous!" a playful realist counters. "Look at corkscrews. You could stab yourself opening the bottle!"

I introduce myself to Marie-Claude Delahaye, the museum's curator, and France's leading historian of absinthe. We sit on a bench in the garden, planted with hyssop, fennel, and mint. Clad in an elegant but simple summer dress and a pearl necklace that sets off her coppery-red hair, Delahaye doesn't correspond to my image of a scholar of debauchery. She is petite, precise, pedantic—and intensely possessive of her obsession.

"One day, at the flea market at Clignancourt, I found this strange slotted spoon," she recalls. "The dealer said it was used to drink 'absinthe'; and explained that it was an alcohol that had been forbidden because it drove people crazy. These two words interested me: 'forbidden,' and 'crazy.'" Delahaye bought the spoon, which became the basis of the museum's collection, and in 1983 published a social history of absinthe. Ballasted by research skills she gained as an instructor of university-level cellular biology, her book was a surprising evocation of a lost episode in French cultural history.

"I was the first one to start talking about absinthe again," she insists. "It's thanks to my research, the connections I made between the artistic and political milieux, that people today say absinthe is 'mythical.'" Delahaye researched the story well: In 1805, Henri-Louis Pernod, who had inherited a recipe for an extract of wormwood from his father, set up a distillery in Pontarlier, a town in the French Jura. His team of salesmen spread it through France; it was particularly appreciated in hot southern cities such as Marseilles. In 1830, the first boats of the African Battalion left to conquer Algeria, with casks of absinthe in their holds: the regimental doctors hoped a strong alcohol would purify the local water and stave off malaria. Once they'd picked up the habit, the officers brought it back to the capital, where they'd meet at cafés on the Grands Boulevards. The Parisian bourgeoisie, in awe of the mustachioed conquerors of Africa, aped the elegant officers and took to ordering the alluring emerald drink.

By the 1860s, absinthe had became the ultimate symbol of sophisticated languor, and *l'heure verte*—the green hour, absinthe time— came to stretch from five to seven o'clock. Much of the appeal lay in the ritual. At military hangouts like the Café du Helder, on the Boulevard des Italiens, spidery-limbed absinthe fountains adorned the circular tables of the sidewalk terrace. Drinkers turned a spigot, and cool water trickled from a cylindrical upper chamber made of glass through one of four drooping spouts. At the rate of one drop a second, the water fell on a sugar cube poised on a pierced and filigreed spoon (an implement usually more spatulate than concave) that spanned the rim of a tapering, short-stemmed glass. As each drop of sugared water hit the shot of clear, 140-proof absinthe at the bottom of the glass, the essential plant oils—soluble in alcohol, but not in water—went opaque, streaking the liquid with opal or emerald meteoric trails. Gradually, as the ideal proportion of five parts water to one part absinthe was attained, the preparation went completely opaque. (This was the *louche*, or clouding, a term that in English still describes somebody whose background is a little murky.) It was slow, seductive alchemy, accompanied by the complex exhalation of the intermingled essences of anise, fennel, hyssop, and melissa. Beneath it all, like a toxic toadstool in a pine forest, lay the titillatingly maleficent odour of acrid wormwood. It was a ritual as irresistible as bitter Vietnamese coffee dripping over sweetened condensed milk; only, as the paraphernalia in Delahaye's museum suggests, far more aesthetic and intoxicating.

"It was an effect of fashion," says Delahaye. "It was the first time women, who didn't consume much liquor until then, really started drinking in public. It was also the first time people had tasted fresh plant flavours in an aperitif; the first time they added cold water to their drink. The whole ritual—the spoons, the fountains, the tall glasses—corresponded to a century of new technologies, of new creativity." In the 1870s, as the phylloxera aphid chewed its way through the nation's grapevines, the price of wine shot up, and absinthe, at three sous a glass, became the official beverage of Bohemia. Toulouse-Lautrec mixed his with cognac, a cocktail he called the "*tremblement de terre*"—the earthquake—which he hid in a vial in his walking stick. Edmond de Goncourt, the boulevardier and diarist, liked to mix his with tincture of opium. Alfred Jarry, author of *Ubu Roi*, and inventor of 'pataphysics, the science of imaginary solutions, took his neat, starting with a shot at ten in the morning. A complete aesthete, Jarry once dyed his face and hands green, and boasted of finishing the day with an absinthe spiked with vinegar and a single drop of ink. (He considered one absinthe the equivalent of a loaf of bread, two the equal of a steak. And, if one is looking for a moral, died at the age of thirty-four, of alcohol-aggravated tuberculosis.)

If impoverished artists could afford absinthe, then so could working people. The real drinkers asked for doubles, and gradually reduced the amount of water they added, until, like Jarry, they were drinking the dreaded *purée*: virtually pure, 140-proof absinthe. If it had all been Pernod, which was made with high-quality alcohol distilled from grapes, the consequences might not have been so severe. But popular absinthe was also cheap absinthe, made with industrial alcohol rendered from beets or molasses, and distillers—there were almost a thousand different brands by the 1890s—added toxic adulterants like cupric acetate (to provide the green tint) and antinomy chloride (to encourage the *louche*). Doctors started to notice manifestations of a new disease: *absinthisme*. Its symptoms included delusions, tremors, and epileptic fits. From a modern perspective, their diagnoses look a little shaky. In a famous experiment, a guinea pig, injected with the equivalent of 7 litres of absinthe in a single shot, went into convulsions and died. (But in another, a frog, given a choice between aquaria filled with distilled water, salt water, and one spiked with absinthe, chose to live in the booze. A natural affinity for green, perhaps.) A pair of intrepid empiricists ingested a gramme of wormwood oil—the equivalent of 200 shots of pure absinthe—on empty stomachs, without ill effect. Nonetheless, absinthe was fingered by temperance groups as "epilepsy in a bottle." Supported by the wine industry—which by the turn of the century was suffering from overproduction and an inability to move its product—they made absinthe the scapegoat for all of the problems of alcoholism. There was no question that in the France of Zola's *L'Assomoir*, alcohol had become a huge social problem: in Paris alone there were 33,000 bars and drink sellers (five times as many as in London or Chicago) compared to only 17,000 bakeries. But absinthe was rapidly and unfairly convicted: what really should have been on trial were the social conditions—monotonous factory labour, overcrowded and insalubrious homes, lack of affordable organized leisure activities—that drove people to the cafés and bars in the first place.

The Belgians were the first in Europe to ban absinthe, in 1906. A horrible crime sealed its fate in Switzerland: after drinking two glasses of absinthe, a day labourer killed his pregnant wife with a rifle, then shot their two infant daughters. (The fact that he had downed 5 litres of homemade white wine before he started on the absinthe was ignored by local officials, probably because the crime had occurred in the Vaud, a wine-producing region.) Though hardly consumed outside of Jean Lafitte's Old Absinthe House in New Orleans—except as a key ingredient in Antoine's oysters Rockefeller—the drink was banned by the U.S. Department of Agriculture in 1912. By the time the first posters declaring the absinthe ban were plastered on the walls of France's prefectures on August 14, 1914, the prohibition almost seemed superfluous. Two weeks before, a far more efficient killer of the working class had come along: France had entered the First World War.

One
Glass
and
You're
Dead

147

"Absinthe doesn't make you crazy," sighs Delahaye as she sells tickets to another wave of straw-hatted tourists. "I've dug up forty years' worth of medical papers, and none of the serious ones mention any 'hallucinatory effects.' It's true, the plant itself, wormwood, isn't entirely innocent. It was known to produce epileptic-style crises; but that was in extreme cases, of very heavy drinkers." She tells me she was shocked when she learned that Green Bohemia was passing off the Czech brand Hill's to the ravers and lads in London as the real thing. "It was pure commerce! That horrible fluorescent-green color . . . I've tried Hill's, it doesn't even louche when you add water!" When George Rowley, a beer importer and one of the founders of Green Bohemia, paid an unannounced visit to the museum, Delahaye went for his throat.

"He didn't speak French, but his wife translated," recalls Delahaye. "I told him it was utter intellectual dishonesty to superimpose all of French cultural history on a product that clearly had nothing to do with absinthe. His wife seemed to agree. Three months later, I got a call: he'd thought about it, and agreed." Rowley and Delahaye decided to collaborate on a French-style absinthe, one based on a nineteenth-century recipe. Today, the Green Bohemia crew still sells Hill's via the Internet, but they've added Delahaye's 68% La Fée Absinthe—with a psychedelic image of a single aureoled eye on the label—to their Web site. Delahaye sells a lower-alcohol version, La Fée Verte, in the gift shop of her museum.

Among many other absinthe-related items. "If you see it here, that means it's for sale," she's constantly reminding visitors. In addition to the six different volumes she's authored, Delahaye sells postcards, absinthe spoons, and reproductions of vintage posters to the never-ending stream of day trippers. I buy one of her books, as well as a small bottle of La Fée Verte, and wait for the offer of a tasting. It never comes. Before I leave, I ask her, as a connoisseur, whether she's noticed absinthe affects her differently from other alcohols.

"I've never had enough at one time to feel the slightest effect." She pauses for a girlish giggle. "Apart, maybe, from feeling a little warm behind the ears. I own some nineteenth-century bottles, but there's no question of opening them—they're collector's items. However, one time, this fellow brought me a bottle of vintage Jules Pernod, and there was still a little left in the bottle. We tried it. It was very aromatic, a beautiful colour, and there was a very strong aftertaste of plants. I didn't necessarily like the flavour—there was too much anise. The pleasure was mostly intellectual."

Delahaye's definition of authenticity is quite specific: the only real absinthe is a high-quality absinthe, made to a specific recipe. It is, after all, a symbol of French cultural history, of a bygone era of elegance and creative fervor. "I approached the whole nineteenth century through an absinthe spoon," she told me. And now, as a vendor and a museum creator, she cultivates her own interest in the myth. To settle for a cheap, inferior brand—as most impoverished artists of the nineteenth century were forced to do—would be a betrayal of its heritage as an elegant aperitif of the boulevards. And to confess to an interest in its potential for intoxication—well, that would be vulgar sensationalism and thrill-seeking.

Back at my hotel, I pour myself a shot of La Fée Absinthe. It clouds minty green, and fills the room with the smell of lemon, anise, and hyssop. As it contains less than the infinitesimal European maximum legal levels of wormwood, a couple of drinks leave me something less than tipsy, and somewhat more than weary. Perhaps this is what Delahaye meant by "intellectual pleasure."

The next morning, I explore Auvers-sur-Oise, a village totally given over to promoting another myth: the tragedy of Vincent van

Gogh, the genius-unrecognized-in-his-lifetime. (The area, it turns out, is also a centre for Marxist opponents to the current regime in Iran. A few days after I leave, 1,200 policemen and gendarmes in bulletproof vests swoop down on Auvers-sur-Oise and arrest 159 moudjahidin. In spite of her elegant efforts to make of her past *gloire* a vast museum, France can't quite conceal her present reality: she is a twenty-first-century nation inelegantly coping with a large and vibrant immigrant population.) I queue with a dozen tourists and pay €5 to spend ten minutes in the miserable attic room where the artist died on a narrow, straw-stuffed mattress. Then I walk down a long straight road through a cow pasture to the enclosed cemetery where his corpse lies buried. Set against a stone wall, the simple headstone reads: ICI REPOSE VINCENT VAN GOGH 1853–1890. Legend has it that when he was exhumed, to be buried next to his brother, Theo, the roots of the white cedar—also known as the thuja, a tree known for its high levels of α-thujone—were found entwined around his coffin. One of the German terms for wormwood is *Grabkraut*—the plant of the tombs.

One
Glass
and
You're
Dead

149

Van Gogh wouldn't have been able to afford quality Pernod absinthe, let alone Delahaye's La Fée; he drank rotgut, and apparently had to be restrained from gulping down his own turpentine. Over the soil next to his grave, I upend what's left of Delahaye's version of "authentic" absinthe. I'm confident Vincent wouldn't have refused a shot of the expensive stuff. But I'm pretty sure he would have complained it lacked kick.

Leaving the Autoroute du soleil, which bores southeast from Paris through Burgundy, I find myself flashing past the trunks of the larch, spruce, and pine trees of the Jura—an area that, thanks to ongoing rural depopulation, is actually more forested now than it was in the nineteenth century. I'm not surprised to read in my Michelin guide that the Jura was not only an international centre of pipe-carving and wooden toy–making, but also the birthplace of a certain Charles Sauria, inventor of the matchstick.

What strikes me as stranger, though, is that the Jura—the coldest part of the country—is also the French cradle of absinthe and

Pernod, drinks more associated with café terrace life and summer afternoons than Alpine eaux-de-vie. In 1905, there were twenty-five absinthe distilleries in the town of Pontarlier alone, producing 10 million litres a year, and one-third of its residents made their living in the manufacture of absinthe. After the ban, the Pernod factory was commandeered as a military hospital, and wounded soldiers recovered on makeshift beds made of empty absinthe crates. Today, it is owned by a Swiss multinational, and turns out millions of packages of Nesquick instant breakfast a year.

On this particular June day, the region is suffering through a heat wave, and I figure an absinthe sipped on one of the terraces of Pontarlier's long, boutique-lined main street would be a civilized end to a long drive. I glimpse absinthe fountains in local shop windows, slotted spoons and vintage glasses in the antique stores. At the Brasserie de la Poste, when I ask a waiter in a white shirt and a broad black tie for an absinthe, he curtly replies: "We don't have any absinthe."

I'd forgotten. Strictly speaking, absinthe is not yet legal in Europe. Hence the euphemistic nomenclature: it is imported from the Czech Republic as Absinth, ordered as Absenta in Spain, and sold under brand names such as Oxygénée and Absente in France. I change tactics, and ask instead for a "François Guy." The waiter shows me a bottle labelled "*Spiritueux aux extraits de plantes d'absinthe*," and I nod my head. The Pontarlier version is made without sugar, which means it qualifies as a bitter, and can contain—under European law—over three times the amount of thujone as other brands. Even Marie-Claude Delahaye acknowledged the excellence of François Guy, and compared it to vintage absinthe. On the terrace, I'm presented with a shot of transparent, yellow-tinged liquid in a tall glass and all the requisite paraphernalia: an absinthe spoon, a Perrier glass full of ice cubes, and a bottle of water.

Ordering a François Guy in Pontarlier is as close as you can get to drinking an old-style absinthe in public in France. To my left, a pair of Tour de France wannabes are working on plates of steak frites, their thighs and calves burnt as pink as the rosé they're sharing. To my right, the waiter stoops to give a plastic water bowl to a panting terrier at the feet of a well-dressed *dame*. I unwrap a sugar cube, strain water through it, and watch the liquid louche creamy white. The taste is slightly bitter, highly herbal, with an appealing menace lurking beneath the anise. I am pleased; I feel like I'm tasting something authentic; I briefly bathe in the aura of a long-forbidden indulgence. The anachronistic mood is ruined as a girl in a headscarf walks down the sidewalk, and a teenager in a slow-moving car leans out the window and yells: "*Couvre ton visage!*"—"Cover your face!"—instantly recalling me to the France of the racist Front National, chauvinistic xenophobia, and the twenty-first century. And another detail gnaws at my mind: François Guy contains only 45 per cent alcohol—far below the proof of its venerable ancestors.

The next morning, I'm sitting before François Guy, the man. "My great-grandfather, Armand Guy, started making absinthe in 1890," he begins. "And now I'm making absinthe exactly the same way he made his." Guy grew up in this distillery—a cluster of houses with peaked tiled roofs and white facades on a quiet residential street—and we're in his office, a slightly intimidating setting, as the wall behind me is festooned, from floor to ceiling, with swords, rifles, and helmets. Guy himself, his head shaved to stubble, six foot three in loafers, with powerful forearms, and a prominent chin, exudes the kind of self-assurance that must come from belonging to an industrial dynasty in what was once a one-industry town. He dismisses Czech absinthe: "Attention: Poison. That stuff is pure shit. There isn't a single gram of wormwood or anise in it. You might as well put it in your gas tank." He mocks the European Union's laws on thujone content: "It's utter hypocrisy. You can only call it absinthe if it has 35 milligrams of thujone a litre or more. But if you do call it absinthe, it's illegal." He makes short work of nineteenth-century claims of toxicity: a conspiracy between doctors and the wine merchants. "You'd have to drink 6 litres a day before you started having problems with thujone. The issue wasn't the wormwood, it was the percentage of alcohol. People were drinking 60 millilitres of absinthe at a go, at 68 per cent! And this was after work, on an empty stomach! It's the equivalent of drinking six modern aperitifs in a single glass. No wonder those artists were completely cracked." And while singling out thujone as inoffensive and alcohol as the harmful ingredient—hence his brand's modest 45 per cent by volume—he also boasts the thujone content of his brand is higher than any other on the market. "We're currently at 33 milligrams a litre. Any more, we'd be in trouble."

I'm given a quick tour of the factory. In one corner, nylon sacks filled with Spanish anise are stacked to the ceiling. Employees in blue overalls seal crates of cherries preserved in alcohol. We come to the heart of the distillery: a copper still, connected by a swan-necked pipe to a refrigerating unit. "We load a vat in the centre of the still with alcohol, wormwood, anise, and other herbs, heat them and let them soak overnight," explains Guy. "Then we boil them, and the essential oils evaporate and pass through the pipe with the alcohol, where they gather and pass through water-cooled condenser coils." From a pipe, a clear liquid trickles from the bottom of the cylindrical condenser into an oak cask: it's pure, high-proof absinthe, and the odour is intoxicating. "I've already distilled 2,000 litres this morning. Most of the Spanish brands don't even bother to distill. They make what we call *absinthe-bâton*." Absinthe made with a stick. "They add ready-made wormwood extract to alcohol and stir. That's why they taste so bitter—and it's the acidity and impurities that give you a headache the next morning."

Up a flight of stairs, Guy flings open a door to a sunlit backyard. A garden is planted with peonies, rhubarb—and hundreds of wormwood plants; it's the first time I've seen the living herb. For all its attendant mythology, it's a dowdy-looking leafy shrub that rises no more than waist high. "Rub one of the leaves," insists Guy. Grey-green on top, whitish below, the intricately lobulate leaf feels silky between my finger and thumb. "Now smell your thumb." The medicinal odour, of the toadstool hidden in the pine forest, emanates from my pores. I touch the tip of my tongue to the leaf, and can feel my face contract; it is as bitter as earwax. "This is just a show garden," says Guy. "I have 55,000 plants in a nearby field. We use goats to keep the weeds away; they won't touch the wormwood, it's too bitter."

Guy's claim on authenticity lies in these plants. By growing his own wormwood—a fact prominently proclaimed on every label—he's hoping to make Pontarlier's absinthe a veritable product of the Jurassien *terroir*, and thus reclaim from Iberian savages and Balkan cossacks a drink that is quintessentially French. I ask him if he plans to make a demand for an *appellation d'origine contrôlée* (AOC), the official designation that means a genuine Roquefort can only come from the caves of Roquefort, a real Champagne from the vineyards of Champagne. "It's already under way. We put in our request a year and a half ago. Strictly speaking, an AOC wouldn't be possible, because some of the ingredients—the anise, in particular—can't be grown here. It would have to be an *appellation d'origine réglementée*, an AOR. Either way, it's a guarantee of quality. Say you come from another country, you know nothing about absinthe, you want to buy the best. All you'll have to do is look for the AOR label. It's like a business card; it puts a necktie around every bottle." It would also relegate foreign absinthes—the Spanish and Czech brands that Guy despises—to second rank. The absinthe of the French Jura, made according to ancestral recipes with wormwood grown in Pontarlier, would be the only acceptable brand; all others would be imitators—the equivalent of vulgar Polish *méthode champenoise* versus a true Dom Perignon.

We repair to a corner of the distillery, where a young couple, part of a prematurely jolly crew of bus tourists, are enjoying a late-morning tasting. Their baby, planted on top of an upended oak barrel, knocks a lump of sugar off a spoon into a glass of absinthe; I'm surprised she's not reeling from the fumes. François Guy proudly pulls out a bottle of his eponymous aperitif, and shows me how it veers from transparent yellow to milky white with the addition of water. I praise the louche, but confess my mission is to seek out a bottle of La Bleue. Which leads me to the question I've been saving: Wasn't absinthe first made in Switzerland? And if so, how can he possibly hope to claim it for France?

"Listen," he says, abruptly. "The absinthe that was known the world over didn't come from Switzerland. It came from Pontarlier." He goes to his office, returns with a book published by the Pernod distillery in 1896, and reads aloud: "'In spite of the name Swiss absinthe by which it often goes, the famous liqueur is of French origin. At the end of the last century, a French doctor, Dr. Ordinaire, exiled in Switzerland . . . did not scorn panaceas, [and] employed one in particular, the elixir of wormwood, composed of aromatic plants whose secret only he possessed.'" Guy closes the book with satisfaction. "Even if it was first made in Switzerland, the inventor himself was French." Nonetheless, Guy reaches behind a row of bottles of his own *spiritueux*, and brings out an unlabelled litre-bottle of clear liquid. "I bought this in Switzerland. Look, when you add water, it turns blue. French absinthes, real absinthes, turn green or opal." He's right: when I hold the glass to the light, I immediately notice a captivating bluish tinge.

I also can't help noticing that Guy keeps his bottle of Swiss absinthe on the top shelf.

The rivers of the Jura are as elusive as the mythical *vouivre*. They appear dramatically in mist-filled mountain caverns, meander elaborately through narrow valleys, and disappear abruptly into the karst—to re-emerge, dozens of kilometres away, often with completely different names. The Doubs (from the Latin *dubius*, or hesitant), which arcs through the centre of Pontarlier, is one such river. In 1901, the Pernod factory was lashed by lightning, and the bolt cracked in the basement warehouse, igniting a hogshead of absinthe. A quick-witted employee, fearing an ethyl alcohol–fuelled hecatomb, opened the vats, emptying a million litres of Pernod's highest-quality absinthe into the Doubs. As the factory burned, the river took on a distinctly opaline hue, and between turns at the hose, firemen filled their helmets with a premixed dose of the Green Fairy. Two and a half days later, a geologist rushed several kilometres downstream, and discovered that an entirely different watercourse was redolent of anise—proving definitively that the River Loue was merely a resurgence of the Doubs.

While the Jurassien waters dip into grottoes and slip beneath frontiers easily, crossing the border isn't always so easy for humans. Suddenly, on the road east from Pontarlier, I come to the Swiss border post, and a grim-faced customs agent with the bluest of gimlet glares motions me to the side of the road and demands my passport. A German shepherd on a leash approaches, sniffs my tires. The guard has me empty my trunk, and carry my bags into a narrow room, where a younger colleague watches as he pats down the legs of my pants and probes the seams of my backpack with nimble fingers. I'm instructed to turn my pockets inside out. And then, in another bag, he discovers a bottle of absinthe and a spoon, a gift from François Guy.

"Ah!" The slightest of smiles crosses his face. "You're doing the absinthe trail!" The tension lifts. "Go ahead: you can close your bags." Outside, I wait until a stocky woman with a utility belt finishes reattaching the door panels she's unscrewed from my car.

"Welcome to Switzerland . . ." I mutter to the customs agent, a little wryly.

"You have to understand," he counters. "You're a young man, in a rented car, with a Paris licence plate. We get a lot of drug traffic here."

In Switzerland, French absinthe obviously doesn't qualify as anybody's idea of a drug.

As I pull back onto the highway, I remember I have left Europe; Switzerland never joined the Union, and has its own constitution, its own laws, its own quirks. I haven't driven more than half a kilometre along Swiss roads before I glimpse my first mythical creature: a rosy-cheeked gnome.

It's Happy, planted outside a gas station, flanked by the Walt Disney version of Snow White.

After the adrenaline rush of crossing another frontier, euphoria sets in: I've finally made it to the birthplace of La Bleue. I'm in the Val-de-Travers, literally, the valley that lies athwart, crossways, its bottom carved from east to west, rather than the Alpine standard of north to south, by the eccentric course of L'Areuse. It is part of the French-speaking canton of Neuchâtel, whose relationship with the rest of Switzerland is a troubled one. The Traversines call the Swiss Germans the "*Neinsagers*," or "no-sayers." In 1992, their compatriots said "No" to joining Europe—which was perhaps their right. A century ago, however, they said "No" to absinthe—and for this, the Traversines will never forgive them. The Val-de-Travers styles itself an autonomous republic; once, they even set up barriers outside the tunnel that leads to Neuchâtel and demanded to see the passports of Swiss Germans. On the Val-de-Travers Web site, Article 7 of the constitution of the *République Autonome du Val-de-Travers* enshrines both the freedom to complain and the right to distill.

Had I been on this road a century ago, the entire valley bottom would have been coloured greyish-blue with wormwood. The herb has always grown wild in the valley's upper meadows, and, like many rich and intoxicating substances—opium poppies, milk chocolate, LSD, Gruyère—its potential was first developed by the industrious and inventive Swiss. In spite of the spurious evidence of Gallic origins shown me by François Guy (surely a national impulse to assume that all that is civilized in the world is French), more serious scholarship shows absinthe probably first trickled from the still of a certain Henriette Henriod, from the Traversine village of Couvet, in the mid-eighteenth century. The French-born Dr. Ordinaire was aptly named: he invented nothing more extraordinary than a tonic made of chicory—an ersatz coffee extract.

The first written recipe for absinthe—probably purchased from Mme Henriod—which dates from 1794, was found in the record books of the Swiss Abram-Louis Perrenoud, who changed his name to Pernod when he set up his first distillery in Couvet. (The Pernod factory in Pontarlier was established a decade later, to satisfy French demand and circumvent customs duties.) For over a century, the Val-de-Travers owed its prosperity to the planting, harvesting, and drying of wormwood, and the distilling of some of the world's best absinthe. With the prohibition of 1910, the Swiss government ordered the absinthe fields plowed under, and the more pedestrian industries of dairy farming and clockmaking took over. The blue liquid went underground—yet another Jurassien stream disappearing into the karst—only to burble up again in stills hidden in barns, broom closets, and attics. For 250 years, this has been the one place on earth with an authentic, uninterrupted history of absinthe making. Add to that a century-old tradition of clandestinity, independence, and the camaraderie born of flouting a prohibition generally and gleefully acknowledged to be absurd, and you get the Val-de-Travers—a microstate that lives up to its name: the valley where everything is a little askew.

As long as you speak a bit of French, and don't look like a cop, it's not too hard to track down a bottle of La Bleue in the canton. After a dinner of fried lake perch, I head into the hills north of the village of

Couvet. I've been advised to avoid the establishments on the main road; they tend to be wary of strangers and tourists. A half-dozen cars are parked outside a modest, brown-roofed restaurant that backs onto a lake. The dining room is empty, but a group of sun-pinkened farmers seated at a corner table watch me approach the tall, dark-haired woman behind the bar.

"*Une petite bleue?*" I venture.

The room goes silent. The barlady looks me up and down—notes my longish hair and foreign accent—and seems to make up her mind. Disappearing into a cupboard behind the bar, she returns with an unlabelled litre bottle, and pours a shot into a Duralex glass. I take a seat at the table next to the farmers, and they watch my technique as I pour chilled water from a ceramic yellow container into the liquid and observe its louche. I glimpse the telltale aura of blue around the edges, the guarantee that I'm about to drink the world's most authentic and deadly absinthe.

Slowly, I lift the glass to my lips.

*A Brief Digression on the Neurotoxicity of Thujone

The active ingredient in absinthe, α-thujone, is a convulsant neurotoxin, which in low doses can provoke trembling, vertigo, and headaches. At high and repeated doses, the symptoms include memory loss, irritability, depression, loss of motor control, convulsions, irreversible nerve damage, and, eventually, death.

But then, as the Russian chemist Dmitry Mendeleyev noted: "There is no such thing as a dangerous element, only dangerous quantities." Taken in high enough doses, sugar (the active ingredient in marshmallows) can be a fatal toxin.

The most extreme, and widely quoted, contemporary estimate of the quantity of thujone in nineteenth-century absinthe, at 260 milligrams per litre, comes from a biochemist named Wilfred Arnold at the University of Kansas Medical Center. When I asked Dr. Arnold how he'd arrived at this figure, he told me he'd based it on an 1855 book that gave the total amount of dried wormwood in a typical recipe. Other scientists have questioned Arnold's estimates; they believe that it's unlikely all of the thujone in the dried wormwood would make its way into the final distillate. Actual gas-chromatography analyses of unopened bottles of vintage absinthe show as little as 6 milligrams of thujone per litre. Even taking Arnold's estimate as accurate, the amount of α-thujone in an average serving of vintage absinthe would only be 7.8 milligrams per glass. To put this in perspective, the no effect—in other words, safe—dose of thujone in an average-sized human being is 8.75 milligrams per day.

Dr. Arnold referred me to the work of B. Max, a retired pharmacist, as bolstering his research. However, when I looked up the recommended reference in the journal *Trends in the Pharmacological Sciences*, the author estimated that there was probably only 2 to 4 milligrams of thujone in a glass of vintage absinthe, adding this was "far below the level at which acute pharmacological effects are observed." Even the intrepid pair of nineteenth-century French scientists—the ones who consumed the equivalent of two hundred glasses in a single sitting without ill effect—acknowledged that wormwood essence was present in absinthe in only "homeopathic doses."

The most recent, and intriguing, research on thujone comes from the environmental toxicology lab at the University of California at Berkeley. According to a study supervised by John E. Casida, thujone can block a receptor called GABA-A, which normally inhibits the firing of neurons. Thus, thujone, by blocking the blocker, allows neurons to fire more freely. This provides the stimulating effect, that sense of lucidity within my drunkenness I noticed—or thought I noticed—on my pub crawl in Spain. There is some speculation that alcohol and thujone may have a synergistic effect, boosting the sense of stimulation.

Dr. Casida's paper concluded that "current low levels of α-thujone . . . in absinthe are of much less toxicological concern than the ethanol content." In other words, the booze will knock you out before the wormwood will touch you. However, he believes that there may have been enough thujone in some nineteenth-century absinthes to have a discernible neurological effect. "A friend of mine picked up a bottle of Pernod at auction," he tells me. "It probably dated from the 1880s." Did you open the bottle? I ask. "Oh yes,

I had a glass, for purposes of a celebration with my friend. You could almost smell the thujone in it . . ." He declines to comment on how it made him feel.

Having soberly reviewed the current literature on thujone research, my conclusion is the following: over a hundred years after they first started, scientists are still injecting mice with ludicrously massive doses of wormwood, and the mice are still convulsing and dying.

And, more to the point: if a senior toxicologist is willing to belt back a shot of high-test absinthe, then so am I.

I finish my first glass of La Bleue: it is slightly sweet, with a strong flavour of anise, but also an aroma of freshly cut flowers I've never encountered before. The farmers, who are looking through a flag catalogue, talking tractors, and vaguely following the score of a lacklustre Neuchâtel football game, watch me closely. I ask the barlady for another.

One
Glass
and
You're
Dead

159

As she pours a second shot, the old guy next to me nods approval: "It's better for your balance if you have two. After all, you have two legs!"

"Unfortunately," I tell him, "I also have four wheels. I have to watch out tonight."

"Absinthe helps you drive better!" another farmer shouts, and there's laughter from the next table. They start talking among themselves, and I catch snatches of conversation: "He'd have to drink five or six of them before he really felt it . . . yes, but then he'd have to sleep in his car . . . the key is the thujone, the French stuff doesn't have any . . . Do you remember Jean? He'd start each day at 9 a.m. with an absinthe . . ."

I ask my neighbour if it's difficult to get your hands on a full bottle in these parts.

"You want one now?" he says, *sotto voce*. "I can get you some tonight . . ."

But I refuse his offer. I figure I should ask a few questions, do a little shopping around, before I start filling my trunk with full bottles. I bid adieu to the room; and they watch me leave, a little disappointed, I think, that I don't lurch into the door jamb as I leave.

The drive back to my hotel along the lonely, winding road is slow and spooky. Thick tufts of fog have descended on the dark mountain meadows; entering one, I feel like I've driven straight into a glass of cloudy absinthe. In my peripheral vision, I glimpse spectral beings lining the roadside. No *vouivres*, though; only sleeping dairy cows, collapsed and folded for the night.

I have an appointment at the Blackmint Distillery in Môtiers the next afternoon. Yves Kübler, the scion of a distilling family who is making the only legal form of absinthe in the Val-de-Travers, meets me in the garden. He is a stocky young man in his thirties, as distracted and emphatic as François Guy.

Switzerland, one of the first nations to suppress absinthe, is now cautiously moving towards legalization. The latest revision of the constitution removed Article 33, which until then had banned its production. But Switzerland's agriculture laws still prohibit its sale, and set the maximum legal limit of thujone in any drink at 10 milligrams per litre; for the moment, Kübler is forced to sell his product as an "*Extrait d'Absinthe.*" It is essentially a commercial version of moonshine La Bleue. I point out that even the legal French absinthe has three times more thujone than his.

Kübler responds by promulgating his own definition of authenticity. "François Guy's absinthe is not absinthe! All he uses is wormwood, fennel, and anise. And a real absinthe has at least seven different ingredients. It's proven historically. I use nine plants in mine!" He pours me a shot from a half-litre bottle; there is indeed a complex herbal bouquet, though it's less heady than the glass of La Bleue I had the night before. Kübler has launched his own attempt to claim the absinthe of Val-de-Travers as intellectual property, lodging a demand for an IGP—an *indication géographique protégée*—the Swiss equivalent of an AOR. "Our historical dossier is solid as rock. The Pernod family was Swiss; the first distillery was in Couvet. My great-grandfather founded this distillery in 1863. We're going to call it 'Fée Verte de Val-de-Travers, Veritable Absinthe.'"

François Guy is growing his own wormwood, I point out. Where does yours come from? "There are now four growers in the Val-de-

Travers, and I bought their entire crop of wormwood last year. I also import wormwood from Germany, which I resell to the pharmacies. Anybody who makes moonshine absinthe here is using German wormwood—and since it's grown in greenhouses, where there's no need for the plant to struggle against the cold and the heat, it produces less thujone. I've had clandestine bottles analyzed—they have ten times less thujone than mine does!" Kübler leans back in his chair, satisfied. Not only is the French version inauthentic; there's nothing especially interesting about the legendary, underground Bleue. He's confident that the Swiss authorities—disgusted by the fact that the French pinched the name Gruyère centuries ago—will vote to abrogate the law, allowing absinthe to become a product of the Swiss *terroir*. His final obstacle to selling his *extrait* as "Absinthe" will be removed; authenticity will be his.

One
Glass
and
You're
Dead

161

"Kübler?" says Pierre-André Delachaux, with a grimace. "What he makes isn't absinthe. *This*, this is absinthe." He waves his hand towards a green bottle embossed with a skull and crossbones (an antique bleach bottle, he explains) on the picnic table before us. We're sitting in his backyard, sipping absinthe from short-stemmed goblets. Tall, blue-eyed and yellow-bearded, with a balding pate lightly beaded with sweat on this hot afternoon, Delachaux stands up, raises a pottery pitcher above his head, and lets a long stream of water trickle from a narrow spout sculpted like a tiny boar's head. This, he explains, is the authentic Traversine method of preparing one's absinthe; it ensures there's more oxygen in the mix.

Delachaux, a teacher of high school French and history, is infamous in the canton. When he was a socialist deputy in the early 1980s, he had François Mitterrand, then president of France, served a soufflé glazed with absinthe at a dinner in one of Neuchâtel's leading hotels. A head of state had consumed a forbidden substance at an official function; the uproar was enormous. Delachaux survived (the next time he saw Mitterrand, the president said: "That matter of the absinthe—liquidated?"), but it's made him a public champion of the Traversine absinthe-making tradition. He runs the local museum in the town of Môtiers, where a room is devoted to absinthe, and has written several books and studies on the subject. When I mention all the claimants to authenticity I've encountered so far, Delachaux is scathing.

On François Guy: "It's absinthe in a hoopskirt. It's as if you decided to prance around in a top hat, with a cane and a cape. That's what the French like: folklore. They're trying to recreate old recipes, whereas here we have an uninterrupted tradition that goes back over two hundred years. And our tastes have evolved; our absinthe has changed over time. That's why we don't use a sugar cube; we've slowly added sugar to the mix." On Kübler's claims that his is the only authentic brand: "That guy says whatever suits his needs. Sometimes he says his stuff is the real, old-time absinthe; but when the authorities ask, he says it isn't absinthe at all, just a harmless liqueur. I call it decaffeinated absinthe." Delachaux, it turns out, is opposed to legalization. "If absinthe is legalized, two or three brands—probably Pernod in France, maybe Kübler here—will dominate the market. Right now, there are between sixty and eighty clandestine distillers in the Val-de-Travers, and they all have their own distinct recipes. Everybody here has their favourite. Legalize it, and gradually all that will disappear, and we'll be left with a single standard—the Coca-Cola of absinthe." It's a compelling, if familiar, argument: like the champions of Slow Food, he is defending gustatory biodiversity against standardized alcoholic monoculture.

But I sense that what Delachaux really values in his absinthe is its clandestinity, a trait intertwined with the history and character of the Val-de-Travers. "Some people say the Traversines are closed, but it's not true. We were always open to the world. Rousseau sought refuge here after he was exiled for writing *The Social Contract*. We always traded with France; later, we exported watches to China. But we are *résistants*, and our resistance expresses itself in one important form: absinthe. When absinthe was forbidden, this canton had only been part of Switzerland for sixty years. Until then, we had been independent. And all of a sudden, these Swiss Germans, who are still constantly messing with us politically, come along, launch a rigged trial against absinthe, and ban our drink! So quietly, absinthe went underground—and it's this resistance that interests me. For people here, absinthe corresponds to the pleasure of transgressing, the pleasure of offering. I'd be ashamed—and I'm not alone on this—to offer a visitor a glass of legal Kübler." I suggest to Delachaux he's being a little elitist. Before the prohibition, absinthe was a popular drink, cheap and widely available—like soft drinks today. "Perhaps," he says, "there is an elitist side to this. But not economically. The clandestine absinthe here is cheaper than the brands that Guy and Kübler are selling. I concede, however, that I'd like it to remain a little mysterious, a little underground. I think one has to merit one's absinthe."

I seem to have merited mine, because Delachaux pours me another long shot. "But frankly," he says, frowning, "I'm a little disappointed they served you absinthe at that bar last night. They should have refused you." I take his point. I am a tourist, after all—albeit one on a mission—and thus an agent of globalized culture, another potential underminer of local tradition. "Then you would have gone away, still intrigued, with the myth intact."

The myth, as it happens, is getting a little blurry in my mind—Delachaux's Bleue is mounting to my head. I can sense that I'm losing my command of the French subjunctive model, mixing up the genders of my nouns. But if there are only minute traces of low-quality German wormwood in the local hooch, as Kübler contends, is there anything, apart from the high degree of alcohol, that makes La Bleue any different from vodka or gin? "Nobody will tell you this," says Delachaux, lowering his voice, "but there is an effect in absinthe that you don't find in any other drink. And believe me, I've been drinking it for a long time now. After three whiskies, I feel stupid. After three absinthes, I feel more intelligent. It's no accident that so many artists were interested in absinthe. It didn't turn anyone into a genius; but it could help stimulate the genius they already had."

Delachaux disappears into his house to dig up a treatise, leaving me alone with the bottle of absinthe. I top up my glass, and find I'm feeling, if not more intelligent, then certainly more receptive to the beauty of this pastoral summer afternoon. Shaded by an overhanging tree, I look over the wildflower-flecked cow pastures, which the sun is painting in hues of fluorescent yellow and absinthine emerald, towards the Chapeau de Napoléon, a clifftop castle perched on one of the low mountains that rise from the valley floor towards the French border.

The mountain vista calls to mind the echo of a quote. "If, while resting on a summer afternoon, you follow with your eyes a mountain range on the horizon or a branch which casts its shadow over you, you experience the aura of those mountains, of that branch." These were the words that Walter Benjamin—another mystic intellectual of the left, a collector with a taste for the unique, the rarefied, the hard to obtain—used to qualify the concept of aura, which he further defined as "the unique phenomenon of distance, however close an object may be." Here at this table, I feel I am basking in the aura of authenticity: of an absinthe made according to a centuries-old tradition; rather than some modern ersatz created for the night-club circuit. And though the sought-after object is sitting within reach—and its molecules are currently coursing through my bloodstream, binding to my neurons—I still can't help but perceive a phenomenon of distance. Even now, the aura of absinthe, like its myth, remains ungraspable.

When Delachaux returns, an article in hand providing further proof of absinthe's Swiss origins, I sympathize more with his prickly distaste for those who seek to collect, commercialize, and possess the myth that was born in his valley. He's right: there is a pure pleasure in offering, and the *belle époque* revivalists, spoon vendors, and elixir peddlars who are profiting from the current revival are missing the point, the heart of the attraction. At the core of the myth lies the idea of danger and transgression; and the attraction of the Val-de-Travers is its underground culture of resistance. Speakeasy passwords, sly euphemisms, over-the-bar winks: in clandestinity lies community, and in any underground community, formed out of the resistance to a mainstream perceived as oppressive, you'll find exclusiveness, coded language, irreverence, and ritual.

Delachaux pours me a final shot of La Bleue—aka *un lait de Jura*, aka *un thé de Boveresse*, aka *une couèchte* (Swiss absinthe has as many coy nicknames as Californian cannabis)—repeating the demonstrative ritual of pouring from on high. It's delicious, I tell him—the best I've had yet, more flowery and complex than the shots I had in the bar—and I compliment him on his taste.

Naturally, he won't tell me where I can buy a bottle of it for myself.

As much as I appreciate Delachaux's hospitality—and his Bleue—the experience was dissatisfying. The historian, though he is quick to exempt himself from vulgar commercial motivations, is in his own way guilty of laying claim the myth.

But I'm determined: I won't stop until I have a bottle of my own. I spend a leisurely afternoon driving down narrow dirt roads, with sheepdogs chasing after the tires of my car. At one dairy farm, I track down the owner on the threshold of his cheese room.

"Absinthe?" he says. "I have a few bottles for myself, and my wife uses it to glaze her soufflés. If you'd like some Gruyère, though, I can sell you all you want."

A little discouraged, I stop in an antique shop. As I browse through the vintage Swiss Army knives and crystal vases, I come across a shelf of old absinthe spoons and glasses. "Are you interested in absinthe?" says the owner, a slender woman with auburn hair, wearing a becoming, polka-dotted dress. "Well," I say, "I'm not that interested in old spoons. I'm actually looking for a bottle."

After a glance outside the front door, she says, "Follow me," and leads me into the back of the shop. She pulls an uncorked bottle from the bottom drawer of her desk, and pours me a shot, which she fills with water from a glass coffee pot. "Do you like it?" Indeed I do—it's as smooth as Delachaux's, only a little less sugary. "I can sell you a bottle, if you'd like.

"You know," she continues "the inspectors of the *Régie des alcools*"—the local version of the Appalachian revenuer men—"know perfectly well we're making absinthe here. The stills are hidden in abandoned buildings, in the forest; nobody will ever tell you where they're hidden. The distillers buy the alcohol from the *Régie*; myself, I can go to a pharmacy and buy several litres of pure alcohol. And if you know the pharmacist, you can even ask him for premixed packages of absinthe herbs: 'Give me a Number 3, with hyssop and melissa,' for example." I give it a try a little later in a drugstore in Couvet: a fresh-faced young pharmacist pulls out a shoebox full of wormwood. "Some people use it for tea," she tells me. "To settle their stomachs. But if others want to mix it with alcohol . . . The Val-de-Travers consumes as much raw alcohol as the rest of Switzerland combined, so clearly it's going somewhere. The only time they make arrests is when somebody is importing a larger amount of cheaper, lower-grade alcohol from Germany or Italy. Then the *Régie* isn't getting their cut, there's a denunciation, and they close down a still or two. It's all a bit of a game." I tell her I'd love to buy a bottle, and she directs me down the street to a bank machine—"It's right by the police station." My first bottle costs me 50 francs; she wraps the unlabelled litre in newspaper with practised hands.

Farther along, at a bend in the road, I stop in a roadside restaurant—empty except for a solitary drinker, and go through the now-familiar ritual.

"*Une absinthe?*" I ask. The waitress starts to reach for a bottle of Kübler above the bar, but I protest. "No, a real one," I say. "*Une petite bleue.*"

"Kübler," she mutters, "nobody wants to drink Kübler." She leans beneath the bar, pulls out a bottle with a colour-photocopied label of a lowing cow marked: "*Le lait, un produit naturel de chez nous.*" I ask her whether drinking a lot of the stuff can be dangerous. "Well, if you drink it all day, of course it is." she says. The bar's only other patron, an old man with his own cloudy glass before him, shouts: "It's healthy! It's good for the lungs."

And I'm offered another litre of absinthe, this one at only 42 francs. She asks her gangling teenage son to search for a label, and he glues it onto the bottle before me—the image shows a skeletal temperance worker, pointing a gloved hand to a clock nearing midnight, next to the date October 7, 1910: the day absinthe was banned in Switzerland. A green-skinned beauty lies at his feet, a knife with a handle in the shape of a blue cross plunged into her heart.

"You know," the barlady tells me, "my great-aunt was famous around here. She sold absinthe from her kitchen, just down the street." Delachaux had alluded to this legendary figure: as a child, he used to go to the house of the infamous Berthe Zurbuchen, aka

La Malotte, where his father liked to knock back a glass in her kitchen. La Malotte made her own absinthe for eighty years, and when an overzealous liquor commissioner decided to crack down on clandestine distillers in the 1960s, she was the victim of a celebrated show trial. At the moment of the sentence—a 3,000-franc fine—she famously asked the judge: "Do you want me to pay you right now, or when you come by my house to pick up your weekly bottle?"

The barlady still remembers her with admiration. "The trial didn't stop La Malotte from making absinthe. In fact, she painted her house green—like the Green Fairy." And her clients—many local gendarmes among them—continued to bring bottles of alcohol to her, which she'd transform into absinthe by mixing it with the necessary herbs in her still, and serve them in her kitchen. "It's illegal to make absinthe, it's illegal to transport it, but not to drink it! So she risked nothing."

I remember the fable of the canny grasshopper—camouflaged among the green blades of grass, watching the showy butterfly being netted. *"Pour vivre heureux, vivons cachés."*

But fuck fables: the myth is what interests me. And today, June 14, the traditional beginning of wormwood harvesting season, is my last chance: it's the Sixth Annual Absinthe Festival in Boveresse. The chief tourist attraction in this town of 350 is the Drying Shed, a three-storey wooden structure where bundles of wormwood were left to desiccate before being sent to the distilleries. I begin my search for refreshment with a *soufflé glacé à l'absinthe*, the same frozen dessert that got Mitterrand in trouble in Neuchâtel. It's sweet and bitter ice cream, but just a confection, hardly more than an amuse-bouche. The main street is lined with stands selling Val-de-Travers T-shirts, rusty absinthe spoons and piles of reprinted labels, potted herbs that go into the making of absinthe. In a tent behind the town hall, a band is playing "Johnny B. Goode" and "Barbara Ann," as the villagers dance stiff versions of "le rock." The only thing for sale, besides sausages and french fries, is Kübler's legal absinthe, though a wormwood-macerated rum called "Le Décollage"—the name means "blast-off"—offers me a bit of a lift. I wander to the upper floor of the town hall, a basketball court that has been turned into a kind of bazaar for absinthe collectors. Marie-Claude Delahaye is seated at a table, too busy signing books to notice me. Another dealer is trying to peddle a vintage fountain for 2,150 francs. Most of the vendors are French. For all the overpriced memorabilia, there's not a drop of Bleue to be found.

I wander back to the main stand, where I mutter to a man with a sprig of just-picked wormwood in the pocket of his plaid shirt that I didn't come all the way from Canada to drink Kübler. A slight, mop-topped man with stooped shoulders and hangdog eyes overhears me.

"Are you looking for a real bottle?" he says. I nod. We shake hands; he introduces himself as "Pierrot." "Come with me," he says. Along the way, he mutters something to Serge, a broad-shouldered man with a booming voice, in plaid pants; and we are joined by the mustachioed Marcel, in a burgundy singlet, whom I recognize as one of the French paraphernalia dealers. We walk past a vacant lot planted with a stunted patch of wormwood, into a gabled house with two sculpted cats above the entranceway. In a spacious kitchen we sit at an Arborite table; I am flanked by Pierrot's teenage son, in a Nike sweatshirt, and his aged father, in a pressed white shirt. A bottle is uncapped, the absinthe is poured, silence descends. Whispers, passwords, reverence: I am at the heart of the ritual.

Ice-cold water drips onto the liquid. The flowery bouquet provokes exclamations; exploratory sips are taken. "Ah, *magnifique*," says Serge. "Not too much anise, not too much sugar. What's in your recipe?" Pierrot is evasive: "I've experimented with several mixes; this is my favourite. I'll tell you one of my herbs—hyssop. It's about 54 per cent alcohol by volume."

Marcel, jocular, blurts: "And where do you keep your still?"

"That," says Pierrot gravely, "I'll never tell. In any case, it's not here—it's in a nearby village." It turns out he's a pharmacist—not a bad day job for a distiller—and he has a position to uphold.

As the glasses are refilled, the anecdotes begin. Serge specializes in obscure absinthe collectibles, and talk turns to the issue of the Swiss border guards. "Once, I went to visit François Guy's distillery in Pontarlier; but it was closed that day. So, when I was driving back to Bern, I told the Swiss customs man, quite frankly, that I'd been trying to buy some French absinthe. And he says: 'Why would you go to France to buy their garbage, when we have the best clandestine absinthe makers in the world here?'"

I ask whether I risk much bringing a couple of bottles of Bleue over the border. "Well," says Marcel, "they could fine you and seize your car. Just do like I do. Pour your Bleue into a wine bottle, and stick the cork halfway in, like you've just come back from a picnic. They never check."

I'm halfway through another glass—and this, ably mixed by a Traversine pharmacist, is the bitterest and best I've tasted yet—when I dare to ask the barbarous, reductive question. Apart from the exquisite bouquet, apart from the sublime mixture of herbs, is there any difference between a half-dozen glasses of Bleue and a half-dozen glasses of vodka. "*Oui!*" comes the unanimous response. Marcel says of Bleue: "After six of them, believe me, you feel euphoric. If you're feeling depressed . . . it's gone. I'm diabetic, and I feel it drives my diabetes away."

Serge is more diffident, only saying: "Keep drinking, you'll see." But he's so impressed with Pierrot's Bleue that he buys a dozen bottles. Marcel buys several himself, then stands and excuses himself: "I have to go back to selling my antique glasses and fountains. If I don't come home with enough money, then no *boum-boum*"—he mimes a couple of pelvic thrusts, as though sodomizing a barnyard animal— "from my wife tonight." I buy a bottle myself; Pierrot wraps it in newspaper, gives me a supermarket bag, and charges me only 40 francs.

By now, Oscar Wilde's famous dictum is starting to make sense. "After the first glass," he wrote, "you see things as you wish they were. After the second glass, you see things as they are not." And after three glasses, I return to the main street, which seems to be full of happily inebriated village folk, unselfconsciously feting their beloved drink. But I make the mistake of pouring myself a shot of Pierrot's absinthe under a picnic table in the party tent, and the last phrase in Wilde's apothegm returns: "Finally, you see things as they really are, and that is the most horrible thing in the world." I look around, and see salespeople, mostly from France, all seeking to lay their claim to a myth; and this is indeed a horrible sight. Every year, the prices of the collectibles go up, the greed increases, and the myth turns to folklore. The *vouivre* seems fated to become Happy the Harpy, as anodyne as any ceramic Disney garden gnome.

There is nothing for it but to continue drinking. As dusk falls, menacing clouds move in from the south, and thunderclaps compete with the clashes of cymbals as a marching band describes endless ovals in the main street. I find myself standing unsteadily in the middle of the street, staring, as a full moon, louched with mist, yellow as Pernod, rises over the rounded mountains. Pierrot's father, catching me wavering, walks by and gives me a wink: "It was good stuff, *non?*"

My grasp of sequence gets shakier at this point—absinthe, for all its stimulating qualities, can play havoc with the memory—but I was apparently coherent enough to strike up an acquaintance. I remember being invited to the apartment of Nicolas, who lived across the street from the House of the Cats. He was my age, in his mid-thirties, modest and bespectacled, and eager to chat with somebody who had crossed an ocean to try his favourite aperitif. We sat on his tiny back porch, and he poured glass after glass. "This is the same kind the Baron of Rothschild—at least one of the barons—has sent to him in Geneva."

And Nicolas talked, honestly, about life in the Val-de-Travers. "This is one of the poorest cantons in Switzerland," he said. "Since quartz killed our watchmaking tradition, all of our industries have disappeared. It's impossible to keep young people here."

I remember Nicolas pulling out a guitar, and singing an ode to absinthe, of his own composition, as his sandalled feet tapped beneath the kitchen table. I can just barely decipher the lyrics I insisted on scrawling down:

Dans ce coin de pays	(In the corner of this land,
niché dans une vallée	nestled in a vale,
s'écoule une rivière	flows a river
telle le breuvage des fées.	that runs with the nectar of the fairies.
. . . Vous, gens de ce pays	. . . You, people of this land
vous ne m'en voudrez pas	won't blame me if I forbear
de ne pas dévoiler	from revealing to you
le nom de ce breuvage.	the name of this elixir.)

Of course its name is best left unsaid. Nicolas, as far as I can recall, didn't try to sell me an antique spoon, a T-shirt, or his own favourite brand of absinthe. He vaguely hoped I could set him up with poets and singers in my hometown; perhaps I could find someone to collaborate on a CD on absinthe for next year's festival. That night, in Boveresse, I felt like I'd gotten to the heart of clandestinity: a wink on the main street beneath a full moon, a wholehearted invitation, the shared flouting of authority, and, a bonding ritual: cold water clouding a sacred liquid. In its purest form, such ritual fosters connection and friendship.

The trouble with many modern rituals, of course, is their chemical and materialistic nature. For all that is positive in the creation of a counter-community, too often at its centre lies a herb or a liquor, a powder and a needle, which ends in the solitary oblivion of intoxication, addiction, and isolation: fistfights and stash-grabbing, severed ears and sanatoriums, the hollow gaze of the ravaged Paul Verlaine at the end of his career.

And, in my case, a rising of the gorge and a too-abrupt adieu to Nicolas. Followed by a long stumble down the main street and back to my hotel. No hallucinations, no sudden bursts of poetry, no transfiguration of the starry night into Vincent van Goghesque swirls. Just a brief brush with the festival mascot: a woman dressed as a green fairy, wearing a pointed cap and carrying a yellow magic wand, skipping through the crowd. Then, the familiar consequences of besottedness: a slow ricochet up a Caligarian staircase, *Lost Weekend* bed spins, and nightmares of blue-eyed water snakes chewing at my liver. The next day, all echo of leprechaun laughter had faded; all that was left were the ogres of hangover stalking my path.

My quest for a bottle of "authentic" absinthe—spurred by doubt and annoyance at a bogus ritual in an expat bar in Barcelona—is a rebellion against the age of mechanical reproduction, the era of Coca-Cola Classic, of Limited Edition Original Prints, of Exclusive Director's Cuts. In a time when very little seems sacred, when industry's capacity to reproduce and distribute has pried the cult value from the original object, then any search for the authentic is an impulse to resacralize, to track down the original and reattach its aura.

If decadence is symptomatic of alienation from tradition and community, then I suppose my pursuit of authentic absinthe has been a decadent one. Urban hipsters, weaned on sophisticatedly marketed semblances of authenticity, are particularly susceptible to this syndrome, the hyperactive fetishization of mythic commodities. If it had been gin and vermouth, rather than absinthe, that had been banned since the era of the Volstead Act, people would be paying fortunes for Jazz Age–vintage conical glasses, and reverently quoting Dorothy Parker and Dashiell Hammett about the narcotic qualities of the fabled martini. In the case of absinthe, a century of prohibition has created a similar myth. A simple truism, ignored by legislators worldwide: ban something, and you make it stronger and more attractive.

In the nine decades since absinthe was banned, psychopharmacology has come a long way. We've developed amphetamines that can make your neurons fire like pinwheels; blotter hits of acid that will leave you melding with the spirits in the oaks; and ecstasy so strong it will convince you that techno is the classical music of the new millennium. In the final analysis, it is perhaps unwise to put too much stock in the rapturous declarations of unstable, impoverished, undernourished debauchees of the nineteenth century. Baudelaire thought absinthe a harmless tipple, but considered hashish jelly the most sublime shortcut to artificial paradise. Me, I was bored with hot-knifing hash by the time I was seventeen.

In some versions of the *vouivre* story, the seductive serpent tempts its victims to the water with a diadem that turns out to be a twig. But when the desideratum is authenticated as genuine, as original, as chemically pure, its aura still holds us at a distance. Though by writing this essay I've indulged an urge to appropriate the misty water sprite of the Jura, I hereby renounce all trademark, copyright, and authorial claim. The truth is, I never even came close to grasping it. Authenticity, it turns out, always proves to be the most persistently elusive myth of them all.

I made it through Swiss and French customs with only the most cursory of passport checks, my bottles of illegal Bleue hidden in a clear plastic garment bag of reeking socks and underwear. There's a bottle of La Bleue sitting on the table in front of me, the last one left from my trip. The fact is, I still don't know exactly what I'm looking at; there is no list of ingredients on the label. Though it's transparent, I can at least say with confidence that it is not water, "that terrible poison," as Alfred Jarry put it, "so corrosive that out of all substances it has been chosen for washing and scouring, and a drop added to a clear liquid like absinthe troubles it." Perhaps it's just high-proof alcohol charged with a few aromatic mountain herbs. Or maybe this particular bottle is so laden with α-thujone I'll wake up in an asylum, my face dyed green. Short of subjecting it to a gas chromatography analysis, there's no way of knowing.

Since I'm no collector, I suppose I'll uncap it one day and get around to drinking it—as an offering to friends who are also suckers for transgression, ritual, and myth.

One Glass and You're Dead

The Ballad
of Big
and Small

John
Vigna

You woke me on December 25, a rifle across your knees, barrel pointed towards the flickering Christmas tree. I shook my head, closed my eyes and opened them again to see if you were still there. I didn't know you owned a gun. Instinct told me it was loaded. Your breath reeked of booze, but your voice was calm, reassuring.

"Bro, let's go out and shoot some shit."

I was caught off guard by your conspiratorial tone; it signified an intimacy we shared only when we were getting along, which was rare. I hadn't seen you in a few years; you were twenty-eight years old and you'd done time, lived on the streets, drifted in and out of rehab. And then, spending Christmas at Dead Man's Flats with our family, I reeled with how our parents, your twin, Mark, and our youngest brother, Peter, felt foreign to me, but not nearly as much as you did, Paul.

You said you wanted to go outside and shoot squirrels and birds.

I glanced at the bedside clock: 3:41 a.m. "Let's go in the morning, okay? In the daylight."

Your lower lip bulged with Copenhagen, your ball cap was pulled low. "I'm going pro," you said. "I've been working out." You scratched the side of your face, placed your hand back on the rifle.

I sat up. You hadn't played hockey in a dozen years. I hid in the dark, asked how your workouts were going. You sniffed mistrustfully, like I was conning you. And I was. I recounted your goaltending feats, steered you towards a lighter moment; we chuckled about games of Showdown in the cul-de-sac where we grew up in the Calgary suburbs.

"I've got this buddy, see, and he's been talking to some guy in North Dakota who's with the farm team there. He says they need a goalie." Your eyes sparkled with the lie.

I said, "That's great news. You should go for it."

You sniffed again. "Okay, bro. You'll see. I'll prove you wrong." Your voice was bitter. "I need some air," you said. The rifle hung loosely in your right hand.

Your body blocked the Christmas-tree lights briefly before fading into the dark. I lay down and stared at the ceiling. I couldn't wait to go home.

"GRANDE CACHE: Your Escape Into the Wilderness." I consider the sign on the outskirts of the Alberta company town built in 1966 by the McIntyre Coal Mine, the same year my younger brother, Paul, was born. Closer to the prison, another sign greets me: "ATTENTION: You are entering a Correctional Service Reserve. Any vehicle or person on this site is subject to a search. No loitering or photographs. RESTRICTED AREA."

A low brick building with peaked black roofing and large windows, the Grande Cache Federal Institution resembles the Catholic elementary school St. Vincent de Paul that Paul and I once attended in Calgary. But twenty-foot fences of barbwire and razors surround this minimum-security prison. Light posts loom throughout the parking lot, a camera perched atop each, scanning in slow 180° arcs. A large German shepherd paces back and forth in a pen. Outside the fence, two gazebos, and a lawn neatly clipped like a putting green.

I park my rented car, unload my duffle bag, six bags of groceries and walk towards the main entrance of the prison, past an empty bike rack and an inukshuk with a plaque that reads: "May the Inuk be your guide for a safe journey through life's travels. This is a symbol of leadership, confidence, and encourages the importance of friendship: a reminder of our dependence on one another."

Inside the waiting area: a couch, Coke and candy machine, and a trophy case, jam-packed with softball and golf trophies presumably for the prison staff's extracurricular activities. I put down my bags and wait.

Paul is thirty-six and has been an injection cocaine user since his late teens. I am his older brother by a year, here to support him while he serves a two-year sentence for credit card fraud, theft under $1000, breaking and entering, and possession charges. As part of the Prisoner Family Visit program, better known as the conjugal visit, I'll stay in prison with him for seventy-two hours. I hope to reconnect with him, which won't be easy. I've tried to escape Paul's reign of terror, shame and pain, by avoiding him for years, to no avail. I haven't seen him since two drug dealers nearly beat him to death a couple of years ago. What will we talk about? Will we argue and fight? Will we speak plainly about his cocaine addiction? I have no idea who my brother is anymore. I'm not sure I've ever known him.

A male guard with dark grape-coloured lips and a mouth packed with misshapen yellow teeth emerges from a booth with tinted windows, blinking in the daylight. When I tell him I'm here to see my brother, he grimaces, flips through pages on a clipboard, picks up the phone, murmurs a few words, returns to the booth. A heavy-set woman enters, snaps on a pair of latex gloves, rummages through my duffle bag. She removes the multivitamins, ballpoint pens, cellphone, laptop. I'm annoyed by the mess she makes of my clothes. She asks for my car keys. I hand over my wallet and check for anything else that might reveal my address; like everyone else in our family has tried to do, I can't have Paul know where I live. I walk through a metal detector. She pushes my bags through an X-ray machine, hands me a clip-on badge with a large "V," motions me to put it on. The guard buzzes us through two separate doors leading outside and the woman escorts me to a miniature house covered in grey siding, the same dreary slap-it-up-quick style that characterizes much of Grande Cache. Unit B202. She unlocks the front door and leaves.

Two brothers, Big and Small, stood in a field. A gopher lay at their feet with a marble lodged in its jaw. The gopher made a faint shrieking sound and its tail twitched over their sneakers. Small jumped back first. Big glanced at him and knew Small would cry because he felt the same himself. But Big was eight, a year older, and therefore tougher than Small; he knew that crying revealed weakness.

"What are we gonna do?" Small said. "We can't just leave it, what if Father finds out?"

Big held the slingshot in his left hand. It was a fluke he'd hit the gopher. He turned away. If he blinked it was all over. Older brother crying. Other kids would hear about it.

The gopher twitched again. Small didn't want to shoot gophers. Big had stolen the slingshot from Woolco, made Small promise not to tell.

"What's Father going to do when he finds out?" Small said.

"He ain't gonna find out, unless you tell him. So shut up," Big said.

The gopher whimpered. Tiny red-and-white bubbles grew and popped from his mouth with each quick, sharp breath. Flies buzzed near the mouth. Small began to cry. Big handed him the slingshot, found a large rock, held it above his head. As he stared at Small, Big flung the rock down, smashing the gopher into the dirt.

Small stopped crying. They looked at one another.

"Hey, bro," Big said. "We should make sure it's dead, eh?"

Small didn't answer. He knew what Big was up to when he called him "bro." He knew that he wanted something from him.

"Bro, why don't you lift up the rock?"

Small was silent.

"Bro, c'mon. If you lift it, I won't tell Father you stole the sling-shot." Small stiffened.

"It will help you be a better goalie," Big said.

The flies buzzed around the rock. Small rolled it aside with his foot. The gopher lay still, face crushed into the dirt, the marble no longer visible. Two teeth poked through a mess of blood. Small looked at the gopher and then at Big with ice in his eyes. Big saw the respect that Small once held for him grow cold and distant. Big turned away.

Small dug a hole with both hands, used two twigs to roll the gopher in the hole, covered it up gently.

As they walked home together, Big made Small promise not to say anything.

At home, Big told Father that Small had stolen a slingshot, killed a gopher.

Father slid the belt off his khaki shorts, grabbed Small, pushed him up the stairs to the bathroom, slammed the door. Big grinned at his cleverness and his ability to lie to Father, who believed him since he was the oldest. Big listened to the sound of leather smacking skin. He wondered if Father would strike Small's hand and wrist with the buckle, as he often had done to Big. He listened for a confession but heard only wails. He knew Small wouldn't tell Father. He also knew that Small would brace himself for each stinging blow by telling himself that he'd be a better goalie.

The
Ballad
of Big
and
Small

179

Within the confines of the prison walls, a low chain-link fence surrounds unit B202, creating the illusion of a tiny suburban yard with freshly cut grass. A two-person swing set. Slate picnic table bolted down to cement supports on the ground. Filthy, rust-covered barbecue, chained to the side of the house. Large dump truck tire filled with sand, plastic pail and shovel. I'm a little surprised that the toys aren't chained down as well.

I had expected to see bars on the windows, cots to sleep on, cold cement floors. Instead, the master bedroom has a queen-sized bed and night table stuffed with condoms. The smaller bedroom has two single beds, a chalkboard, crayons and paper. Coloured sheets adorned with comic-book heroes. Wall-to-wall carpeting. An open-style kitchen and living room with faux leather couch, large-screen TV, DVD player, CD player, chair, coffee table. Four chairs around an Ikea-style dining room table. It's much nicer than my own home. I glance out the master bedroom and see a camera on a post fifty metres away. I check the other windows. Cameras trained at every angle.

A stocky woman strides quickly towards the house. Paul shuffles behind her, limping, all attitude. His hair is long, stringy, receding; a triangular soul patch beneath his lower lip. Broad shoulders. Well-defined, tattooed, muscular arms. A large mesh sack slung over his shoulder. My first thought is, *My god, he looks like a thug.*

Inside the house, he greets me with a "Hey, bro," as though we had seen each other last week rather than two years ago. We embrace each other with one arm, lightly, awkwardly. His face is pasty white, slightly pockmarked with recent scars, not clear and tanned as I remember. But his brown eyes startle me. They jitter back and forth, bloodshot, anxious.

Big boxed with Best Friend when he was eleven. Small pestered them; he wanted to watch. "What's up with Small?" Best Friend said, who was taller than both Big and Small by several inches. He grew up with two older brothers who took turns beating him up.

"Get lost," Big said. Small looked as though he might cry.

"Aw, shit, he can stay," Best Friend said. Small's face lit up. "But he can't just take tickets. He's gotta box, too."

Small locked the garage door. Best Friend threw Big a pair of gloves to pull on. They circled one another, gloves held up to protect their faces. Best Friend moved in, jabbed with a left-right. Big, head snapping back, continued to circle and keep away from Best Friend's long arms. Best Friend's next punch glanced off his ear. Big's face flushed. He swung wildly, missed Best Friend's shoulder. Best Friend laughed. "What kind of pussy are you?"

Big felt Small's silence burning into him. Best Friend faked a left jab and smashed a right on Big's nose. It bled.

"Don't get any blood on the gloves; my brothers will kill me," he said.

Small ran into the house, came back with a box of Kleenex, handed one to Big, who tore it from his hands, wiped his nose, grabbed another and stuffed it up his nostril.

"I gotta wait for this thing to stop bleeding," he said.

"Can I play?" Small said.

Best Friend shook his head and smirked. "Just don't come crying to me when I beat you to a pulp."

Small pulled on the gloves. Best Friend circled, looking for an opening. Small held up his gloves like he saw Big do. His first punch surprised Best Friend, landed on his forehead.

"Jesus Christ," Best Friend said. He rushed in and swung at Small, who blocked the punches, and returned one that stopped

Best Friend cold, opened a small cut above his eye.

"Okay, you little fucker, that's it. Time to get serious." Best Friend unleashed a flurry of punches, battered Small's body and head. Best Friend paused for a moment to take in some air. Then slammed Small's face hard, dropping him to the concrete.

Small quietly writhed on the ground.

"He's okay," Big said, secretly pleased that Small was in pain because it meant he wouldn't play with them anymore. Best Friend knelt down to help Small up. Best Friend pulled his gloves off and tossed them aside. "We need to get him some ice."

Small's eyes watered. He had a red welt that would turn into a bruise. Big's mind turned towards creating a lie to explain this to Father. "He's fine. He just needs some rest."

Small wobbled into the house, upstairs to his room, up the ladder to the top bunk; the bottom bunk belonged to his Twin who was watching TV in the Family Room with Smallest Brother.

"Maybe we should call someone," Best Friend said. "He might have a concussion or something. We shouldn't let him go to sleep."

Small lay still, curled in a ball.

"He's fine. He's just got a little headache," Big said. He didn't care if Small fell asleep, as long as he didn't hang out with them anymore. "I'll check on him later," he lied.

Best Friend leaned towards Small. "If you need anything, call us, okay? You're a tough little guy. You did good."

Big remained silent, feared Best Friend liked Small more than himself. "It's a good thing he didn't fight you," Best Friend said. "He would have kicked your ass."

Paul's parole officer addresses him like a stern parent, in the same tone Dad often used to control us, promising violent consequences if we didn't toe his ever-changing line. Dad was an only child of Italian immigrants who came to Canada to work in the southern Alberta coal mines. His father had a harsh temper, beat him with wooden spoons and belts. Dad studied hard, escaped to university but continued the cycle with the four of us.

"You make sure you clean up after yourself and leave the house in the same shape you got it in," the officer said. "Do you understand?"

The
Ballad
of Big
and
Small

181

"Yes. I understand, Mrs. Shore," Paul said. He keeps his head down. She spins out of the room.

"What's the deal with her?"

Paul shrugs, wanders through the house to check out the rooms. He insists on taking the children's bedroom. I object half-heartedly; he should have the master bedroom, but he's firm.

"It wouldn't be right, John." He says the room is too big for him; he doesn't need the comfort and luxury. It will only make it harder for him to return to his cell.

On Grey Cup Sunday, Big and Small's Parents drank cocktails and watched the game at the Neighbour's house. Big and Small defied Father's orders to stay at home, went to the nearby university to play basketball; Small wanted to stay home but Big persuaded him to join him. Big was thirteen and played basketball every moment he could, the freedom and spontaneity of the game thrilled him and offered an escape from his family. They ran up and down the hallways, tossing each other bounce passes, ricocheting the ball off the walls and dribbling to blast past one another. Big liked to trash talk Small; he needed the audience of his younger brother and his younger brother loved playing with him and in this way they both got the approval they sought from one another. "Yo, yo, bro, you wanna get beat left or right?"

"Left," Small said, giggling. And that's what Big did, laughing and mocking him.

"Your turn."

"I'm going to beat you right." Big stopped him easily. "Nice try, buckaroo. Better work harder on that move."

Small ran down the hallway, leapt up to try touching the ceiling, fell short. He tried again and missed.

"Rise, yeast," Big said. "Nice try, little man. You're getting close."

He threw Small the ball. Small dribbled between his legs, spun around in glee. On a crossover the ball squirted off his foot, hit a metal locker. An alarm blared, surprising the boys.

"Holy shit. What the fuck did you do? We're screwed," Big said. They bolted down the hall, burst through the doors, sprinted home. They stopped a block from the house, Small hyperventilating. "I didn't mean to do it. You saw. It was an honest mistake," he said.

"That's okay, bro," Big said. "Don't sweat it."

They got home and told Mother the story. She looked nervous, reassured them it was an accident, not to worry about it, but not to tell Father it, at least not right away. Father came in from the Neighbour's all smiles. His cheeks were red. Big knew to avoid unpleasant topics when Father drank. Even sober, his mood could flip from light to dark quickly.

Small didn't like secrets. He didn't like how they made him feel inside. He blubbered out the story.

"Is this true?" Father said, the red spreading from his cheeks, his forehead, ears and neck.

Big nodded. "It was an honest mistake. We were just messing around. No harm done," he said.

Father glared at them.

"The kids were just playing," Mother said. "They didn't do anything wrong. It was an accident. He's telling the truth."

"Telling the truth doesn't make it right," Father said. "He should have been minding his own business. He should have stayed home." He ordered Small to go upstairs and wait for him in the bathroom where he would strap him. As he slipped off his belt, he glared at Big and said he would deal with him later.

In the months that led up to our visit in prison, Paul, you called me collect, usually on Sunday evenings, sometimes on Tuesdays, or not for several weeks. You never knew how much I grew to detest the sound of the phone ringing in my house, especially in the evening, a shrill call to your drama, one I could not resist. Each time the phone rang, I braced myself for the news of your death. I lived like this for most of my adult life, haunted by the sound of a phone ringing, whether it's mine or someone else's. You requested two black Pilot rollerball pens. Questions agitated you, so I refrained from asking how you would repay any of our relatives, family or friends you had scammed over the years. Do you remember that one bad night, before you landed in prison, when you called from Sylvan Lake at 2 a.m.?

"I need some bus fare, bro . . . I just need fifty dollars for bus fare. I start a new drywalling gig in a couple of days . . . I need some

The
Ballad
of Big
and
Small

183

cash to eat . . . Man, I gotta get outta here. You can send it on the Greyhound. I'll pay you back . . ."

I asked again where you were calling from. You accused me of wanting to turn you in. You were on the run. I asked if you were high. You hung up. I waited. You called again. I said you were throwing your life away. You replied that I didn't do enough for you, that I was always looking to hurt and keep you down, like when we were kids. I wanted to point out that it had been nearly twenty years since we were those kids, that I still felt guilty for my lies, but I couldn't mention any of this because you were upset and I was afraid that you would use my guilt against me another time. A weakness to exploit. You hung up. Called again. Said you once saw Dad hit Mom as she cowered in the broom closet. "What the hell am I supposed to do with that?" you shouted and hung up. I had never seen Dad hit Mom but now as your words burrowed into me, I wasn't sure anymore.

"You have no idea what it's like to be me," you said in the next call. "I really don't like myself. It's probably better for all of us if I just went away." You hung up. I was deeply shaken. I traced the call through the operator—it came from a pay phone. There was no answer. I called again, and again. Still no answer. I couldn't sleep. I badly wanted to drink a bottle of wine and smoke a joint but feared getting altered in case you called again. I sat in the dark and stared at the wall and although I'm not religious I prayed that you were okay, that I'd be a better brother to you if you were safe tonight. Much later, to my relief, my phone rang at 6 a.m., your voice barely audible, a lazy whisper. You had scored a fix. You said I was a good man, the only one in our family who still spoke to you, who still cared about you. Your forgiveness hurt me even more. But after I hung up, I felt angry and exhausted. I despised the sordid world you kept me tied to. I was tired of riding your roller-coaster nightmare of hope, fear, and danger. I could try helping you, but I really couldn't help you. I disconnected the phone.

As Paul eats enthusiastically, enjoying a spicy stir-fry I cooked for him, I'm pissed off remembering that phone call and how the terror of it hollowed me out. But I was always glad when he called, that he reached out to me. I was addicted to the drama because it felt like atonement for how I had treated him while we were younger and because more than anything, I hated the silence, the not knowing if he was safe and alive. Now, I feel awkward, at a loss for what to talk about, reach for the obvious, ask him what it's like in prison. He considers the question for a moment.

"What do you think it's like?" he grunts. I say it must be tough and lonely and scary having to watch your back all the time and not know who you can trust, that I could never do it. This seems to soften him.

Although the lights are all on, the unit is dim. He unscrews a light bulb to prove it's 40 watts. The unit is full of low-wattage bulbs to prevent inmates and their families from cooking speed. Paul pulls a bent, scorched spoon from the cutlery drawer to demonstrate. He holds up steak knives with blackened tips, presses them together. He lists the ingredients to cook a few ounces of crystal meth: pseudoephedrine pills like Actifed or Sudafed; ammonium nitrate fertilizer, lighter fluid, AA Energizer lithium batteries, Red Devil lye, water, salt, and Liquid Fire drain opener. This is his moment to teach me something about his world and I lap it up, deceiving myself that his honesty has signalled a shift, a new intimacy between us. He shines with knowledge I will never have and I believe he thinks it gives him power over me, which is the truth. But once the details thin, the power deflates and all that's left is a sad story. He's still in prison for drug-related charges while I'm not. Yet, he pats my shoulder and snickers, inflated with an exaggerated sense of himself, boasts that his life would make a great book.

We plug in *Ocean's Eleven* and make microwave popcorn. The phone rings, startling us so that I nearly shout out. Paul picks it up. "Hello?" He hangs up, opens the door, and waves towards the control booth. A flashlight flicks on and off, confirms that he's been seen. Counted. He tells me that they can call anytime. We finish the movie and watch *Pearl Harbour* next, snack on Oreos, sip on colas. Fall asleep at 3:30 a.m.

At twenty-five, I had just graduated from university and prepared to fly to Europe to play professional basketball. You'd moved back in with Mom and Dad after being evicted for trashing your apartment

The
Ballad
of Big
and
Small

185

and skipping rent payments. You had a knack for sneaking up on people. You woke me without a word. I hate being watched in my sleep and you'd been sitting on the edge of my bed, your face in mine, stinking of booze and burnt matches.

"Bro, she's the wrong one for you," you told me. The lines of your mouth were tight. You spat into a Pilsner beer can. "It's a bad idea. She's going to bring you down, bro."

It was strange for me to be at home in the small room I grew up in. I asked what you didn't like about my girlfriend. You were both in the same high school class and she'd always been nice to you.

"She only cares about herself," you replied. "I've got a bad feeling about her." You bobbed back and forth. I wish I could've laughed in your face, told you how ridiculous your ideas were. I rarely had an argument or disagreement with her; there had been no trouble on the horizon. But I was afraid of you when you were drunk or high. You were unpredictable. After I'd returned from playing a game in Lethbridge, you listened to my re-enactment with envy, your eyes darkening. You said I thought I was better than you, that because I had achieved some success in a sport I thought I was above you. You kept taunting me with it, goading me, and you were right: I did think I was better than you, how could I not? After you punched me in the chest and knocked the wind out of me, I defended myself. We fought bitterly, as we did often, but you were stronger, possessed by a violence I couldn't match. You punched a hole in the door and screamed obscenities as I struggled to keep it closed with my shoulder, my socks slipping on the carpet beneath my feet. You wanted to kill me. I believe if you'd busted down the door, you would have killed me.

"You could do better. She'll make you unhappy."

Your low voice unnerved me. You'd been arrested, and attempted suicide by downing sedatives.

The last time we saw each other you were in that condo you shared with Wayne, bent over a kitchen chair, shirtless, your back muscles twitching as you waited for him to stick a needle in the muscle of your ass. You told me you needed steroids to help you compete with the big guys. I didn't know what you meant, didn't ask, didn't care. You'd stopped playing competitive hockey and football in high school five years earlier. You loved alcohol and opiates more. You were always injured anyway. Fractured your nose playing basketball. Dislocated your collarbone in football. Broke fingers playing hockey. When you were five you threw yourself down the stairs with a Fisher Price popcorn maker, split your lips, bawled your eyes out, then did it again. You rushed into the middle of every dangerous situation. It was how you got attention.

The raw smell of your snuff wafted up from the can. I wanted to ask if you were still hanging out with Wayne, what you'd been doing for work. But I didn't ask because my questions always made you belligerent, created more opportunities for you to lie and for me to judge you. And perhaps I was. Although I remained silent and lacked the courage, there was only one question I wanted to ask: Did you make lurid, revolting phone calls to my girlfriend in the middle of the night? She told me she had seen you lurking in the alley behind her condo. I told her it couldn't be true since you lived in Red Deer, last I heard, working as a drywaller.

"Bro, you gotta dump her. She's a slut."

The
Ballad
of Big
and
Small

187

Four packages of cacciatore sausages sat on a shelf in the wine cellar, one each for all four brothers. Stocking stuffers for Christmas. Small looked at Big, who lifted one in his hand and held it towards the light. Hunger stabbed Big's stomach.

"We could replace it," Big said. "Easily."

"You open it first," Small said. He was thirteen and had begun to challenge Big more often than he had before. Small had learned that consequences weren't to be feared as long as the lie held up. Big had taught him well.

The dare caught Big by surprise.

"No way. You open one. I'll buy you an extra pack if you do."

Small shook his head. He knew it was a lie. He returned the package to the shelf.

"Are you sure you want to do that? We could eat it right now, and replace it. No one would ever know."

"You're always lying to me," Small said. "Trying to trick me into doing things you don't have the guts to do."

They turned out the light and locked the door.

Later that week, Father chased the Brothers into the house from their road hockey game in the street. "Who ate them?" he bellowed. His ears were red. He marched Big and Small into the family room where their younger brothers, Smaller and Smallest, stood looking down at their slippers.

"None of you are leaving until you tell me who ate them."

Big glanced towards Small for a clue; Small's mouth curled slightly. Big knew that Smaller and Smallest would never steal. One by one, Father asked them each if they had stolen the sausages. He claimed that he wouldn't punish them for telling the truth. The Brothers knew that was a lie because they were always punished, sometimes violently, for telling the truth, regardless of assurances to the contrary.

Father asked Small, who looked him in the eye, replied self-defensively, "Why do you always blame me? I didn't do it. That's the truth." Small avoided Big's gaze. Father turned to Big and asked if Small stole them.

"I have no idea. I just know it wasn't me," Big lied. Father grounded all four Brothers for two weeks.

The phone rings for count at 7 a.m. It continues ringing; Paul has always been a heavy sleeper. I roll out of bed, stumble to his room. The door is open. I watch him sleep with his arms extended over his head. His curled fingers are clean and soft. After Paul was born, Grandpa saw his infant hands for the first time in the nursery and told Dad, "Watch him. Those are the hands of a thief." Grandpa passed away before I could ask him why he had said such a thing. The phone continues to ring. In the comic-book-hero sheets Paul looks like a child sleeping in on a Saturday morning. He looks like the image of my little brother I have carried all these years and I feel enormous tenderness towards him, shake him gently on the leg. He doesn't move. The phone rings. I shake him firmly. "Paul, you gotta answer the phone." He wakes, looks at me strangely before leaping out of bed. He opens the door, waves weakly, staggers back to bed.

Later, a guard drops in with Paul's artwork, which had to first be cleared by his parole officer. Paul hands the pictures to me. "Bro, I made these for you." I flip through exquisitely detailed drawings of wolves, foxes, bears, and eagles. I have trouble believing that he created them. I didn't realize he could draw. I hold up a picture of a wolf howling at the moon and ask him how long it took to make this. "Eight hours." He created the picture using the technique of pointillism, dot by dot, with a Pilot pen. I ask him how he learned to do it.

"Bro, I got nothin' but time," he grinned. I'm bedazzled by his skill; feel guilty for assuming a lie and yet still cannot fully believe him.

You started bareback bronc riding at twenty, when you moved to Cochrane. You wore Wrangler jeans that fit snug in the crotch, a faded snuff-box ring on the back pocket, a big-ass shiny belt buckle, neon-striped shirt, a wide-brimmed cowboy hat, UPS-brown cowboy boots.

You befriended Brownie, an old-timer who taught you to ride. Grace and agility from days as a hockey goalie served you well. At your persistence, Brownie enrolled you in the Calgary Stampede as a novice.

You asked me to come along. I expected an elaborate sham. It was a sunny July day at the rodeo and we were both stunned into silence at the sight of the Grandstand and Infield crammed with 28,000 fans. We sauntered beneath the bleachers where other cowboys squatted in the dirt among the detritus of peanut shells, gum wrappers, snuff tins, Labatt's Blue plastic cups, french fry trays smeared with ketchup like blood clots. Your initials were monogrammed on the cuffs of your shirt. You nodded to the other cowboys. No one returned your greeting. One cowboy walked past, clenched his teeth, his dislocated shoulder poking out at a strange angle. You flashed me a grin, proud to show me this part of your life. I had underestimated you.

In the chutes, a cage of thick metal bars, the most dangerous place to be in the rodeo, you climbed high onto a gelding that shifted impatiently. You were all business, a study in concentration as you fidgeted on the horse's hot flesh, tightened your grip again, tried to get it right. Brownie cinched the flank strap across the gelding's stomach; it bucked fiercely, rattled you against the chute. You nearly fell off. You used your left hand to push down your cowboy hat, winked at me, nodded to Brownie. The gate opened and you burst out atop a crazed bucking bronco. Brilliant sunshine cut through the grainy haze of kicked-up dust.

You rode spectacularly. Left hand held high in the air, your spurs gliding back and forth along the horse's shoulders, your balance impeccable. Cowboys perched on the fence cheered, lifted their wide-brimmed hats. The crowd was animal: grunted, howled with excitement. But it ended. All too fast. You hit the ground when the buzzer sounded. Less than one second from recording the best ride of the afternoon and a cash prize. Your hat stayed on, your face shadowed by the brim. You stood, shook yourself off, lifted your hat to the crowd's cheers, set it back firmly. It was as though you already knew you wouldn't ride again because your life in that moment was a singular achievement, one that you could live with and hold tight over the years, tell to comfort yourself and see you through the most difficult, unpredictable times ahead.

Our first full day together, Paul shows signs of irritation and boredom. This is the version of him I expected. Belligerent. Pouting. Demanding. He opens and closes the fridge incessantly and it's getting on my nerves. I snap when he barks, "There's not enough food here." I tell him how much I spent on a plane ticket and car rental just to get here, what I spent on groceries, purchasing items I thought he might enjoy. As though the amount of money I spent was proof on the ledger sheet of our relationship detailing how much I cared. He says Oreos are available in the canteen, that he buys them with his salary, $6.90 a day for chores that involve tutoring prisoners or cleaning the commissary. With a wink he reminds me that this salary is part of his reason for wanting to get locked up in a federal institution, rather than a provincial one.

The cost for incarcerating male offenders in a minimum-security federal prison in Canada is $53,634 per year. Paul says that he receives better health care here than on the streets, including routine dentist visits, three squares a day, bedtime snacks, counselling, Valium or Diazepam for anxiety, a well-equipped weight room, a music studio, and a variety of programs geared towards helping him learn new skills if he so chooses. As a taxpayer, I'm supporting his lifestyle, one that is in some ways better than my own.

He looks in the fridge again, and closes it. "It's a sweet deal," he says.

You were twenty-seven and living with Grandpa and Grandma in a sleepy community in southwestern Alberta. You needed a change of scenery to help you kick the drugs. Besides, Mom and Dad's patience was wearing thin—they didn't know what to do with you. You took a job as a labourer at a sawmill in the town of Frank, beneath the shadow of the Frank Slide. I came to take you hiking and see if you were actually living clean.

The
Ballad
of Big
and
Small

191

"He's working hard. Making good money," Grandpa said. "There are no drugs here. If there were, we'd know about it." The phone rang—again for you. It hadn't stopped ringing that morning. Likely, you owed people money.

We prepared to leave. "You work at 1 p.m. Don't be late," Grandpa said.

You laughed at him, told him not to worry. He waved you off with the back of his hand.

We drove in a blue Ford Blazer with bald tires. You told me it was your buddy's, you were paying it down, bit by bit. I sensed a lie since you became defensive when I asked questions. The drive took twenty minutes. Crowsnest Mountain loomed before us like a sore thumb. You leaned forward, looked upward. "Bro, I can't believe we're going to climb *that*."

I couldn't either. You were scared of heights and in poor physical shape. You parked, we slipped on our knapsacks, began hiking. We passed through a dense aspen grove, came into an opening where the air was crisp, trees gave way to tough shrubs and wildflowers and a long, steep scree slope. I asked if you needed a rest. You shook your head. "Keep going, studly." I realized that you saw this as a competition. I wondered if I had unintentionally given that impression and that made me anxious.

We reached a switchback and stopped for a rest. I offered you water. You declined. Your breath was heavy and laboured, your face slick with sweat. You turned around to see how far we had come, wavered for a moment, reached for my shoulder to steady yourself.

"Whoa, it's steep," you said, frightened. We approached a narrow chimney. I advised you to follow my line. I climbed first, easily, chewed up ground until with a final thrust I was at the top. I turned around and watched you climb tentatively, testing each handhold, gingerly stepping up, grimacing. As you approached, I offered my hand to help you up. You ignored it and pulled yourself up beside me. I warned you not to look back until we got farther on top.

A cold, harsh wind blew in from the west. I pulled on my windbreaker, you reached for a sweater and toque. You were smiling. I handed you the binoculars and pointed towards Grandpa and Grandma's house in Blairmore. You waved and laughed. It had been your first summit. I couldn't help myself, told you it was a fairly easy climb compared with some of the others I had done.

Your happiness was genuine; mine felt contrived. I mentioned that it only took one and a half hours to get to the top; the guidebook said it would take longer. Still, I worried about getting you to work on time.

"Bro, we're kings of the hill," you said. "You thought I'd never be able to do it." You were bang on. But I said that I never doubted you, which was another lie. We made plans to climb Turtle Mountain next so we could peer over the edge of Frank Slide, down those hundreds of tons of rubble to where you worked and clearly see Grandpa and Grandma's house. At one time, I didn't doubt your intentions but I suspected you were fleecing our grandparents out of a small fortune as you had already done with my friends, our brothers' friends and our parents' friends. I watched how a lie settled over you. How it gave you strength, a false sense of self, the same thing lying gave to me. You had grown accustomed to that feeling. I had, too. I believed your lies because I wanted them to be true, and because when I lied I wanted them to be true, too.

Paul grabs an apple and bites into it. "So, John, is there anything you came to talk about?"

My family has learned to reveal as little as possible to Paul because he has always found ways to exploit the information. His addiction has been a painful family secret that we've managed privately by not actually facing it honestly, by not looking to ourselves as being in any way culpable only to watch it explode publicly as friends and family became involved. But I'm sick of the shame, the lies, the secrets. Everyone has disowned Paul. I'm the only member of our family still speaking with him. I feel a sense of duty to tell him everything I promised myself I wouldn't. I want to forge a new bond between us, one built on honesty. But it's a tenuous bond because I manage the information, delivering it in small but volatile calibrations, knowing that I ultimately hold the power of information over him.

The
Ballad
of Big
and
Small

193

I talk about Peter's wedding and his newborn child. I speak about his fraternal twin, Mark, who's battling alcoholism and severe weight problems, and how his fiancée left him, citing, among other reasons, a lewd pass Paul made at her one evening. Paul shrugs as if he doesn't remember. He says that he's got enough problems; he can't worry about Mark. I tell him about Mom's new boyfriend and how happy she seems to be with him. Paul's face darkens. I pause. I feel a sense of righteousness through these revelations, vindicated in gauging Paul's reaction. I reveal my suspicions about Dad; that he's been keeping another life hidden from all of us for years. Paul's brown eyes are wet and his lips waver. I am careful to reveal very little about myself because I don't trust him and because I am managing the way he gets to see me: strong, ambitious, honest, got my shit together. He paces back and forth, opens the fridge, slams it shut. Disappears into the bedroom for a few minutes. Goes outside for a smoke.

When he comes back he looks me in the eye and says, "The nice thing about getting to know someone, John, is that you get to know some new things about them, and you get to remember the old things that you loved."

"I just thought you should know," I said. "It's been killing me for you not to know who your family is. I know I couldn't handle it."

"We're different people. There's nothing I can do about the past. I can't think about it. I have to move on and live one day at a time." He pauses for a moment. "I try to look for the good and positive in everyone. And I think that you do, too, John."

I don't know what to say to that. His response is based on misrepresenting myself, deceiving him even in this extraordinary opportunity to be open with him. He flicks on the TV while I make dinner. We fall asleep to *Mr. Deeds*.

Big and Mother stood on the front porch of their Home with Small who just turned in a baggie of pot. Father was away on another business trip to San Francisco. Both Policemen had their hats off. Skinny Cop had a neatly trimmed moustache; Fat Cop had grey hair.

"Can you tell us again what happened?" Skinny Cop said.

"I was walking home from the mall, cut through the playground and found the bag. At the bottom of the slide. In the sand," Small said.

"What were you doing in the playground?" Fat Cop said.

"I saw the bag when I walked past."

Skinny Cop glanced at Fat Cop.

"Was there anyone else around?"

"No."

Skinny Cop held the baggie in his hand. The contents were bright green. It was nearly empty.

Big had seen the same baggie in Small's room yesterday. Full.

"Is there anything else we should know?" Skinny Cop said.

"No."

"Do you have a friend named Wayne?" Fat Cop said.

Big knew Small hung around Wayne at high school, a known drug dealer. Small once brought him home to eat watermelon because he thought that's what black guys liked.

"Yes. He's a friend at school. Why? What's wrong?"

"Nothing. We'd like to talk to him," Skinny Cop said.

Small's dilated pupils skipped from cop to cop.

"I'm telling the truth," he said defensively. "Why don't you believe me? I found it in the playground. That's the truth."

"I'm sure it is," Skinny Cop said. "We'd just like to talk to Wayne for a few minutes. Can you let him know that?"

Small was quiet.

"You did a good thing by turning this over to us," Fat Cop said, looking at Small. "It's disturbing to think what would have happened if some kids found it."

Big looked at Mother. She forced a smile. Her mind seemed to be elsewhere.

Day two, I wake at 8 a.m. to the ringing phone. I'm already aching to go for a run, a hike, a drive. I'm tired of staring at chain-link fences, my movements monitored, listening to the phone's disquieting ring. Paul wakes in the early afternoon, makes a pot of coffee, finishes the leftover pasta. He compliments me on the meal, chats about his prison band, Bitches Crew. He's the drummer. The lead guitarist is Steve, who's in for drug-related charges, as are over 80 per cent of the inmates here. When they are released, Paul plans to move to Montreal with Steve, make a go of it with their band. He slips in a CD of some songs they recorded in the prison music studio and watches me. An assault of metallic noise without any sense of rhythm or melody, caterwauling guitars, indecipherable vocals. It's bloody awful. I feel mean and selfish, unable to be sincere. I say it sounds good, and try to keep reading. I'm caught in my deception. Paul turns off the CD, heads outside for a smoke.

Life passed by in a blur after I saw you in the Crowsnest Pass. You enrolled at a local college, majored in criminology, talked incessantly about your classes. I moved away, tried to distance myself from you and home. Mom and Dad told me they were hopeful. Near the end of the first semester you were expelled for your erratic behaviour; you got caught with a rig plunged into your arm, in a bathroom stall, on a ten-minute class break.

You took up snowboarding with Peter, who idolized your fear-lessness. Peter provided the audience you needed and a role to fulfill: you were his big brother. When you and Peter were children, you used to show your love for him by squeezing his arms so tight that his fingertips would turn blue and he'd cry, and that made you cry because you had hurt him. Snowboarding didn't work out though, Peter was more dedicated than you and kept at it while you dabbled and moved on to other pursuits. You quit the army reserves after a brief stint, found the discipline too difficult, didn't like being yelled at all the time. You moved around and ended up at home again where you recuperated from an ulcer brought on by the drug use and debts you had amassed. You recovered from a second suicide attempt and later, baked Mom and Dad apple pies, providing them with hope that you were on a good path before vanishing again once your strength was back.

I continued to hear fragmented reports through Mom and Dad. You spent time in correctional facilities and remand centres. You moved into 1815, a halfway house in Calgary, to dry out. Here, you befriended Ron, an older man who was a chartered accountant. I kept my distance from you.

After you and Ron were released, he invited you for dinner to meet his wife, Jackie, and his two boys. They lived in a large house in northwest Calgary, a sterilized neighbourhood of culs-de-sac and five-bedroom stuccoed homes that reminded you of where you grew up, a mere ten minutes away. The kids loved you because you played road hockey with them. In the basement, you had set up a net so they could practise their wrist shots on you, much like we did while grow-ing up. Ron paid you to do jobs around the house: paint the fence, insulate and drywall the basement. These tasks reminded you of how Dad used to keep all of us busy during summer holidays with job after job, until we began to loathe him for monopolizing our time according to his needs.

Jackie enjoyed your charm, your kindness, your wild streak. She loved her blow. Ron moved out. You moved in. You tried playing Dad but as the daily responsibility of family life dragged on, you realized the only thing you learned from our dad was employing the strap and enforcing punishment to get to the truth. The boys grew fearful of your unpredictable moods and your belt, and, occasionally, your fists. Jackie financed your expensive cameras as you embarked on a new career as a photographer. You started with pictures of deer and small birds, snapped on hunting trips, later switched to promo shots of strippers. You continued to rack up Jackie's credit cards sup-porting your $300-a-day habit before you fled, with promises to pay her back. You sold your cameras for a few hits. The drywall in the basement never got finished.

You lived on the east side of Calgary, stayed in shelters with mattresses covered in plastic that crinkled each time you shifted as though you lay on top of potato-chip bags, the smell of urine in the dorm rooms, men who coughed up phlegm and wheezed all night. You supported your habit by contacting friends and relatives of the family, began with Grandma and Grandpa, Mom's brothers and sisters, Mark's girlfriend, high school teachers, my friends. The same story: they called to say they would help you out, why did we turn our backs on him? We warned them not to give you money, that you would scam them by copying bank account numbers and credit card slips. We were branded as heartless and uncaring but when their next calls came, they demanded repayment for the money that you stole. These phone calls were how we monitored your whereabouts like push-pins on a wall map, your decline, an ever-tightening net. After you robbed him, your twin, Mark, was the first to disown you. Mom and Dad installed an alarm system after you robbed their house of small change and beer, the empty cans sat on the kitchen counter, the kitchen window left ajar, your not-so-subtle calling cards. An elderly handicapped woman claimed you stole money from her.

The
Ballad
of Big
and
Small

197

You said you had hit rock bottom again, and that you needed a healthy environment to beat the drugs, that you needed your family. Mom and Dad were wary, but in the end they relented beneath your tears and you moved back into their home. Your mood swings terrorized them even more. You harassed Dad, called him "girly," "faggot," "liar." He was scared of you and spent more time in Puerto Vallarta. He disowned you next. Mom put you to work at her bookstore, to watch you. She discovered tea candles, baking soda, and bleach jugs at the back of the store. She deflated the tires of her car in the garage before going to sleep so you wouldn't steal it. You threatened her life, called her names, pummelled her with caustic words. I continued to avoid you.

While working at Mom's store, you broke in to Peter's house and trashed it. The hardwood floors were a mess of broken Jim Beam and Jack Daniel's bottles, overflowing ashtrays, syringe wrappers, pools of puke and spilled paint; the screen door was torn off the hinges. Your brother Peter, who once idolized you so intensely, pressed charges and cut off communication with you. Maybe you wanted to get caught. You confessed relief because prison time would help you avoid the mounting debts, the dealers hunting for payback. You skipped your court date. An uncle saw you downtown. Someone heard you were in Edmonton. You phoned me from Sylvan Lake. You were seen in Vancouver's downtown eastside. None of us knew whether you were dead or alive and I couldn't stand not knowing so against my better judgment I e-mailed you to call me collect anytime. You then phoned at odd hours, often desperate, violent and suicidal, always abusive. Your dream was to move to Vancouver "where the coke is pure." I considered getting an unlisted number like Peter had already done.

When Paul comes back inside from smoking his cigarettes, he's silent again, morose. I'm on guard. I regret dumping the family news on him yesterday. He has no escape from any of it after I leave. The words and memories will ferret a place in him only to agitate him later and lock him up with a shame I don't want to imagine, one I can't since I've learned to block it out myself. I feel selfish for even being here, questioning whether it's been of use to him, or whether it's only a ruse to ease my own guilt for abandoning him as an adult, being cruel to him as a child. Did I come here to make myself look better? Perhaps I did, perhaps I am indeed that selfish. He turns on the boom box, plays his CD, draws in his notebook.

   I flee outside. Stifled, boxed in, unclear of what I should do. I walk along the chain link, fantasize about hopping it, dashing for the taller fences, climbing them and running as far away as I can, from Paul, from my family, from myself. But there's nowhere to go and I head back inside. Paul turns off the music, walks through the unit, sniffles loudly. I'm grateful for having three days alone with him, and yet I can't wait to get away from him. Spending this intensive time with him only mirrors my own life, one of struggle and deceit, one that is just a bad decision or two away from being like Paul's. His wasted potential upsets the discipline I've developed from years of playing basketball but have since lost in a series of poor life decisions and irresponsible behaviour. I can't understand why he won't just get his shit together, stop using, choose a better life. He coughs, turns the TV on and off, opens the fridge, closes it. He blows his nose. Pisses in the toilet. Flushes it. Answers the phone. Steps out to wave, mutters, "Fuckin' screws." I love his voice—soaked with mischief, tinged with pain. He'll always be a tragic man, as though the path he's led is the one he was meant for. Since Grandpa's prophetic nursery observation of Paul's hands being like those of a thief. I've been preparing for his death for over fifteen years. If I don't hear from him for months at a time, I have no way of finding out if he's dead or alive, as if he's missing at sea. But when I see him again, no matter how long the absence, I am grateful for our rare moments of connection and immediately feel guilty for having conjured so many negative possible outcomes. It's a complete mindfuck: I live haunted by our familial past that ties us together, fearful for his future. Yet, in prison together, in the present, as we try to make sense of our family, ourselves and our relationship to each other, I feel closer to him, better able to see him as my brother struggling and scared, not the drug addict, or that horribly demeaning term we once used to separate ourselves from him, "junkie." This is the most time we've spent together since we were teenagers, since he started using drugs. Still, I can't wait to get out of here, and go home. The more time I spend with him, the more responsible I feel for being part of his addiction and the more shame I feel towards my own life.

The
Ballad
of Big
and
Small

199

Paul, do you remember lying on the floor in a room at the York Hotel? You tried to get up, but Brad drove the knife into your hand, pinned you down. Remember how Justice flogged your face with a bike lock? You promised yourself if you survived you would quit doing coke, live normal. You blacked out and came to as Justice kicked you in the ribs again, his nostrils flared, his eyes blown wild. You feared him more than Brad. Justice wanted you dead.

They shoved you in a van. "Dial the number, motherfucker," said Brad. You dialed and asked how Mom was doing. She hadn't heard from you in months; she sensed trouble. Brad grabbed the phone and demanded that she pay him $200 or they would cut you up. You shouted, "Don't listen to them." Justice busted your nose. Jennifer, the driver, called Mom a bitch-whore, you heard her tell Mom that you were a worthless piece of shit, a dead man. Was it worth scoring with Jennifer even though she was Justice's girl? Drilling coke into each other's veins, fucking the afternoons away before she peeled off her clothes for raucous frat boys and fat oilmen at the French Maid? Was it worth stealing a few dime bags from her?

Mom heard you scream, "Don't give in to them." She hardly recognized your voice. Jennifer shouted, "Your son's going downtown. Say bye-bye," and hung up. Mom called the Calgary police, the same cops that had been looking for you, the same cops that had kept a file on you for the past fifteen years since, as a teenager, you turned in a bag of dope during a fit of paranoia, remember?

The trio drove you back to the York. Brad made a call. A well-dressed man had walked in wearing shades. Just like in the movies, you thought. Your life was one long dramatic reel you could never stop and start over again, clean, and perhaps this is what prevented you from trying harder. He shook his head, handed Brad something, slammed the door when he left. Justice jumped up and down, shouted, "Let me do it, let me do it." Brad urged him to relax, flicked the Bic lighter, cooked the junk in a dirty spoon, siphoned it into a syringe, handed it to Justice. You were seconds away from an overdose, a certain ignoble death. What did you feel in that moment? Regret? Sadness? Fear? Relief? And just like in the movies, the police smashed the door open, arrested them, saved your life. Did this make you happy?

After the beating, you laid in intensive care with a broken nose, broken ribs, broken hand, broken leg that required several pins to hold it together, numerous lacerations to the chest and abdomen, torn eye; your head was shaved in two spots where you were stitched up from knife wounds. Do you remember telling Mom and Dad that you wanted to kick the habit? They offered a strong united front for your benefit, but they were mainlined for a divorce. They called me with the news. I flew to visit you in Calgary as soon as possible. You said: "Bro, I need some help. I gotta get out of this life." I was devastated by your admission and physical deterioration; shattered, wished I could have been a better brother to you. Do you remember how I vowed that I'd quit drinking as a small gesture of brotherly support? I immediately broke that promise at the airport, waiting for my flight home, drinking one beer after another in the flight lounge.

Months later, I returned to Calgary and sat in a courtroom with Peter and watched you testify against Brad and Justice. You refused to look at us. They were convicted for seven years. You asked me to save the newspaper clipping. Three short lines. Buried in the city section. Your name mentioned. This made you smile.

At your request, your legal-aid rep petitioned for you to be moved to a federal facility where you could receive proper and regular medical care, and drug rehab, while serving your time.

You got your wish: you were headed to Grande Cache Federal Institution.

The
Ballad
of Big
and
Small

201

On the third and final day, there's no phone call for count. Neither of us want to eat as we wait for Paul's parole officer to come. Paul says he will be discharged in three months. An unmarked white van will pick up released prisoners and drive them to Edmonton, drop them off downtown, leave them on a street corner to begin their lives again. I tell him I'd like to be here when he gets released, drive him myself, and stay with him for a week or two to help him get his feet on the ground. As I make the offer, I imagine how it will all play out, how I will ultimately save my brother. "That would be good, bro," he says. "But I'll be fine." I realize that he doesn't want my help. He's probably already got a scheme in place for his release. The truth is, he doesn't believe me.

With little time left, I try to get closer by asking direct questions I am afraid of hearing the answers to, questions that only encourage him to lie. Are you using? He looks me in the eye. "I've been clean since January." His defensive tone suggests a lie. It's what he thinks I want to hear. And I do.

Are you nervous about getting out? He can only take it one day at a time, he says, "the good Lord will take care of me." He adds, "Let bygones be bygones." That's the closest he comes to expressing regret or apology.

How will you resist the street when you get out? "I can't think about it because it makes me anxious and I have enough anxiety being locked up, paranoid that inmates are plotting against me."

Finally, do you have any intention of repairing relationships within the family? He stares at me with a mocking grin. "Sure, John, whatever you say."

His parole officer walks towards us. I hug Paul; awkwardly say that I love him and I'll be here for him when he gets out. The intention is genuine, but the moment I say the words I sense it won't work out in reality. I ask that he write, that he save the letters for when he gets out, but stop short of offering my home address.

In high school, when Paul first began experimenting with drugs, he used to steal my basketball T-shirts and wear them, pretending to be a recruited athlete before he sold them for dope money. My parents thought I had taken things too far by putting a lock on my bedroom door. They thought I had been exaggerating these thefts until, after my room was locked, other items throughout the house began to disappear. Now we exchange T-shirts. He hands me his plain white prison issue with a name tag that simply says: Vigna. We exit unit B202 together and shake hands. His parole officer locks the front door and closes the gate while Paul waits on the sidewalk. Paul gives me that everything's a-okay smile, turns and limps towards the main building, his mesh bag slung over his shoulder.

He does not look back.

Postscript:

Paul died alone in his rooming house on June 1, 2007. He had been dead for over a month before my family found out—we didn't receive notification until the first week in July.

The manager of the rooming house told us that he had found Paul in his room, slumped against his locked door as if to block any entry. There were spent syringes on the ground and the room was in complete shambles: the furniture turned over, shelves emptied and torn apart, clothes strewn everywhere, broken glass scattered on the floor, his sketchbook and journal nearby. Paul was such a neat freak, so clean and orderly that it was devastating to see in graphic detail the squalor of how he had spent his last moments. I asked the manager if he thought Paul's death was a suicide; he declined to offer his opinion. He said we had the facts and that it was up to my family what to do with them, how to interpret them. What was important, he said, was that Paul was released from a life of pain. I pressed the manager further but he did not budge, suggesting that I wait for the coroner's report.

Word from the coroner wasn't expected for a few weeks. In the meantime, we held a quiet memorial in the Crowsnest Pass. Afterwards, I carried a small container of Paul's ashes and climbed Turtle Mountain, the mountain Paul and I had made plans to climb the day we peaked Crowsnest, over a decade ago. It was a flawless, searing-hot, blue-sky day. On Turtle Mountain, you can peer over the edge at Frank Slide and witness the destructive swath of rubble that spread across the land for hundreds of metres, burying the town of Frank and everyone within its path. But it's hard to imagine that even if Paul and I had climbed the mountain together, he would have looked over the lip.

There are all kinds of scientific measuring devices on the peak, devices that measure the slightest movement, as the mountain is still considered unstable. In the distance to the west, Crowsnest Mountain. In the foreground, my grandparents' house, sold after they had passed away, now inhabited as a recreation getaway by Calgarians. Across the highway and train tracks, the graveyard where my grandparents and great-grandmother and other family members on my father's side lay in rest. I am careful to keep away from the edge; it is here that I scatter Paul's ashes.

I returned to Vancouver but the sound of the phone ringing still startles me and I suspect it will for some time yet. A couple of weeks later the coroner's report finally came in. Paul's death was officially ruled an accidental overdose.

The Blue
Jewel of
the Jungle

Andrew
Westoll

I WAKE at 6 a.m. to the soft murmurs of the *Trio* language. Outside, my crew is gathered under the overhang of my thatch-roofed hut, inspecting the insides of our motor. The sun is slowly rising. The village of Kwamalasemutu is beginning to glow.

"*Cuday mana*," I say, the *Trio* morning greeting, the only words I know. The men look up at me nervously.

"*Andu!*" yells Ipiroke.

"*Fa yu sribi?*" asks Lukas.

Mawa drops his wrench and walks towards me. The Basha just smiles his goofy smile.

"We have problem," says Mawa.

"I see that."

"Man we pay for motor not happy. Now we use my motor. First we fix."

"How long?" I ask.

"Not long."

"We still leave seven o'clock?"

"Yes. Seven o'clock."

At ten-fifteen, Lukas and Mawa screw the engine casing back into place and we ferry our equipment down to the river. Three water-proof barrels filled with cassava bread and *farine*, 300 litres of gaso-line in six black jerry cans, two old detergent buckets overflowing with *casiri* beer, a bright blue jug with 100 litres of rainwater for drinking, 50 kilograms of rice, two huge tarps, two metal storm-lanterns, six life jackets, two rifles, one bow, a quiver of arrows, an extra outboard motor. And all of our personal gear, hammocks and clothes and boots stashed in countless garbage bags. We will be gone for a week. Aside from our staples, we will eat whatever we can kill.

As we push off and the crowd onshore yells their encouragement, I see the extra outboard motor sitting in the grass.

"Lukas," I say. "*Yu frigiti motor.*"

"No problem," says Lukas, yanking on the ignition cord. "Motor good now." After the seventh pull, the engine roars to life.

Five minutes upriver, we stop at a small collection of huts on the opposite shore, the equivalent of a Kwamala suburb. Lukas jumps out of the boat with a bag of fresh diapers and runs up the hill to one of the houses. While he's gone, I watch a young girl roll a huge round of cassava bread beside her like a Hula Hoop. The bread is as tall as she is. When it catches the sun I can see right through it, an orb of golden-brown with the shadow of a girl in its centre. A young boy waves at me from a nearby hammock. He makes a series of threatening hand gestures and points to the east, as if we are crazy to be headed that way. As if danger lurks upriver.

We are about to disappear into a secret wilderness, in search of its crowning jewel.

Perched above Brazil in the middle of the Guiana Shield, Suriname is the least-travelled country in South America. Though many untouched places have been called the Last Eden—Patagonia in Argentina, the Okavango Delta in Botswana, the Ndoki region in the Democratic Republic of Congo, the wild island of Borneo—this unassuming republic has a legitimate claim to the title. Ninety per cent of the country is covered in thick neo-tropical jungle, the largest percentage of rain forest cover of any nation on earth, and only 430,000 people live here, with a population density similar to that of Canadian Nunavut and Russian Siberia. Consequently, the jungles of Suriname are the most pristine left on the planet.

Five years ago, I lived deep inside these jungles for a year, at a remote anthropological field station where I worked as a monkey researcher. Ever since then, I've dreamed of returning. Late last year this dream came true, and I've now been travelling here for five months.

My curiosity has led me to Kwamalasemutu, the land of the Trio Indians, in the remote south of Suriname. In 1968, a young Dutch herpetologist named Marinus Hoogmoed discovered a remarkable new frog species while exploring the valleys of the Four Brothers of Mamia, a modest set of hills near Suriname's border with Brazil. He called it *Dendrobates azureus*, after its stunning azure-blue skin. The Trio Indians, who had known of this frog's existence for centuries, already had a name for it. They called it *okopipi*.

The
Blue
Jewel
of the
Jungle

207

Okopipi is revered by the Trio for its rarity, its iridescent blue skin and the extraordinary strength of its poison. Each frog contains an average of 200 milligrams of toxin; 2 milligrams on the tip of an arrow is enough to kill a man. The Trio used to catch *okopipi* and sell them on the exotic-animal market, but laws have recently been passed banning their trade. Today, *okopipi* is considered one of the most vulnerable amphibians in the neo-tropics. The total population is thought to be no more than three hundred individuals.

Having spent so long travelling this obscure nation and searching for its quintessential soul, *okopipi* seemed the perfect quarry—elusive, rare, endangered. So three days ago, I left the capital city of Paramaribo aboard an ancient Russian Antonov bound for the south. Since arriving in Kwamala, I've rented a boat, rented a motor, hired a crew, and spent every penny I have on gasoline. Granman Asongo, the Paramount Chief of the Trio Nation, has given me permission to travel by boat to find *okopipi*. He says it will be the first expedition of its kind in recent memory. Accompanying us will be the Basha, a representative from the Trio government who will report back to the Granman on what we find upriver.

Asongo has set just two conditions. First, I am not to take *okopipi* home with me to Canada. Second, I am to bring the Granman as many red-footed turtles as I can find.

At our last meeting, I asked Asongo how long the trip would take. He peered up at the ceiling of his office, thought for a moment and then gave a broad smile.

"Sunset, sunset, sunset, arrive."

Along the shore of the Sipaliwini River the jungle is thick and seems to brood. Young cecropia trees poke their necks out over the water like curious children, their crowns of convoluted leaves drenched in sun. A white heron-like bird with a bright blue beak watches us pass and then plunges its head into the river.

Soon the river narrows and the rapids of *gruni keni* appear. Mawa stands in the bow and directs Lukas through the stones. We get stuck on the bottom a number of times and the motor chokes when Lukas cranks the gas. Up ahead, another boat approaches in the opposite direction. Inside sits a Trio family, the husband at the motor, his wife and two small children in the bow. Their boat is as heavily laden as ours but is a better vessel, shaped more like an arrow compared to our broad, ungainly dugout.

As they speed between the rocks, aided by the current, Lukas yells something to the husband, who quickly turns his boat and meets us at the shore. The family has agreed to switch boats with us. The husband laughs at the thought of our attempting this journey with our current canoe. His family unloads their possessions onto the shore, a menagerie of dead or dying animals. A turtle with a stick through its armholes, alive but in severe discomfort. A baby kinkajou with a rope around its neck. A selection of river fish strung through the gills with a piece of wire. Two blue-and-green parrots, their feet tied together with string. An adult spider monkey, his eyes closed, his hands limp and haunting, a single bullet hole through his chest.

Lukas lifts our faulty motor onto the stern of our new boat as we load our gear into the hull. Within minutes we are back on the water and the family has disappeared up the hill into the jungle. We make it up *gruni keni* despite our engine's complaints. Then the river calms. Fist-sized balls of cotton fall from the *kankan* trees and drift on the river's surface. We pass several orapendula colonies, the dark birds flashing their yellow tails as they dive for cover into palm-thatch nests, each one hanging like a blackened teardrop from the branches.

Half a mile up ahead, the river becomes a field of boulders and whitewater. This is *ewana tepu*, or Iguana Falls, the largest series of rapids on the Sipaliwini. There is no way our engine can handle this, I think. As if in agreement, Lukas steers us to the right-hand shore, where a small side-channel empties into the river.

We enter the channel and become enveloped by a close, green darkness. Our route is less than 5 metres across, a shallow jungle stream that will surely go dry in a week or two. Our motor echoes against the tangled underbrush and thick canopy. At an especially tight section, a tree boa drops from its perch beside my head and knifes into the water.

Now the channel is dotted with floating mangoes. I grab one out of the water and hold it up like a trophy. Then Lukas cuts the engine and lets out a moan, and we come upon the source of the fruit. An enormous mango tree has collapsed and fallen across the creek, completely blocking our way.

We jump out into knee-deep water and hack through the tree. It takes us two hours to cleave a space for our boat to pass. Just as we're pulling it through, Mawa whispers something and the Indians suddenly stop moving. Mawa's eyes are wide as he points at something over my shoulder.

Behind me, stretched out on one of the mango branches, a massive green anaconda sits sunning itself. Its body is perhaps 15 feet long and more than a foot thick. I stumble back towards the boat, shocked that this snake has been there the whole time. I expect the others to laugh at my fear but nobody laughs. Instead, everyone leaps into the boat and Lukas cranks the motor. At the sound of the engine, the snake slowly slinks back into the water, the yellow-and-black spots on its hide glistening as it disappears beneath the surface.

We spend the rest of the day crawling upriver and struggling through rapids. Our morale sinks as the motor worsens and we snack on dry *farine*. I am beginning to think this trip was a mistake. We've hardly made any progress today and we're wasting precious litres of gasoline.

Finally, at six o'clock, we limp to shore, where the remains of an ancient hunting camp sit rotting among the trees. Ipiroke and I jump

The
Blue
Jewel
of the
Jungle

209

out with our gear and the others continue upriver to work on the motor and catch dinner. Twenty minutes later, the fire is roaring and we've hung our hammocks beneath makeshift palm-frond shelters. This camp has been used for centuries by Trio hunters, but Ipi says no one has slept here for at least five years. This is prime hunting territory, he says, but no one can afford the gasoline required to get here.

The sun drops beneath the canopy and the jungle closes in. Ipiroke sings to the animals. He impersonates three species of monkey and four species of bird. As a cool evening mist descends on the river, a lone bird responds to Ipi's call from perhaps a mile away.

An hour later, the men return with a boatload of meat. Two 40-pound tiger fish sit in the bow, their striped flanks glowing orange in the dark, their mouths spilling out with vicious teeth. In the stern sit two 20-pound *sipali*, or electric stingrays, the primeval namesake of this river. Lukas hefts a *sipali* from the boat and hands it to me, his fingers plunged through its eye sockets.

Fireflies dance around our camp as Lukas cooks the fish in pepper water and Mawa smokes the remaining meat. We gorge ourselves on the rich, oily flesh. Then the Basha retrieves an old detergent bucket and lifts the lid, revealing a familiar pink sludge. It is time to drink *casiri*.

The Basha adds a few cupfuls of river water to the brew and we chug it down. Above us, the moon is reflected by the leaves in the trees, the green of the jungle giving way to the black and white of the night. My crew tell jokes I don't understand and giggle among themselves. The Basha lets loose a series of spectacular farts. Exhausted and drunk, we soon retreat to our beds.

As I stumble into my hammock the crossbeams of my shelter creak ominously. Then the whole structure collapses. I fall to the ground with an awkward crash, the splintered timbers landing on top of me. The men roar with laughter but within seconds they set to work. Lukas and the Basha disappear into the jungle while Mawa and Ipiroke cut new saplings and arrange them in a lean-to fashion. From somewhere in the darkness I hear a strange ripping sound, and then Lukas and the Basha appear from the dark carrying long strips of bark. They use the bark as rope, tying the new timbers together, and soon my shelter is rebuilt. I hang my hammock and test it out. The timbers are sturdy and will last perhaps another hundred years.

The men return to their hammocks and chat as a light rain trickles down from the canopy. I fall asleep to the whispers of their dying language.

Prior to the 1960s, the Trio lived in small, semi-nomadic villages scattered throughout southern Suriname and the northern regions of Brazil. Their territory followed the watershed divide between the Sipaliwini basin, where the rivers flow north to the Atlantic, and the Upper Amazon Basin, where the waters flow south to the world's largest river.

The Trio are a multi-ethnic tribe made up of several previously distinct Amerindian groups. At some point, likely long before the New World was discovered, these peoples began referring to themselves inclusively with the term *Tareno*. Over time, outsiders evolved this word into its current usage, *Trio*. *Tareno* simply means "the people here" and reflects the tribe's loose geographic and cultural histories.

In 1954, the protestant West Indies Mission established the Suriname Interior Fellowship, a new hub for missionary work in the Guianas. In 1960, the Surinamese government began Operation Grasshopper, opening up the country's tangled interior by building forty new airstrips. These two events marked the beginning of the end for the Trio's traditional way of life.

The Trio have no words for measures of distance. Instead, distance is expressed in terms of the amount of time it takes to travel it. For this reason, Trio estimates of distance are always vague, highly subjective and related to the course of the sun. We have travelled one sunset so far. We have two more to go.

I roll out of my hammock at 4:30 a.m. It is dark and so time still sleeps. The wooden posts of my shelter creak and I brace myself for a fall, but somehow it holds and I walk to the smouldering campfire. I am anxious to wake the crew and get on with the day. Our trouble with the motor coupled with the unexpectedly low water has set us back at least six hours of travel time.

Ipiroke is the first to rise. He emerges from beneath his palm-frond roof wearing only a blue Speedo-style swimsuit.

"Andu!" he yells, as he makes his way to the river by flashlight. "Andu!"

We are on the water by seven. The motor is better this morning and we let out a cheer as our fears of another day spent crawling upriver are dispelled. The river winds as if carved into the earth by a child. We pass a pile of boulders in the middle of the river and a colony of bats bursts out, enveloping the boat for a few seconds in a squeaking black cloud. The back of Mawa's T-shirt declares he is "Proud to be plunger-free."

After pulling the boat through the first set of rapids, the sun finally breaks above the canopy and washes the river in light. To my left, a thick bamboo stand turns translucent in the sunshine, green and see-through like the filaments of insect wings. We pass a *kankan* tree that leans over the river with the weight of more than fifty orapendula nests. Then Lukas cuts the engine and Ipiroke stands with his rifle. Mawa jumps out of the boat, wades to shore, and disappears into the bush.

Ipiroke aims at a branch-fork near the top of the majestic tree and fires off a round. The gunshot echoes up and down the river and a huge mass of green plummets from the branch. It lands with a thud in the underbrush and Mawa yells excitedly. A chase ensues. From the boat, all we hear are Mawa's yelps and frantic footsteps. Suddenly, the injured animal crashes out of the bush—an iguana, its prehistoric body more than five feet long, desperately trying to save itself. Just as it stumbles to the water's edge, Mawa bursts out of the forest behind it and snatches it up by the tail.

He hands the writhing reptile to Ipiroke as Lukas starts the engine. Ipi digs the blade of his machete into the iguana's chest and I hear the whoosh of life escaping its body. He splits the animal open from neck to tail, its innards splashing into the water as he cuts them loose. In ten seconds the animal is empty, nothing but meat on bones, its lifeless fingers long and wrinkled, its gorgeous rack of blue-green spines slumped into its gaping body cavity. Ipi tosses the corpse into the hull and rinses his hands in the river. Lukas taps me on the back.

"*Ewana switi*," he says. Iguana tastes good.

We pass *agarapi kreeki* and the river begins to narrow. We pull our boat up a series of rapids, each of us up to our waists in rushing water, struggling to keep our footing as we pull on the gunwales. Lukas decides to motor up a particularly rough patch so we climb back in, and as the engine struggles against the current a 3-foot *anyumara*—the oily river fish built like a tank—leaps into the bow. With a flash of steel, Mawa pins the fish to the hull with his machete. In seconds, its liver, intestines, and air bladder are floating past me.

We are travelling through an uninhabited jungle teeming with life. During the dry season, hardly a soul travels these waters, and even when the rains come it is rare for anyone to make this trip. Consequently, the region is stocked like a supermarket. We come upon a forest turtle swimming across the river. Lukas aims straight for it and Mawa simply scoops it out of the water and places it in the boat.

I ask Mawa how much farther it is to Sipaliwini. He looks up at the sky and draws a slow arc in the air. As he does this, he keeps count on his fingers. Then he closes his eyes, as if remembering past trips on this river, or perhaps asking the sun for the answer.

"*Kande wi go doro sixi yuru*," says Mawa. If we travel well, we'll arrive in Sipaliwini at six in the evening.

Walaba trees line the shoreline, their seed cases like thick boomerangs hanging from pieces of string. As we pass beneath a massive wasp nest, 2 metres long and thick as a tree trunk, Lukas yells something in *Trio* and turns the boat down a side creek.

Mawa and Ipiroke quickly reach for their rifles again. They load their guns as Lukas aims the boat at a nondescript section of the shore and cuts the engine. The boat scrapes up onto the rocks and the men leap out. As they scramble up a steep embankment into the bush I scale our piles of equipment and follow them.

The jungle floor is still dark. The men race through the underbrush and I struggle to keep up. When I finally reach them, both men are whispering to each other and staring straight up into the canopy. A lump forms in my throat as I recognize the scene. The men are hunting monkey.

Forty metres above us, an adult red howler monkey sits with his back to a tree trunk. He does not move, just stares down at us through the thick foliage. His maroon fur glimmers gold as it catches the sun that has not yet reached the forest floor. The bearded face is dark and ghoulish. These are the monkeys who howl like banshees, their ghostly wails renowned throughout South America for their haunting depth and power.

Mawa raises his gun but cannot get a clear shot. Lukas strips a young sapling and, hefting it like an axe, bashes it against the trunk of the monkey's tree. Now both men begin to grunt loudly from deep in their throats, impersonating a predator or perhaps a jungle spirit. They are trying to scare their prey into moving, into exposing himself to Mawa's rifle.

In seconds, the monkey is leaping through the canopy. The men continue to grunt as they track the animal. Suddenly, my training in primatology kicks in. I see more flashes of red escaping to the west—two juvenile females, one juvenile male, an adult female with a baby on its back. I almost yell to the others but stop myself. Instead, I watch the monkeys recede into the green, winning their freedom and leaving their doomed patriarch behind.

Time moves in strange circles. I used to study monkeys and now I'm hunting them.

A gunshot shatters the morning stillness. I wait for a body to crash to the ground but nothing happens. Lukas and Mawa share a few words. Then Mawa leans his rifle against a rotting log, grips the blade of his machete between his teeth and begins shimmying up a tree.

Mawa glides up the trunk effortlessly. Far above, the monkey sits slumped over, his prehensile tail instinctively wrapped around a thick branch and keeping him from falling. In less than a minute, Mawa comes level with the dying animal, reaches out, and unwraps the monkey's tail. The monkey slips from his perch, plummets through the branches and lands at my feet with a massive thud. His eyelids drift shut as a last breath exits his nostrils.

I drag the corpse back to the boat, my hand gripping the base of his tail. His crimson fur is softer than I'd expected.

At five o'clock we come upon the first signs of civilization. A small dugout canoe, large enough for a man and his hunting dog, is beached on the riverbank. Next to it, a fishing net is wrapped around a snag of wood. Ipiroke yells a *Trio* greeting into the bush but receives no answer. Then we round a corner and the late-afternoon sun is suddenly blinding, lighting up our boat and the water around it. The jungle on the shore has vanished. We have entered the Sipaliwini savannah.

I stand up and peer over the mud walls of the river. I catch glimpses of a surreal landscape, miles of tall grasses and rolling hills dotted with solitary trees. It looks like the grasslands of Africa. The last five months in the jungles of this country have been a dark and lonely time for me. But now, as Lukas steers us down the middle of the narrowing river and the sky opens up, I begin to see beyond myself for the first time in a long time. I imagine the crush of solitude perhaps loosening its grip, ever so slightly, slipping away with the claustrophobia of all those trees.

An hour later we see a triangular yellow flag fluttering over the river and Lukas cuts the engine. We dock beside an enormous boulder and unload our gear. Then Mawa leads us into the grasses. Two small children emerge from the trees and scurry ahead of us, desperate to deliver the news of our arrival. Their skin is wet with river water and their hair is a glossy black. We pass a family compound, rectangular thatch-roofed buildings with walls of split bamboo. Soon there is more traffic on the trail, men wrapped in towels on their way to bathe, their upper bodies rippled with muscle and riddled with green tattoos.

We stop at a small cooking hut with no walls. Inside, two old Trio women tend the fire and spill the guts of fish into the embers. They wear ancient, torn skirts and nothing above the waist. When they see me they smile and begin to laugh. Ipiroke drops the dead howler monkey at the women's feet and mumbles something softly to them. As we walk away, one of the women chops off the monkey's tail with a single swipe of her axe.

Mawa leads us to a modern-looking building and we climb the stairs to the second-floor balcony. I open the door to one of the rooms and a horde of cockroaches flees to the corners. I set up my hammock in the semidarkness. Through my window, the savannah stretches to the horizon, where a range of hills glistens in the weak light.

Lukas cooks a late dinner of boiled iguana, rice and pepper water. The meat is almost white, very tender and tastes a bit like pork. As I

The
Blue
Jewel
of the
Jungle

215

chew a piece of the animal's forearm, tearing the flesh from its slippery hide, I chomp down on something hard and metallic. I grimace in pain and spit the meat into my hand, assuming I've lost a filling. The men burst into laughter. In the middle of my palm sits a small, grey gunshot pellet.

In 1961, the American Baptist missionary Claude Leavitt arrived with his family in the south of Suriname. Upon entering his first Trio village, the people told Leavitt they had seen only three *pananakiri*, or outsiders, before him: Lodewijk Schmidt, a Surinamese explorer of African descent, and two Americans searching for a pilot named Redfern, whose airplane had crashed nearby.

Leavitt quickly realized his task of bringing the word of God to the Indians would be much easier if he could convince the scattered Trio to settle in a single village. Leavitt promised free health care and education in this new mega-village, and soon the Trio agreed to amalgamate in an indigenous metropolis on the Wiumi River. The new village was called Alalaparu, which means "place of the brazil nut" in the *Trio* language.

Acculturation of the Trio began swiftly with the move. The people now had access to steel tools such as machetes, axes, and knives. A medical clinic was established and village hygiene was improved, resulting in greater life expectancy for the residents. A new airstrip reduced travel time to the towns on Suriname's coast from two weeks by paddle to two hours by air. The Missionary Aviation Fellowship began an air ambulance service, transporting seriously ill Trio to Paramaribo for treatment. Teachers were flown in to instruct the children and literacy flourished. A small store was set up, offering a range of material goods. Within a few years, the population at Alalaparu grew from one hundred to more than four hundred as Trio emerged from the surrounding jungles to take advantage of this new-found wealth.

But as is true of missionary work the world over, the real societal gains brought about by Leavitt were accompanied by long-term cultural losses. There are pictures from the late 1960s of Granman Asongo in traditional Trio garb—his hair in a bowl-cut, his face painted for the hunt, wearing nothing but a maroon loincloth. Soon after these pictures were taken, traditional Trio dress was outlawed and Asongo was sent to Texas for theological training—now he wears a suit and gold-rimmed glasses. The traditional system of government, in which a charismatic elder oversaw a community held together by kinship ties and marriage, was replaced by hierarchical, centralized rule. Customary song and dance rituals were replaced by fervent Christian music and ceremonies. Shamanism was forbidden, as was polygamy, body scarification, and the recounting of Trio mythology. All of these practices were punishable by flogging.

The incessant evangelism of the Baptists slowly overwhelmed the Trio. As the people revelled in the surface benefits of western culture, their own ancient culture began to disappear. Perhaps the only social tradition to survive Leavitt's influence was the ritual drinking of *casiri*.

The
Blue
Jewel
of the
Jungle

217

Alalaparu continued to grow and soon the population was hit by severe food shortages. With their newly acquired rifles, the Trio quickly exhausted the surrounding jungle of game. The Wiumi River ran dry for months at a time and fish populations dwindled. Gardens had been built too close together and a plague of ants decimated the crops. Agricultural land was replanted too soon and the tired soil failed to produce.

Fifteen years after it was founded, Alalaparu was abandoned in 1975, the same year Suriname gained independence from Holland. The Trio relocated to virgin land on the Sipaliwini River. This new village was called Kwamalasemutu, or "place of sand and bamboo."

Sipaliwini wakes. The ancient ladies have started their fire and the roosters have begun to bawl. A small Indian child, his legs crippled by some ferocious disease, crawls from a nearby hut and heaves himself up into a hammock. Bees hum from somewhere beneath our building as the village dogs emerge from the grasses. The sun is up and time has begun to flow.

Before we leave, we drink *casiri* at the house of Mawa's friend. The brew is fresh and potent, stronger than the batch we brought with us, and soon my vision is swimming. We load the boat, taking only the necessities and leaving the rest behind. Today, if we are lucky, we will reach the grasslands of Mamia, the homelands of *okopipi*.

For some reason, a villager has given us an old rice sack with an 8-foot boa constrictor inside. The Basha sits with a small birdcage containing a chestnut-bellied seedfinch, or *picollete*. The poor turtle on a stick has shit during the night. As Lukas guns the motor a torrent of brown water comes sloshing past my feet. Our boat is now a modest zoo.

Lukas decides to run the first set of rapids, the steepest ones we've seen besides *ewana tepu*. Like the rest of us, Lukas is very drunk. Halfway up, we hear a sickening sound—metal grinding on stone—and the boat lilts and begins to drift backwards. We jump out, the water up to our chests, and pull the boat to a small island of rocks to inspect the damage. Our prop is still there but one of the blades has sheared off.

No one speaks. Instead, the Basha digs through our piles of gear and emerges with a pot and the barrel of cassava bread. Inside the pot, chunks of boiled howler monkey sit in a congealed sauce. The men dig in but I wait for them to eat their fill. Then I reach reluctantly into the pot and pull out a severed hand, the fingers webbed with grease and onions. I nibble the primate palm, rip a piece of stringy flesh from it and feel the revulsion rising from my stomach. I give the hand to the Basha, who tears the fingers off one by one and sucks the meat from the bone. I take a piece of breast instead, choking down my breakfast as the monkey fur tickles the back of my throat.

We spend the morning hauling our boat up an endless series of rapids. The motor is almost useless now and we crawl against the current. Amazon kingfishers dive into the river beside us and emerge with foot-long fish. We pass beneath a dove's nest, the mother on top of her egg, waiting until the last moment to flee. We have left the Sipaliwini River behind and have joined the river of Mamia.

At noon we pull over, exhausted and baked by the sun. We are used to having the canopy to shade us but in the savannah the heat is relentless. The rainy season was due about three weeks ago.

I assume we've stopped to rest but Ipiroke grabs the axe and wades to shore. He scrambles up the bank to the base of a giant *awara* palm, the crown of which sags with three huge clusters of red fruits. Each cluster contains at least a hundred nuts; this is what Ipi is after. But instead of shimmying up the trunk, Ipi begins chopping down the whole tree. Meanwhile, Mawa asks me for my lighter and I hand it to him without thinking. He wades to the other side and disappears into the grasses.

Lukas and the Basha cast their fishing lines and I climb out of the boat. I watch Ipi work as I crouch in the shade beneath the riverbank, balanced on a slim piece of stone. Then I hear the crackling and smell the smoke. I climb up to the grasses and am almost engulfed by flames. Mawa has set the savannah on fire.

I can see him a half-mile away, holding my lighter to a new swath of grass as walls of flame sweep between us. I scramble back down to the shore but Lukas has moved the boat upriver and there's no way to escape. The crackling gets louder and the air becomes an oven. The grasses above me shrivel and burn and I prepare to leap into the river.

Somehow, the fire fails to catch the trees at the water's edge and it burns itself out. Lukas and the Basha are laughing at me and Ipi continues to hack at the palm. I wait a few minutes and then climb back up to the grasses.

I wander through a scorched landscape. The grasses are gone, replaced by black ashes, and clouds of thick smoke drift on the breeze. The charred earth melts the soles of my flip-flops and bakes the soles of my feet. In the distance, the fires continue to rage as Mawa walks between them, his head bent low in search of something. Lukas has joined him now and is setting his own swaths of savannah ablaze.

Then a cry goes up from the river and the palm tree begins to fall. It drops slowly at first, a shower of nuts preceding it to the ground. Then it disappears below the riverbank and lands with a violent crash. Ipiroke miscalculated. The tree now lies across the river, barring our return journey.

I climb back down and splash into the water. The Basha drifts the boat back and we fill the hull with nuts. As we plunder the palm, Mawa and Lukas appear at the top of the riverbank, covered in black

The
Blue
Jewel
of the
Jungle

219

ash. They carry six savannah turtles, flushed out of hiding by the flames, sticks thrust through their armholes, twenty-four red-soled feet flailing in the air. The Trio treasure these turtles as pets. These six are gifts for Granman Asongo.

By four o'clock, the creek is no more than a foot deep and Lukas has cut the engine. Mawa and Ipiroke use sticks to pull the boat along. Then, from a dark cluster of trees on the riverbank, a lone Indian emerges and waves us down. This must be Winni. We have arrived in Mamia.

Lukas beaches the boat and we carry our gear up a small rise, where a firepit blazes and a makeshift hammock camp leans to the north. As I approach, Winni eyes me and then grabs my hand and shakes it. He is perhaps forty-five years old, with a slight build, weary eyes, and the ubiquitous bead jewelry of the Trio around his neck.

Winni's daughter is here as well, a beautiful teenager with a glossed black ponytail down her back. As we reinforce the shelter and cover it with our tarps, she butchers an iguana. She holds it by the tail and sweeps her machete across its belly as if playing the cello.

Winni asks to speak with me. He has changed his clothes and now wears a white button-up shirt and black pants. Even out here, the ceremonial greeting of a stranger is a high priority. Ipiroke translates from *Trio* to *Sranantongo* for me. When I first arrived in this country, I needed translations from *Sranantongo* to English.

Winni welcomes me to the Sipaliwini Nature Reserve. Granman Asongo had radioed him to tell of the white man and his search for *okopipi*, so he hiked four hours this morning to meet us. Winni will be our guide into the mountains. He is happy I am here and hopes that I will pay him. He also hopes I find what I'm looking for, because without the rains there are no guarantees. He finishes by warning me not to leave Mamia with *okopipi* in my backpack.

I thank Winni, give him his money and promise not to take any frogs. He seems to relax a little and we settle in for dinner. The others have caught a few *dwala* and have boiled them with the iguana. As we eat, the sun sets and the *mopira* flies ease. Afterwards, we hang our hammocks and my crew collapses into them, exhausted and happy to have arrived.

Before bed, I light a smoke and walk out to the savannah. The moon is full and casts a cool, grey light. To the south, the Four Brothers of Mamia rise up, the land's last sigh before Brazil. Mosquitoes have replaced the *mopira*, and fireflies dance among the grasses. Forty years ago, another white man came here to climb the Brothers. He fell off the mountainside and died before help could reach him. The missionaries had just arrived.

The
Blue
Jewel
of the
Jungle

221

Our search begins with a prayer. We gather in the dark at the edge of camp, where the jungle gives way to savannah, where the trail to Brazil begins. Winni asks us to bow our heads. He speaks quickly, efficiently, reverently—the voice of a man who knows faith and timing are of equal importance when you live alone in the bush. He uses a mixture of *Trio* and *Sranantongo*. I pick out sections about God, happiness, white men. As he speaks, waist-high grasses squeak in the morning breeze and the sun still sleeps behind the Mamia Mountains.

We begin to walk. Winni and his daughter take the lead and I follow them closely. After three long days pulling our boat upriver, hiking feels like flying. But Winni goes slowly, bent at the waist, sweeping his machete across the grass in front of him to scare off snakes. He wears ancient rubber boots and his daughter wears $2 flip-flops. She is thirteen and has lived her whole life in the savannah with her father.

The footing is bad, made worse by the pre-dawn darkness. The trail is nothing more than a 3-inch-wide break in the grass, worn into the land by the family of two in front of me, the only people who walk here. Their home is four hours away, on the far side of Mamia, a shack on an airstrip that no one uses. Their lives are defined by the scars they leave on the land—this invisible trail, the blood-red machete wounds on trunks of trees, a pile of charred chicken bones. It is a reciprocal thing, this wounding and scarring. A country leaves marks on its people just the same.

After half an hour we stop on a small rise. The young sky turns red then orange as the others catch up. When the first rays of sunlight sneak out from behind the Four Brothers, Winni's daughter giggles.

"*Okopipi dape*," says Winni, pointing off-trail towards a valley between the mountains. This is where it lives, the only place on earth, nestled between sacred hills in the southernmost reaches of the country.

Now the footing is treacherous. Without a trail we stumble blindly over thick tussocks of grass and sharp rocks the colour of rust. At any moment I could step on a snake and it would all be over. Winni and his daughter pull away as my ankles twist and swell. The others take their time. They tell jokes and scan the horizon for game.

We outrun the sun to the foot of the mountains, where Winni stops in the shade and considers our next move. He confers with his daughter, who points towards a patch of giant helaconia palms, a sinister mass of green that stands at the bottom of the valley. Winni thinks for a moment, then nods and heads straight for it.

Among the palms the air is cooler, the ground soft with black mud. But everything is closer here, darker, and soon it becomes difficult to breathe. My boots sink to the ankles as Winni's daughter seems to float. We find a small creek and follow it up the valley, the shallow water stagnant and still. We brace ourselves against the helaconia that grow along its banks, but soon the water is gone and we hike up the middle of the dry creek bed.

And suddenly we are searching. Without a word, Winni has slowed and begun examining the crumbling walls of the old river, and everyone behind me has fanned out in twos and threes. We are in thick jungle now, the insects howling their morning rhythms, the lizards scrambling for cover. The little water that remains from the last rainy season glistens in the mud as the sun pokes through the canopy.

I stay close to Winni. He goes up one side of the riverbed and I go up the other. I look inside every hole and behind every rock. I lift dead cecropia leaves from the forest floor and flip old logs to peer beneath them. We go softly, quietly, as if meditating. The footfalls of my crew are above us now, the men exploring the steep hillsides that used to feed this river.

After another half-hour, Winni turns to me, his face blank but for a slight frown. "*Watra tumsi saka*," he says. The water is too low. The same problem that plagued our entire journey—the lack of rain that made the Sipaliwini rapids impassable—now threatens our final goal. Winni has never had to search this long before. I don't tell him I've been searching for five months.

The crew keep looking but I take a break. I lean up against one of the boulders that, when the rains finally come, will give this river its shape. I realize I may never find what I'm looking for; the exhaustion that has been building for so long finally descends. I shut my eyes and listen as the Indians scour the bush, the soft roar of the rain forest rising and falling like waves on a distant sea.

And then someone screams. A woman's voice, halfway up the eastern hillside, crackling with fear or excitement or both. The forest comes alive with thumping footsteps. I push off from the rock and scramble up the steep riverbank, *maka* spines stabbing my hands, my backpack catching on low-hanging vines and showering me with ants. Winni races past, unsure of what his daughter has found. I do everything I can to keep up.

Today, the Trio Indians of Suriname face a new kind of threat, a challenge more modern yet equally as insidious as Baptist missions. The Surinamese government, with their eyes firmly fixed on the rich deposits of bauxite and gold that are believed to exist in the southern savannahs, refuse to give the Trio legal title to their lands. The reason, of course, is that the mines in the north are nearing exhaustion. When the extraction industry casts its inevitable gaze southward, the government wants to ensure that the Trio will be powerless to oppose it.

The Trio are taking action. In partnership with the Amazon Conservation Team, a US-based NGO, they are creating the first GPS resource maps of their territory. These maps will be crucial in demonstrating the Indians' cultural ownership of the land. The Trio are also actively courting ecotourism projects to the region, in the hopes that a sustainable tourism economy will be able to compete with the potential of mining.

But no one knows if these projects will be enough to protect the Trio and the entire rain-forest menagerie—from the birds to the monkeys to the blue frogs—from the rapacious impacts of the extraction industry. By withholding legal title to lands the Indians have inhabited for thousands of years, the government of Suriname is merely compounding the cultural and societal destruction already suffered by the people here.

The crew is halfway up the hillside, gathered around a small palm tree. At its base, the leaves and old nuts have been pushed aside, and in the middle of this clearing sits a tiny blue frog. Its iridescence is stunning against the mud and decaying leaves. Its legs are a dark cobalt and its bright blue back is mottled with deep blue spots. I inch closer. I can't believe what I'm seeing. Then Winni puts his arm out to stop me, leans down, and gently plucks *okopipi* from the ground.

He holds the frog out to me. I hadn't planned on touching it—its poison can kill a man, and the oils in my palm might harm it—but I can't help myself. It weighs almost nothing. It is less than 3 centimetres long. And as I feel its frantic heart beat through its cold, moist skin, I experience a moment of sheer and shaking wonder unlike anything I've ever felt before. Mawa offers to take my picture. Ipiroke and Lukas brandish their machetes and pose like buffoons. The Basha says nothing, as usual, his goofy smile perhaps a little wider.

I begin to feel very proud of myself. For a split second, I'm convinced that I've found what I've been searching for, that I am holding the quintessential spirit of Suriname—the soul of the Last Eden—in the palm of my hand.

But as soon as this feeling arrives it is gone. In my mind, *okopipi* is a powerful metaphor. In my hand it is simply an exquisite amphibian. Because this hidden garden is under siege.

I blame everyone. The Baptists, the Surinamese government, the extraction industry, my own monolithic society, the short-sightedness of the Trio themselves. I even blame myself, though I'm not sure why. But then I look at the Trio around me and realize they blame no one. They seem content to be Christian Indians, to be using axes and rifles, to be awaiting the inevitable influx of tourists to their land. They seem cautiously optimistic about what time might bring them, in spite of all they've lost. So who am I to lay blame on their behalf? Sunset, sunset, sunset, arrive. Perhaps the people here blame nothing but the sun.

I lean down, place the frog on the ground, and cover it up with leaves. We find four more as we hike out of the forest. Then Winni leads us to the summit of the Four Brothers, where we look out on the sweeping Brazilian savannah.

The trip home to Kwamala is arduous even though the current is with us. We set more of the savannah on fire and have to chop our way through the *awara* trees. We shoot rapids we shouldn't and almost capsize three times. We happen upon a school of *karari* floundering in a rocky pool and slaughter more than sixty of them, poking sticks through their gills and arranging them in neat sets of ten in the bow. Meanwhile, a nasty blister opens up on my left buttock like a giant bedsore.

The
Blue
Jewel
of the
Jungle

225

We arrive in Kwamala to little fanfare. As we unload our gear a small crowd gathers to watch. In the middle of the river, a young Trio girl stands on a submerged rock. She waves to us and steps into the water, slipping beneath the surface without a splash.

Granman Asongo gives me a bear hug when he sees me. He is happy we are safe and that no one died. He asks if we found *okopipi* and I tell him yes. He asks if I brought any back with me and I laugh and tell him no.

The next day, as I wait for my plane back to the city, I find Lukas, Ipiroke, and Mawa sitting inside an abandoned cookhouse, a half-empty bucket of *casiri* between them. They are celebrating our successful return, but they are also mourning the end of the adventure and their return to unemployment.

I sit and drink with them, show them the photos from our journey. They watch as we drag our boat up the Sipaliwini River, bunk in hammock camps centuries old, and walk behind Winni and his daughter. But then the photos go dark and lose their focus. Indian faces, flashes of jungle, men with a blur of blue in their hands. I wait for the photo of me with *okopipi*, the blue jewel of the jungle.

The photo never comes.

Mr. Tree

Jeremy Klaszus

WE SPEND a lot of time together lately, Opapa and me, mostly on his treed acreage southeast of Edmonton where he lives with my omi. Cloistered by the aspens and poplars surrounding the blue two-storey house, we visit another distant forest together, looking down from outer space on a sandy patch of land 40 kilometres east of the icy Baltic Sea. "These were mostly Scots pine and spruce," Opapa says, reaching into memory while rolling the rubber wheel on his wireless mouse. The trees enlarge in the Google Earth window, creating a dark green cauliflower-like carpet on his computer screen. Outside, evening grosbeaks and black-capped chickadees flit from branch to branch. "And here is where I planted my first tree, a two-foot Scots pine seedling. That was before the war."

To many, Opapa is known simply as Mr. Tree. He earned his arboreal nickname partly because of his famed love for and knowledge of trees—he's volunteered with Alberta's Junior Forest Wardens, a forestry youth group, for as long as I can remember—and probably because he also looks a little treeish himself. Below his snowy beard and bushy white eyebrows, aged skin hangs off gnarled limbs. Long grey-and-white hairs cover his knobby hands like mossy bark. He even acts treeish at times, like one of Tolkien's ents, giant tree-shepherds that never bother to say anything in their own tree-language unless it's worth taking a long time to say.

Opapa similarly takes forever to tell a story. Often it's too much for Omi.

"Ach, Ernst, get on with it." Omi, going on eighty, rolls her eyes and reaches for her iPod.

"I speak in paragraphs, Laila," Opapa replies coolly, returning to his Google Earth travels.

Opapa has spoken often of "the war" throughout my life but I never really knew what that meant. I knew he was on the German side and joined the Hitler Youth. I knew he fled his home, travelling from house to house across Germany with his mother and sisters, all of them starving, but I never understood why. As a boy I listened politely to his stories and went back to playing *King's Quest* or some other computer game.

What I did know, or thought I knew, was that the war had somehow made Opapa a very stern and serious person. How else to explain his countless lectures? Opapa was always scolding us grandchildren about something, whether it was our "horseplay" or our feeble knowledge of chemistry. "You don't know the chemical elements? That is very basic knowledge . . ."

"I tolerate absolutely no horseplay in my home, especially on Sundays . . ."

"Absolutely no wearing of hats indoors. There are rules . . ."

I found Opapa's severity both terrifying and amusing. We all usually escaped his judgment having endured only the tedium of his lectures, though I also remember getting whapped once or twice for the crime of "horseplay."

These memories are eclipsed, however, by happier ones. On Easter Sundays, we hunted for chocolate eggs in the raspberry bushes behind my grandparents' brick-and-brown bungalow in the Edmonton suburb of St. Albert. On Christmas Eve, we'd gather around Opapa in the living room after church, our young faces lit by the white lights on the tree, as Opapa read the Christmas story from the Gospel of Luke in his hybrid German-Wisconsin inflection that makes words like "not" sound a bit like "nat."

"And it came to pass in those days, that there went out a decree from Caesar Augustus, that all the world should be taxed . . ."

When I was about twelve, my grandparents moved to their acreage where Opapa is completely surrounded by his beloved trees and birds. Nostalgic sounds and smells are everywhere: the chorus of a Handel oratorio on the radio—locked always onto the CBC—and the inviting aroma of Opapa's red cabbage simmering on the stove.

And then there are Opapa's stories. The older he gets, the more he talks about Nazi Germany, often in sharp and harrowing detail. In the twilight of his life—he's now seventy-eight—he seems to find more and more comfort in his childhood narrative, even though much of it is bleak.

I've spent most of my life vaguely embarrassed by my German heritage, acutely aware that the Nazis perpetrated some of the most heinous crimes of the twentieth century. In school, history lessons were accompanied by those flickery black-and-white videos of Hitler's frenzied speeches at rallies. Opapa is my direct link to that history. As a writer, I pride myself on telling untold stories, but I had never learned this part of my own story. Now I was being given a second chance in my mid-twenties, an age by which many people have already lost their grandparents, and with them, all their grandparents' stories. I still had access to everything.

"I want to tell you about my home city of Tilsit . . ."

Opapa takes me with his words to East Prussia, Nazi Germany's easternmost province. Like carpet that changes shade with each pass of a vacuum cleaner, Opapa's homeland changes colour on the map each time the machine of war rolls overtop. The Russians kept much of East Prussia after the Second World War and wasted no time in purging the land of German names, German culture and, in one of history's lesser-known ethnic cleansings, Germans themselves. Hence Tilsit, which sits on the southern bank of the gentle Neman River across from Lithuania, is now called Sovetsk. The city is part of Kaliningrad, a small Russian exclave sandwiched between Poland and Lithuania. "A forgotten part of the world," Opapa says.

I pull from my pocket the digital recorder I use in my work as a reporter and set it on the arm of his black leather chair. Then I listen as Opapa's deep, gentle cadence—"the Morgan Freeman of German men," says my wife, Colleen—takes me over spire and shingle, into another time and place, some sixty-five years ago . . .

Tilsit-Bendigsfelde, East Prussia, 1944. Dusk after a warm summer day. A German boy of fourteen bounded out the front door of his brick house. A lock of blond hair across the boy's bony forehead danced with each step. Ernst, the youngest of five children, ran past the fruit-laden apple and cherry trees in the yard towards the dirt road where a steady stream of people—Germans, Estonians, Latvians, and Lithuanians—already moved west towards the forest. He fell into the column, his mother and two sisters close behind.

This exodus of neighbours and refugees felt both familiar and tense. It had become routine, like eating breakfast or brushing teeth.

The coniferous forest took them in one by one. Within minutes, the entire troop had funnelled itself into the sandy paths between the trees, the same paths where Ernst's biology teacher regularly took his class, telling stories about each plant while smoking his flint-and-steel-lit pipe.

Running into the forest, even now, was oddly reassuring for Ernst. He enjoyed being among the needle-filled boughs in the dark. He certainly preferred it to huddling in the basement, the shelter his family used if they didn't have time to clear the half kilometre between the house and the forest.

Ernst and the others pressed deeper into the trees.

Silence.

This waiting period always stretched and shrunk in later conversations; one person recalled it as half a minute, another remembered it as ten minutes. Ernst used the time to think of his father who was shovelling coal on a train north of Tilsit. The enemy often targeted trains and Ernst felt pangs of worry whenever his father was away.

"Papa is very brave," Ernst thought to himself. Friedrich, his papa, always risked trouble. Before the war, when he manned railroad crossings at night, Friedrich would sing hymns into the hand-crank phone in the stone booth by the crossing. He sent his baritone all the way to Insterburg, 50 kilometres down the line, entertaining other sleepy railroad workers with his songs. The voice was forever a mystery to the other workers.

Then came the war. Friedrich was drafted into the Bahnschutz, the German paramilitary railway police, and sent into occupied Poland to oversee a stretch of railroad. Ernst later overheard his parents talking heatedly about the experience in their adults-only tongue of Lithuanian. He made out bits of the conversation and his older sister, Gustel, translated the rest.

His father had been standing on the station platform in Poland one afternoon when he heard voices coming from inside a locked box-car. Confused, Friedrich realized there were people inside. The voices weakly asked him if he could open the door so they could unload dead bodies.

Stunned, Friedrich offered to check with his superiors. He strode into the station, picked up the phone and made his request, but the officer hung up on him and the train chugged away, doors still shut. Within hours, the officer he'd spoken with drove to the station and literally stripped Friedrich of his rank, angrily tearing the epaulette from his shoulder.

Shortly afterwards Friedrich was dismissed as "politically unreliable." It was an accurate label, given his quiet opposition to Hitler. Friedrich went back to shovelling coal on locomotives, stunted in his career because of his refusal to join the National Socialist party. The mayor of Bendigsfelde, a Nazi, always regarded Friedrich suspiciously, and Ernst worried that his papa might one day get sent away.

A high-pitched wail jerked Ernst from his thoughts. The warning siren. A minute later, white flares illuminated the city, drifting from the sky as slowly as fuzzy aspen seeds. The siren stopped its screeching but the anti-aircraft flak guns barked out their challenge to the enemy planes above, creating a deadly hail of shrapnel in the forest. Ernst threw his arms around a pine for protection.

"Look out!"

A chunk of metal ricocheted off a limb above, shaking Ernst's tree like a badly hit baseball vibrates a bat. The young tree hugger clutched the trunk even tighter, his pockets bulging with bits of golden amber he'd collected along the beach in Danzig.

About ten minutes later, the bombers left. Fires burned inside the city but the people in the forest were unharmed. Ernst returned home with his mother and sisters, the pattern of pine bark imprinted on the inside of his arms.

Ernst thought again of his tall, bald father. "I hope Papa is okay."

Dressed in a plaid shirt, a brown wool sweater ("cotton is cool, wool is warm," Opapa always says) and a bolo tie made from a knobcone pine cone, Opapa looks professorial against the backdrop of books covering the living room walls. Many are theological tomes he accumulated as a Lutheran pastor in the fifties and sixties.

Once in a while, I interrupt Opapa's storytelling to clarify dates and locations. But one question gnaws at my mind as he describes his happy childhood in Tilsit: How much did you know?

Did you know of Kristallnacht, when the synagogues in Germany were burned to the ground? What about the concentration camps? Or Hitler's fierce anti-Semitism as revealed in *Mein Kampf*? Did you know of these things when at age ten you joined the Jungvolk, the Hitler Youth's junior branch, compelled by law? How much did you know when you swore an oath to "devote all my energies and my strength to the savior of our country, Adolf Hitler," and declared you were willing to give up your life for him?

How much of the Nazis' anti-Semitism did you swallow? And did you feel any sense of guilt or shame when you learned of the Holocaust after the war?

In my family, questions are seldom asked directly and these questions are particularly difficult to ask, partly because they are loaded with accusation against a kid who was only four years old when the Nazis took power. I look back at Nazi Germany through the lens of the Holocaust. As a boy, Opapa lacked that advantage. I restrain my judgments and move crabwise, taking days and months to get to the questions I really want to ask.

And it's Colleen, not me, who actually utters the big question: "How much did you know?"

Opapa answers slowly. "We were aware that we were not given all the facts. Similar to today. When I look at the CNN news, in the back of my head I always say to myself, 'OK, I really don't know what the true story is.' Are they winning in Iraq? Bush says they are winning. It doesn't quite look that way when I compare that with the German news and the BBC. But the same thing is happening anywhere there is war. The people are fed propaganda."

To get some of the missing facts, Opapa cobbled together a short-wave radio so he could listen illegally to Swiss radio and the BBC at night. The reports he heard through his crackling earphone cast doubt on the always-upbeat German version of events.

People in Germany liked to say that lies have short legs, and Opapa and the other Jungvolk would repeat the joke that if lies indeed had short legs, Nazi propaganda minister Joseph Goebbels would be walking around on his ass. When German radio reported that a British plane was shot down near Tilsit, Opapa and his friends elbowed their way through the bush looking for it. But they never found debris or wreckage. Nothing.

Opapa was aware that Jews disappeared from Tilsit after 1938— "there was no hiding that," he says—though he didn't know where they went. People spoke in hushed tones of concentration camps but it was all considered hearsay. "The Americans knew more than ordinary Germans," Opapa says.

That night, I make *spätzle* noodles for dinner and Opapa, ever the chef of the house, joins me in the kitchen. He hasn't been feeling well lately and he's too weak to prepare meals. But he can't help himself. I'm doing everything wrong. He instructs me on the correct way to slice cucumbers for salad.

"Hold it like this, not like that. It's the only way to do it."

On the way home to Calgary, I complain to Colleen that Opapa drives me nuts in the kitchen. He doesn't trust me with even the simple task of salad making. But when Colleen slowly passes a semi on the four-lane highway, I find myself barking similar instructions.

"Either pass or don't pass. Make up your mind."

She's not impressed. "Thanks, Opapa."

It was June or July 1944 when my great-grandfather restored favour with his ideological enemies, the Nazis.

Friedrich had finished his shift at Tilsit's railroad roundhouse, a frequent target of Soviet air raids, when he heard a loud explosion behind him. Spinning around, he saw a plume of black smoke towards the end of a train destined for the Russian front. The train, loaded with ammunition, blew apart from the back, car by car, like a string of firecrackers.

Friedrich ran to the middle of the train and unlatched a string of cars before returning to the locomotive and pulling it forward, separating the train and successfully cutting off the explosions.

Friedrich's co-workers later celebrated his ammo-saving heroics. A prominent Nazi even pinned an award on Friedrich's uniform. Though he never wore it afterwards, Friedrich felt a weight come off his chest when the award went on; he no longer worried about saying the wrong thing, about getting in trouble for his socialist—and decidedly non–National Socialist—political views.

Weeks later, on August 15, Ernst heard planes overhead, flying eastward from the Baltic Sea. He stepped outside and watched the planes wing their way across a cloudless sky, challenged only by warning sirens.

At the same time, Friedrich shovelled coal on a train headed across the pastoral landscape from Tilsit to Ebenrode, a town 65 kilometres southeast as the crow flies. The Allied planes gained on the train and eventually overtook it, firing a spray of bullets into the locomotive. Friedrich was killed instantly.

He was forty-eight. His son Ernst, fourteen.

As if to ensure Friedrich was dead, the Allies bombed Tilsit again during his funeral. Flak shrapnel fell as a line of helmet-clad mourners followed the horse-drawn hay cart that carried the coffin towards the cemetery. The shrapnel made a singing sound like raindrops on the ocean, but with a louder buzz. One jagged piece landed directly atop Friedrich's wooden coffin with a startling thwack.

Within days of Friedrich's burial, Ernst, his mother, Auguste, and his sister Lydia fled their home and struck westward, joining the stream of refugees fleeing the Baltic States. They could hear the explosions of the Russian artillery nearby and Ernst's mother thought it prudent to leave before they got any louder. Two of Ernst's older sisters, Gustel and Gretel, had already moved west to Erfurt, the capital of Thuringia, where they worked as secretaries in a police station. His sister Anna was also west working as a nurse in Danzig.

Ernst left his homeland for good, the first of his many transplants. He would never see his beloved childhood forest again, except on his iMac, as an old man, some sixty years later.

My cell rings at 7:49 a.m. Friday morning.

Mom. She never calls this early. "Hello?"

"Opapa went into the hospital early this morning. He's asked for Dad, Tante Judith and Tante Christel to come to his bedside. Dad's on his way now."

Soon Colleen and I are racing from Calgary towards Edmonton's University of Alberta Hospital. We speak very little. I'm worried Opapa will leave his story unfinished, a story I've only partly recorded. I don't have enough yet to piece it together.

On the other hand, death is a straightforward literary conclusion . . .

I scold myself silently.

Learning that Opapa is in hospital is nothing new. He underwent a kidney transplant in 1983 and has since suffered from a long list of bodily ailments: glaucoma, prostate cancer, pancreatitis, skin cancer, and high blood pressure, to name a few. He's always recovered well from his hospitalizations. But this one seems different somehow.

When we arrive in the fluorescent-lit emergency room, Opapa is lying on a bed wearing a white hospital gown patterned with blue snowflakes. Mr. Tree looks brittle as a dry branch. His pale skin is stuck with small white patches. A barcoded bracelet hangs off his left wrist and a catheter tube issues from beneath the pink blanket covering his legs. Omi, looking haggard, stands beside Opapa's bed gently stroking his hairy hand. She's been here since two in the morning, worried that fifty-three years of marriage could suddenly end. Fear and exhaustion are etched onto her creased face.

Opapa looks up. His voice, usually deep and strong, is weak and breathy.

"You came. Thank you for coming."

We get a quick update on Opapa's condition. "Angina is when you get out of breath and the chest feels tight," Opapa explains. "At one point I thought I wasn't going to make it."

Opapa's brush with death has made him unusually emotional. He cries often as he speaks. Yet he can't stop talking. Even here in the emergency room, he looks back on his childhood, reflecting on his beginnings as he moves ever closer to his end. "I worked my way up in the Jungvolk and got the rank of *Hauptjungzugführer*. I was a leader. When we marched, I chose the songs. I always chose folk songs."

As his heart-rate monitor beeps and blips in the background, Opapa recalls the process of leaving Germany for an exchange at a Wisconsin seminary in 1952. An agent at the American consulate in Frankfurt took him aside when he applied for his student visa.

"He wanted to ask me a few questions. 'Born in 1929. Were you in the Jungvolk?'"

"'Yes, I was.'"

"'Well,' he said, 'did you enjoy it?'"

"'Yes, I did enjoy it. Very much.' He then stamped my passport. If I had lied and said no, things might have turned out differently."

Our conversation is interrupted when a doctor enters the room to check on Opapa.

"May I ask where you are from?" Opapa asks the doctor.

"Saudi Arabia."

"Saudi Arabia! I go there on Google Earth and I'm always amazed to look at the desert and see those round green spots of irrigation. Beautiful spots of life in the desert."

"Yeah, perfectly round." The doctor grins at this curious patient. "Have you been there?"

"Only on Google Earth. No jet lag that way."

The doctor is the first of a steady stream of visitors: aunts, cardiologists, uncles, more doctors, cousins, nurses. We decide to leave for the day. Opapa's clearly in good hands. On our way out, Colleen kisses Opapa's lined forehead and says words I've never spoken to him. "I love you, Opapa."

Opapa responds, in tears, with words I've never before heard from his mouth. "I love you too."

Auguste, Ernst's mother, was wise to flee East Prussia when she did. Many who stayed starved to death or worse. One of Ernst's childhood friends endured six years of forced labour in a Soviet gulag for stealing a loaf of bread in Lithuania. Ernst similarly stole bread farther west but only had to worry about escaping the red-faced bakers who came after him swinging their rolling pins.

German women had it worst. The Red Army unleashed a ruthless sexual violence as it moved west into East Prussia seeking revenge for Nazi crimes in Russia. Ernst's family didn't escape this horror. Two of his sisters were gang-raped by the Soviets in 1945. As the drunken soldiers took turns with the women, another soldier played the accordion. Others danced.

Many Germans who waited too late to flee the Red Army never survived. For some, the only hope of escape was a treacherous walk across a frozen inlet on the Baltic Sea. Allied bombs tore deadly holes in the ice, and dysentery was widespread. One refugee later described the trek as "an enormously long funeral procession."

German ships also ferried refugees west on the Baltic. In one of human history's worst—yet lesser-known—maritime disasters, a Soviet submarine torpedoed one of these refugee carriers, the *Wilhelm Gustloff*, killing some nine thousand Germans in January 1945—about six times the number of people who died when the *Titanic* sank. Many were East Prussian refugees.

Ernst wasn't one of them. After leaving Tilsit he travelled by rail with his mother and sister Lydia to Iserlohn, a Westphalian city amidst densely wooded hills, where he took premilitary training and stepped up his Jungvolk activity. He worked from morning until night at the railroad station where German refugees from the heavily bombed Ruhr passed through, many with slings on their arms and bloody wounds on their faces. The plight of wounded German refugees affected Ernst deeply, setting alight the adolescent desire to fight and maybe even die on the front.

To this end, Ernst volunteered with the Freikorps Sauerland, a military unit independent from, but supportive of, the German army. Its battalions, made up largely of disabled war vets and ill-trained teenagers like Ernst, dressed in old German army uniforms. Wehrmacht and SS officers trained the recruits on Sunday mornings. Yet much of the Freikorps aggression was ultimately taken out not on the Allies, but on fellow Germans, particularly deserters and after-bombing looters.

Hours after Ernst told his mother of his plans to join the Freikorps, she broke news of her own. "I've just learned that we need to leave Iserlohn right away. East Prussian refugees like us aren't supposed to be here, but farther east in Saxony."

In fact, East Prussian refugees were scattered across western Germany like seeds spread by wind. But it didn't matter.

"We have to leave. Now."

Ernst never fought for the Freikorps. He left Iserlohn and travelled east by rail to Radeburg, a small town near Dresden, where Tante Elsa—Ernst's father's sister—was staying with her family.

Ernst, Lydia and Auguste all arrived in Radeburg safely, but their baggage, loaded onto a separate train, was ripped apart by bombs.

A later conversation with Opapa.

"Where did you get that information about the Freikorps Sauerland?" He isn't convinced by my findings on the Freikorps' activities.

"From a 1999 article in the *Central European History* journal. I'll e-mail it to you if you like."

Opapa doesn't sound keen on it. "I do not trust all of the historians that I have read. And when it comes to wartime, the truth always dies first, so what we get from so-called historical sources may or may not be reliable." Opapa launches into a long lecture about the bias of "so-called" historians. "I rather doubt that children or old men were involved in killing their own. Maybe that was another Freikorps, but not the Freikorps Sauerland."

I push back a bit. "No, it's definitely the Freikorps Sauerland. I don't know if teenagers or adults were doing the killing but much of the Freikorps' aggression was towards other Germans."

He sounds more interested, but still unconvinced. "They wanted to fight the Allies. That's really what it was."

Opapa is in the cardio ward when we visit him Saturday morning, almost thirty-five hours after he went into emergency. Patients are allowed four visitors at a time. Opapa has eight. Within a couple hours we decide to leave again. Before we go, I get up my guts and say what I've never said to this looming, lecturing figure who now lies helpless on a hospital bed. "I love you, Opapa."

"I love you too."

That night, Omi sends an e-mail to her three children. "Tonight while we were alone, Papa for the first time talked about death. He said to me that there are still some things he wants to do—he's not ready. He wants to work with Jeremy on his project. . . . Papa has never opened up either to me or anyone else as he has the last few days. He has never shown how he really felt about things (except when he got angry). Jeremy, your drawing him out has brought out a side of him that I didn't know—after fifty-three years. I thank you for that."

The following weekend, we visit Opapa again. This time Saturday is quiet. Everyone's at church. Two of my cousins, Opapa's granddaughters, are being confirmed in the Lutheran church today after studying Luther's catechism for two years. Opapa badly wanted to attend but can't.

Confirmation—an essential part of any good Lutheran upbringing. I was confirmed in 1995 at age twelve, my dad in 1974 at age fourteen, and, in 1945, Opapa was confirmed at age fifteen. He dug into the catechism in Dresden, Saxony's artistic capital, along with eight other teenagers.

"I appreciate Luther for many of the things he said," Opapa says. "I certainly don't agree with all of them and whenever I say that, people are listening up. 'What, you don't agree with Luther?' Well, no. I don't agree with him on his attitude towards women. I don't agree with him on his attitude towards Anabaptists. I don't agree with him on what he said about the Jews."

In confirmation we never studied Luther's more incendiary writings. In his hateful 1543 tract *On The Jews and their Lies*, the German theologian describes the Jewish people as "a heavy burden, a plague, a pestilence, a sheer misfortune for our country." He goes further, calling them "an incorrigible whore and an evil slut." Christians, he writes, are to "set fire to their synagogues or schools and to bury and cover with dirt whatever will not burn, so that no man will ever again see a stone or cinder of them. This is to be done in honor of our Lord and of Christendom . . ." Luther goes on like this for more than 65,000 words, his words darkly prophetic of the Nazis' crimes.

I find Opapa's struggle with his faith and church, always hidden from me as a child, extremely encouraging. To me he was always a patriarchal symbol of proper behaviour and belief—the very things I wanted to break away from in my adult life after being immersed in religious fundamentalism throughout my childhood. Private Christian schools, all the way through Grade 12. Church every Sunday, and youth group on Friday nights, where we prayed feverishly for the "lost" while listening to lame music drenched in religious slogans. After a while I couldn't believe I was fortuitously "saved" while those not drowning in evangelical kitsch were somehow inferior and "lost."

The exclusionary theology had to go. And by the time I finished college, it did. I found a church with a more inclusive understanding of faith.

Until recently, I never knew Opapa experienced a similar struggle throughout his life. He questions his religious upbringing as much as I question mine, and now I'm discovering a spiritual friend in a man I always regarded as spiritually and emotionally distant. "What bothers me about my childhood is that we were brainwashed," Opapa says. "I hate to use that word, but I have to. We were brainwashed into believing what we were told about other religions, other faiths, other confessions, other denominations." Confirmation was just one step in this unfortunate process.

But Opapa's confirmation classes were violently interrupted on a night burnt into memory for many Germans.

"It was the first time I saw parts of a human body lying here and there . . ."

Radeburg. February 13, 1945. Ernst slept quietly in his upstairs room, sick with pneumonia, his breath making quick white clouds. Frost clung to the south-facing window. There wasn't enough wood to heat the small room.

Outside and above, British planes flew towards nearby Dresden, Saxony's cultural heart and a transportation hub swollen with refugees from the east. The bombers announced their arrival by dropping spectacular flares of green and white that illuminated Dresden's baroque churches and famed art galleries.

Ernst missed the light show happening outside his window. By the time he awoke an hour later, too sick to crawl downstairs, the walls of his room glowed orange-red. Groggily stumbling to the window, he looked to the south and saw only flames.

The British planes had fanned over the city and bombed with mathematical precision, first at about 10 p.m., and again at 1:30 a.m. Refugees in Dresden burned like tinder in the midnight firestorm. Not just refugees—Dresdeners as well. Not only Germans, but also refugees from the Baltic States, and the handful of Jews left in the city. The storm of fire made no distinction between one human being and another. They roasted as equals. Many baked in underground tunnels where they had sought escape.

American planes bombed Dresden again the next day, further stoking the inferno. In the midst of the fire, Ernst's pastor clambered into his church and rescued a stack of documents from his desk, including the certificates he'd written up in advance of the teenagers' confirmation ceremony. Afterwards the pastor added another line, in blue ink, to Ernst's large-lettered certificate:

"This document was retrieved from the burning parsonage during the terror attack on Dresden on the 14th of February 1945."

Opapa and his cousin Heinz visited the city a week later searching for twin girls from their confirmation class who lived in Dresden and often invited the boys over for dinner. As they made their way though the city's Great Garden, the inner-city park to which refugees had fled after the first wave of bombings, the boys saw intestines and other body parts dangling from the charred remains of trees. The park had been set alight in the second wave of bombings. The refugees had no defence and no escape.

"Watch your step," Ernst cautioned his younger cousin. Together they carefully walked past the corpses still strewn throughout the city. Lifeless hands, heads and arms poked from the rubble. A passerby warned Ernst and Heinz not to go where the bodies were being piled.

"It's too terrible for young eyes."

At last the boys found the girls' house. The inside was gutted by fire; the outer four walls were all that remained. The boys searched for bodies but found only ashes.

The death toll from the Dresden bombings is as hazy as the smoke from the fire. Whether it was 40,000 or 25,000 who died, the living were still burning corpses in the city's Old Market nearly a month afterwards, piling the decomposing bodies onto pyres made of iron-girder grates before soaking them with gasoline. Ernst and Heinz were relieved to learn that the twins from their church weren't among those torched. They'd somehow escaped the fire that so many others hadn't.

In his 1962 essay, "Target Equals City," Thomas Merton writes: "There is one winner, only one winner, in war. The winner is war itself. Not truth, not justice, not liberty, not morality. These are the vanquished. War wins, reducing them to complete submission." The Cistercian monk gives the bombing of German cities as an example. I first read Merton's essay—censored by the Catholic Church until after his death—as a nineteen-year-old student who, after years of fundamentalist indoctrination, was discovering a humanist dimension to faith. I never even thought of Opapa when I first read the essay, but as I listened to his story, Merton's words jumped to life. I began to empathize with so-called "ordinary Germans," the ones I never saw in those disturbing Hitler video clips we watched in school.

Germans like Anna, the sister Ernst regularly visited in Danzig when he lived in Tilsit. At twenty-three years old, Anna gave birth to a son, Friedrich, while fleeing from Danzig to the port city of Swinemünde in January 1945. Little Friedrich sucked in vain on his starving mother's dry breast.

After arriving in Swinemünde, Anna took Friedrich to a hospital and called on her mother and Ernst to come visit. Auguste and Ernst answered the call and went by rail. At the hospital, they met Friedrich for the first time. A feeding tube led up his tiny nose. "For the first time, I looked at someone who was starving to death," Opapa says. "His body was a ghastly colour and there was a little bit of blue mixed into his skin. It was like skim milk that has that kind of bluish tint when they don't add colour."

Opapa and his mother returned sadly to the village of Grossbothen, the next stop on their zigzagging journey around an imploding Germany.

The Sunday of the weekend Opapa is hospitalized, Colleen and I return to work in Calgary. Opapa's condition goes up and down in the days following. He talks incessantly—even more than usual—and shows signs of dementia, getting angry when anyone interrupts him. Even an affirming "uh-huh" midway through a story sets him off. He warns the offender, usually Omi or one of his daughters, that they are increasing his blood pressure. He goes on and on about the shortcomings of the health care system, his speech badly slurred. I phone on my lunch break and he rambles uncharacteristically, mashing one idea mercilessly into the next. "I lose the thread so easily," he tells me faintly. "The thread of thought."

We stay abreast of Opapa's condition by talking to my father. My dad and I have never been close. He was always busy with work when I was a kid, either with his construction job or other projects around home. So when I moved out, we never really kept up a relationship. But I now phone my father two or three times a day.

"How's Opapa doing?"

"Not good. He won't stop complaining about the health care system. He treats Omi very badly, and . . ."

Dad breaks down. I've never heard him cry like this before.

"There are some things you want to be able to say to someone before they die . . ."

Struck by my father's rare honesty, I force out a tearful "I know."

The tender moment passes. "But we'll see. He's having a geriatric assessment soon and that should give us a better idea of what's going on."

After I hang up, Colleen tells me she's never seen me talk with my father so much. "It's good to see."

I continue speaking with Opapa, phoning his hospital room every day or two. When I can, I direct his thoughts towards childhood. His memories are crisp, even now, and when he talks about life in Germany, it's as if we're sitting across from each other in his living room, just like old times.

Grossbothen, Saxony. March 1945. The awful screech of metal on metal.

Ernst looked towards the distant hills beyond the town in the valley. He knew what those hills obscured; his heart pounded stronger as the squealing got louder. He'd been prepared for this moment a week ago by a draft board in nearby Grimma. Yet Ernst didn't feel ready to report for duty and challenge the American invaders as he'd been instructed.

By now the war was all but lost. Grossbothen was one of many German towns caught in Allied pincers; Russians to the east, Americans to the west. But Ernst, even now, refused to believe that Germany was defeated, as did his cousins and friends. They often whispered hopefully about a secret weapon they'd heard was in the making.

"What kind of weapon is it?" they asked each other.

"A bomb that could take out a city the size of Berlin." The boys were giddy at the idea. "Or *New York*."

"The fatherland isn't defeated yet."

As the tanks came thundering into view unopposed, like horrible growing insects, Ernst felt less sure of his earlier optimism. The sight of them made him tremble. He had to leave immediately if he was to report on time.

"I have to go."

He ran to the house and had just stood up his bicycle when his mother came out.

"Stay with us, Ernst. You know there's no hope in going down there."

Ernst looked away, torn. He felt obliged to fight but knew it would be futile. Even well-trained teenagers couldn't stop tanks, and he and the other recruits had little training.

"Please, Ernst."

He listened to his mother and decided to stay as the tanks rolled into the village.

That night, one of Ernst's classmates scurried up the hill. The boy, fifteen or sixteen, arrived at the house pale and trembling. He'd deserted, a crime punishable by death.

"Heinrich!" Ernst recognized his friend.

"I barely got away, Ernst. We dug foxholes but couldn't dig fast enough. They handed us guns but I didn't know how to fire mine."

"So what happened?"

"Absolute bedlam. Our bullets did nothing. Theirs did. Half our class is dead." Ernst had just met his classmates two weeks earlier and shuddered to think eight of them were gone.

Once the Americans took over the village, they freed all the POWs in nearby camps—many of them Russian soldiers. These newly freed soldiers were different than the POWs Ernst encountered in Tilsit. Those men were sad and kind. At night, the unusually lenient Tilsit commandant let his prisoners assemble into a choir. The wistful voices, singing Russian folk songs, raised goosebumps on the neck of anyone who heard them.

These soldiers in Grossbothen ran from house to house looting, stealing, and raping. And drinking, always drinking. Stolen watches dangled from their arms.

Ernst had one run-in with the Russians when they broke in to the room he shared with his cousin. The soldiers kicked open the door, shone a light into the bleary eyes inside and jammed a gun against Ernst's temple, barking something in Russian. No one got hurt but the soldiers stole everything of value from the house, including a gold watch.

The Americans were gentler, often leaving half-full cans of meat and other food on the garbage pile behind their camp.

Ernst adjusted quickly to living under occupation. Using binoculars they'd swiped from the American camp, Ernst and his cousins looked down from the same hill where he'd first seen the tanks. This time, however, the Americans weren't far away but assembled in a U-shape on the meadow below. Through his stolen lenses, Opapa saw colours of red and blue bursting from the soldiers' lapels. They began singing, like the Russian POWs in Tilsit, but with less skill.

O! say can you see by the dawn's early light
What so proudly we hailed at the twilight's last gleaming . . .

The boys wept bitterly as they listened to this strange new song. There was no denying it anymore. The fatherland was lost.

"I can't remember if I wept or not," Opapa says, thinking aloud. "I can't remember. I just don't. Why can't I remember if I wept?"

The first time Opapa told me the story, he said he cried. The second time he wasn't so sure.

Many of Opapa's boyhood feelings are holes in his memory. He remembers where he travelled when, and what he did where, but when I ask him what he felt, his storytelling falters. Günter Grass, the Danzig-born novelist and ex-Jungvolk member, describes memory's fallibility in his memoir *Peeling the Onion*: "Memory likes to play hide-and-seek, to crawl away. It tends to hold forth, to dress up, often needlessly. Memory contradicts itself; pedant that it is, it will have its way." Opapa similarly acknowledges the shortcomings of memory and often quotes a line he remembers from Farley Mowat: Old men remember the past the way it should have been.

I circle again to the Holocaust, asking Opapa if he remembers feeling any guilt or shame when he learned about the Nazi death camps. His answer comes surprisingly quickly. "No, I never felt that guilty. I was not involved."

I press further. "Then what was your response?"

"Shock."

A few days later, Opapa calls me on the phone. His answer had sounded final but he's clearly been thinking of it some more. "You were probing about how I felt. Feelings are terribly difficult to describe. How do you feel sixty years later? So much has happened in between."

He has a question of his own. "How did you feel when you found out that the Canadians put all the Japanese Canadians into concentration camps?"

The question catches me off guard. "I wasn't alive at the time, but it was a bad choice."

"Right. You were not involved. I wasn't involved in Hitler's atrocities. Regret is really all one can feel. You can't say 'I'm sorry,' because I didn't do it. Those things just should not have happened."

March 1945. The sea rose and fell as a bitterly cold wind swept over the ship. Restless refugees, chilled and miserable, stood on the deck nervously scanning the brackish Baltic waters for Soviet submarines.

Anna went into one of the cabins below and opened a small compartment where she'd hidden her baby. He was still there, wrapped tightly in an off-white sheet. Friedrich had stopped breathing shortly after boarding and Anna feared he'd be thrown into the churning sea below if his death was discovered. She resolved to get Friedrich to Rostock, the ship's destination, where he could be properly buried.

Once the ship arrived, Anna hid her first-born in her coat and succeeded in bringing him to land. She seldom spoke of the experience afterwards, trying always to forget the horror of hiding her lifeless child aboard the ship that, in a cruel irony, may have saved her life.

Almost three weeks have passed since Opapa first went into the hospital. I've come up from Calgary to give Omi a break for a few days—she's worn out. We immediately get back into Opapa's story, jumping all over the place. When I focus too much on his childhood, he turns to the later years of his life, after he immigrated to America in 1952. "I want you to get a full picture of who I am," he says.

Soon he's spilling regrets about his disciplinarian parenting. Besides having experienced some of his severity first-hand, I'd also heard my dad's stories, like the one about the broken typewriter, when Opapa came home and found one of the keys broken. He lined up his four children and asked who broke the key. No one confessed, so he gave them all spankings. He asked again. No one confessed. More spankings. My dad, getting wise to the pattern, stepped forward and admitted to breaking the key—only it hadn't been him.

"Which key did you break?" asked Opapa. Dad guessed incorrectly. Spankings again.

Omi later revealed she had broken the key.

When I ask Opapa about the incident, he can't remember it. "Maybe that's one of those incidents I wanted to forget."

"When you look back on your life as a parent, are there many things you would change?"

"Oh yeah. But my understanding of child rearing came much too late." Strictness and severity, he explains, are parts of his Prussian heritage. "Don't spare the rod. You want the child to grow up straight, then you have to enforce it manually. Well, that's not the way to do it."

Later that night, while watching CNN with Omi at the acreage, I relay my earlier conversation with Opapa. She asks me to e-mail her that section of my interview notes so she can forward it to my dad and his sisters. She CC's me. "I think you might find some comfort in what is contained therein. I know that I wish that I had stood up to Papa more on your behalf. Some individual scenes are etched permanently on my memory—how I wish I could forget them."

I never heard anyone talk about that e-mail afterwards. Maybe they are hoping to forget, too.

May 1945. Victory in Europe. Liberation for many Europeans, but not Germans. The Allies decided all Germans, including children, were guilty for the crimes of the Nazis. *Stars and Stripes*, the American military newspaper, proclaimed that "in heart, body and spirit every German is a Hitler!" In the following months, the Allies imposed punishing rations on an already-hungry population, waving aside requests by the Red Cross and other relief groups to send aid.

June 1945 is a gaping hole in Opapa's memory. He remembers only that he stayed at a refugee camp in the medieval city of Erfurt. It could have been hunger, he says, that blanked out the details. All he remembers is staying in wooden barracks with his mother and sisters.

His memory picks up again at the end of June, walking south on a dusty road, along with his sisters Anna and Gustel. All three carried rucksacks and blankets on their backs. Their mother had sent them to find a new home in Büsingen, a German village just over the Swiss border more than 400 kilometres away, where the family had relatives. They had left the camp just in time. The Americans pulled out of Erfurt and the Red Army occupied the city in July. There was no going back.

After a long day of walking, the travellers came to a Bavarian village where they found all the doors—even barn doors—shut to them. No one would give them lodging. The young refugees were strangers in a strange land and knew it. They decided to ask at one more house, their last hope for the night, on the edge of town. An elderly couple sat on the porch watching the sun set beyond a potato field. Upon seeing the tired travellers, the couple waved them over.

"Of course, stay with us tonight." The man and his wife were old, probably in their seventies. "Have you eaten? We'll make a meal."

Inside, the three refugees sat in the kitchen and drank tall glasses of water as the woman prepared soup and sliced bread. The refugees stared wide-eyed at the Catholic imagery decorating the walls: rosaries, images of Mary, a cross *with Jesus still on it*. The Lutherans couldn't remember ever being in a Catholic home before.

Then the wispy-haired old man entered the room with a wooden bowl filled with warm water.

"May I wash your feet?" he asked softly.

The three guests exchanged bewildered looks. "If you wish, yes. Thank you so much."

Their feet were dirty and cracked after the day's journey. But the old man knelt down and gently washed each foot with care until all were completely clean.

When I visit Opapa next, he's back at home. Omi is away at a church conference and I take her place in driving Opapa around Edmonton in his Volkswagen Jetta on errands. As we go to pick up *brötchen* rolls and Tilsit cheese, he gives constant orders from the passenger seat: get into the left lane, slow down, get into your right lane, let off the gas a bit, turn here, no, sorry, it was back there, and SLOW DOWN, there are rules. His directions are often wrong and he incessantly asks me to slow down, even when I'm going below the speed limit. "Your driving is bad for my blood pressure."

I try to see how fast I can go without getting him too upset. It's a mildly cruel game that makes his endless instructions somewhat tolerable.

"There's an emergency vehicle ahead. Slow down to 40."

The "emergency vehicle" is actually a concrete truck parked 20 feet off the street. I gently step on the gas, barely topping the speed limit of 60.

"You're not slowing down."

"Yeah."

These days, there's not much Opapa can do when someone breaks one of his beloved rules. I zip past the street parking spots in front of the bakery, irritating him even further.

"Ach, slow down!"

Later, back at home, I ask Opapa more about his relationship with authority. I think I've figured it out, shrunk it down to a sentence. "Let me know if this sounds right to you. It sounds like you discovered the freedom to question authority throughout your life, and yet you struggled to extend that freedom to others, particularly those in your own family." I brace myself.

"That's correct, yes." I relax. "That's where the influence of my childhood comes in. My mother was strict with us, overly so. She would punish us for little things like not being tidy. She pointed out that that's the way she was brought up." Opapa pauses. "You live the life of your parents all over again, to some extent. The problem then is that one learns too late."

His voice breaks. "You have to be seventy-eight before it sinks in."

September 1945. Ernst ran up the gentle green slope, two cartons of cigarettes stuffed in his underpants. The paunchy customs officer followed close behind but the gap widened with each step.

"Get back here!"

Ernst kept sprinting. He usually smuggled cigarettes calmly through the Swiss-German checkpoint but this time he'd decided to make a run for it. Ernst knew if the officer caught him, he'd keep the contraband for himself, trading it on the black market. Ernst had similar plans. He didn't smoke, and in any case cigarettes were too valuable. They could be traded for food. Ernst's main meal each day was a watery, saltless soup—not enough to live, but too much to die.

The trailing officer tripped on a root and fell, unleashing a string of curses and empty threats before returning to his post.

Weeks earlier Ernst had arrived in the French occupation zone with his two sisters. Only Anna could actually live in Büsingen, however, since it was her husband's hometown. Ernst and Gustel found separate rooms in Gottmadingen, a town on the German side of the border, and regularly went back and forth to visit Anna.

The three talked worriedly about their mother and other sisters. Did they get out of Erfurt in time, or were they stuck in the Soviet zone? Were they even alive? No one knew anything. After talking about their worries and reassuring each other as best they could, Ernst and Gustel would cross the border and return to Gottmadingen.

Ernst's last border crossing was by far his best. He'd approached the border like he always did: nervously.

"Anything to declare?" asked the customs officer.

"No. I have nothing. Absolutely nothing." Ernst's bright blue eyes darted away.

"Let's see about that." The officer called him in, confident he'd busted a wily young smuggler. He patted Ernst down but found nothing. He asked the boy to strip completely naked. While Ernst undressed, he emphasized his innocence.

"I had no money when I went into Switzerland. I tell you, I have nothing."

Finally, Ernst stood in only his skin. The officer checked the pockets of his shorts and rubbed his finger along all the seams, desperately looking for something of value. His face was drawn in disappointment.

"I told you I have nothing." Ernst tried his hardest not to grin. It was the only time he'd crossed the border without cigarettes.

Countless oblong boxes of tree seedlings soak in the June rain beside Omi and Opapa's grey tarpaulin garage: pines, spruces, birches, and Siberian larches, their root balls tightly wrapped into bundles of twelve. Every spring, Opapa collects thousands of seedlings from greenhouses that would otherwise throw them out. This year is no different despite his sickness. He gives the young trees away to friends, relatives, colleagues, strangers—anyone willing to pick them up from the acreage.

Opapa's planted hundreds of thousands of rejected seedlings all over Alberta since he arrived here from the United States in 1965, sent to St. Albert to start a new Lutheran church. One day he lets me in on a secret: he's actually a guerrilla tree planter. "My seedlings are planted everywhere," boasts my authoritarian grandfather. "Even in places where they're not supposed to be."

He doesn't want to go into detail "because it will upset people"—Alberta has strict regulations on tree planting in forests, rules Opapa says "must not be bent"—but he explains his gonzo forestry habits by telling a story about a rogue stand of Douglas fir trees in the Rockies near Alberta's David Thompson Highway, trees that drifted east over the mountains long ago, carried as seeds from what is now British Columbia. This is the dominant theory among botanists, Opapa explains. "That theory satisfies them." But Mr. Tree, ever the contrarian, has his own theory and the highway's titular fur trader is the central character. "My theory is that when David Thompson came back from British Columbia, he had bags full of seeds that got too heavy for him. So he spread them in that area. That's my theory, and I may be very wrong."

Like the David Thompson of his imagination, Opapa planted trees where they don't belong. Pine in spruce forest. Spruce amongst pines. Siberian larch in both. When he leads schoolchildren in a planting he follows the rules, but planting on his own he did whatever he liked. He tells me, smiling, that his trees are growing in many of the campgrounds where he's stayed throughout his life. "They're growing there without permission."

The larches, Opapa says, will add autumn colour to a green forest with their yellowing needles, and people will come up with their own theories on how those trees got there: they were planted by the government, or perhaps a logging company.

Or maybe just the wind.

Sometime in 1946. Dates blurred by hunger. Ernst and Gustel moved from Gottmadingen to nearby Murbach, 2 kilometres away, into a house owned by a German farmer stuck in a Russian POW camp. That's where Auguste, their mother, found them more than a year after they parted in Erfurt. But the details of the reunion have gone missing from Opapa's mind.

"I don't have a clear picture . . . There are so many fuzzy times . . ."

Together they made one last move to Randegg, a village a kilometre or so northwest of Murbach. "And then from that time on, it got a little bit better each day, each week, each month." Randegg was home for Opapa until 1952, when he transplanted westward yet again, first to Wisconsin and finally to western Canada. His mother lived in Randegg until she died in 1983.

When Opapa was in the hospital, I asked if he ever found a place of belonging in life. He said he did. Naturally, the forest topped his list. Lying beneath monitors and medical charts, he longingly described his favourite spot on the acreage. "I call it my cove. There's a little bench in the trees and everything's just sitting there, waiting for me."

At the time, we weren't sure he'd see that or any other forest bench again. But less than three months later, Opapa and I are on a campground bench overlooking Alberta's Kananaskis River. I have to give Dad credit. We're here because of him. The last couple years he's arranged weekend camping trips for our family, even borrowing a fifth-wheel camper so Omi and Opapa can come along. We never went camping much as kids—Dad was always away or busy—but now he's the one working to bring us together.

Opapa looks better than he has in months. He easily pushes his blue walker around the campground's paved black roads, no longer the frail skeleton we saw in the hospital gown. His white beard is long and full. His voice has the quality it lost when he was sick. Opapa admits he's still impatient, but Mr. Tree is looking treeish again, here in the forest he loves.

I look up at the mountains across the river, crisp grey stone against the rich blue of summer sky. But Opapa is looking downwards at the earth, at the fallen pine cones and budding wildflowers. Indian paintbrush bursting with red and green leaves. Fireweed with pink petal towers.

The summer sun pounds against the tattoo on my left arm, a work-in-progress sleeve of Alberta forest flowers. I chose it as a way to remember Opapa, to keep his memory alive when he's gone. Of course, when Opapa sees it, he sets into lecture mode. "Do you know you can never get an MRI now because of the metal in your arm? That is very serious. Did your tattoo artist warn you of that? What? You think there is no metal in tattoo ink these days? Do you know anything at all about metal . . . ?" The summer prior, Opapa had given me his copy of *Wildflowers of Alberta*. I decide against telling him I lent it to my tattoo artist as a guide.

Opapa gives me a lot of his stuff lately. Last year, it was a couple wilderness books and his flint and steel. This trip, it's *Plants of Alberta* and a knife he bought when he visited Randegg in the seventies. He opens the knife's saw blade. "This is used for amputating appendages or even limbs," he deadpans. "But it can also be used on wood if need be." He opens the main blade but doesn't have the strength to close it. "Here, you close it. It's yours now."

He swats at a mosquito on his long-sleeved shirt. For a long time, we sit silently on the bench. Woodland birds dance in the rustling trees above until finally, Opapa is ready to leave and together we walk slowly back to the campsite.

Johnny Flynn's Oysters

Margaret Webb

The oyster's a confusing suitor;
It's masculine, and feminine,
and even neuter.
— OGDEN NASH

I first tasted Johnny Flynn's cultivated oysters at the funky Oyster Boy restaurant in Toronto. His were my first experience of eating one raw. My partner, Nancy, who grew up in Nova Scotia, had been urging me to try one for years, seducing me with all manner of cooked oysters, but I resisted this adult rite of passage to a spinsterly age for two reasons. First, it takes but a second to swallow an oyster, but five years to grow one to market size in Canada's chill East Coast waters. Perhaps more alarming, raw means—at least in the case of oysters—that the creature is very much alive. Yes, the plump rise of flesh, which so resembles that part of the female anatomy, meets its death in your mouth. Or stomach if you do not chew. But you must chew, Oyster Boy owner Adam Colquhoun had told me, not only to release the heady flavours but to ensure the creature is still alive and fresh, and therefore not dead and skanky.

Contemplating the half decade of life that would be sacrificed for my one second of pleasure, my mind swirling with images of sex and death, I placed my finger on the sensuous swell of meat. Springy! I raised the shell to my nose and sniffed the ocean liquor. Fresh!

Tipped the tender morsel into my mouth and chewed. And, oh perverse, addictive pleasure.

My partner and I began haunting the top oyster bars in Toronto—Starfish, Oyster Boy, Rodney's. We sampled our way through platters of the luscious libertines—fished from the wild, cultivated on a farm, flown in from the East Coast, West Coast, United States, Europe. To our palates, no other oyster could rival Colville Bay's classic sharp hit of salt, followed by a tingling sweetness and steely clean finish.

We were not alone in our lust for these gems. Adam Colquhoun told us that he is so keen to bring in the first shipment of spring oysters after ice breakup that he has flown down to Prince Edward Island, stayed with the Flynns, donned hip waders and rubber gloves, and helped with the harvest himself.

While passing a lazy afternoon at Starfish slurping up a few of the sweet sensations, I watched a chef and his wife visiting from Chicago polish off a massive platter filled with a sampling of every oyster the bar stocked. After, they each flipped over a shell, declared it their favourite, then ordered a half dozen more of, yes, Colville Bays.

Patrick McMurray is the proprietor of Starfish. He holds a Guinness Book world record for shucking (thirty-three Cape Breton Aspy Bays in one minute) and is uncommonly obsessed with the bivalve. If he were an oyster, he told me, he would want to be a Colville Bay. To the couple from Chicago—growing smugger by the minute for their discerning taste—he waxed on about its beautiful teardrop shape, deep cup, the gorgeous green of the shell, the crisp texture and bright flavour of the meat, even the tiny tuft of seaweed Johnny leaves on the shell, which makes for an eye-popping presentation of half shells on a plate of ice. "It's a perfect little oyster," Patrick pronounced. "You can't get a prettier oyster than a Colville Bay." Across town, there are none on the menu at Rodney's Oyster House, though Rodney Clark, the man who started the oyster-bar craze in Toronto in the 1990s, would dearly love to have them. As Johnny Flynn's American distributor told me, he could sell twenty-five times more Colville Bays than he does—if only Johnny would raise more. But, apparently, Johnny likes to play hard to get.

The more I learned about the Colville Bays, the more intrigued I became. With his cultivated version, Johnny Flynn had managed to improve upon what many consider the world's finest oyster—the PEI Malpeque. But how? I wondered. Was it the water, the breeding, the technique of a slow rubber-gloved hand? When my curiosity reached a fever pitch, I decided to make a date with Johnny, to find out the secrets of his craft.

The shoulder seasons—spring and fall—are splendid times to visit Prince Edward Island. The crowds of tourists drawn to this gleaming pearl of summer heaven are at their thinnest, while the oysters are at their fattest. Arriving the last week of June, Nancy and I are pushing the season, but I have no worries. I did my research. Summer oysters are perfectly safe to eat, though after spawning, which occurs here in late summer, they can be thin and copper tasting. As a conservation measure, Prince Edward Island closes its wild fishery from July 15 to September 15, which may explain why that old English parson's warning against eating oysters in months without an "R" in the name still holds sway, even here. But oysters fished in hot weather need only be refrigerated once out of the water—something the Romans surely knew, packing them back from Brittany on ice.

Yet, when I called Johnny to make arrangements for our visit, he said something about it not being an ideal time, as it would be lobster season, and he still fishes lobster. That information hit my East Coast partner particularly hard, for she thinks the only thing sexier than eating oysters is eating oysters and lobster. We booked a cottage with a full-size kitchen.

Our two-hour drive from Prince Edward Island's Confederation Bridge to Johnny's hometown of Souris, on the southeastern tip of the island, takes us through a sumptuous summer day. Scenery unfolds as if from an *Anne of Green Gables* novel: rolling farmland, shimmering copper beaches, glistening blue ocean. While I drive, Nancy reads aloud recipes from the oyster bibles we have brought along—M.F.K. Fisher's *Consider the Oyster* and Karen Warner and Lonnie Williams's *Oysters: A Connoisseur's Guide and Cookbook*.

Her sensuous reading of recipes I had earmarked suddenly makes me wonder about our relationship. Being two women has nothing to do with my anxiety. We have been growing ever happier during our decade together and have developed a strong partnership, albeit one with rather more defined domestic roles than I had ever expected. While I throw myself into exotic-food adventures and lustily seek out new recipes, she is usually content to remain at home, by hearth and wine fridge, perfecting my first flawed dishes. Ah, but the oyster has changed all that, drawing us inexorably into this adventure together.

And that thought turns my mind to wondering if the little devils (literally called that by the Mi'kmaq Natives of Malpeque Bay) really are an aphrodisiac. Certainly, they have a storied reputation—as a staple at any half-respectable Roman orgy or at the breakfast table of a cavorting Casanova who stoked his libido by sucking back a dozen a day. One PEI bumper sticker we see hails them as "Nature's Viagra."

From my research, I gleaned that oysters are very good for you, but not that there's a direct spark from a wee oyster to, well, let's just say they're packed with zinc, which helps metabolize testosterone, which makes the prostate gland healthy and happy indeed. Their few modest calories are also chock full of protein and a medicine shelf of vitamins, plus iron, copper, magnesium, calcium, and phosphorous. To get your recommended daily allowance of all this good stuff, you need only eat four or five medium-sized oysters a day. My theory is that a famished Roman soldier or starving American colonialist would feel pretty good after eating five, sated with a dozen, and raring to reproduce after a few bushels.

And Johnny? According to one long yarn circulating through a Toronto oyster bar, he saves the shell of every oyster he ever eats—and there's a massive pile of them behind his house in Prince Edward Island. Which makes me wonder, should we be expecting a Don Juan in hip waders?

The Colville Bay Oyster Company crouches on a poetic, windswept stretch of red sand shoreline across the water from Souris. The company sign hangs discreetly on the side of a cedar-shake garage, not on the front where you might actually see it from the road. Inside is a tiny 26-by-32-foot government-inspected processing plant where Johnny and his family grade and pack the catch for shipping two times a week. A few steps down the beach is the Flynns' old family homestead, a small white bungalow where Johnny's eighty-two-year-old mother still lives. And there, standing in a small boat in the turbulent ocean inlet of Colville Bay, is Johnny Flynn himself. He looks every inch the typical fisherman, wearing a sou'wester, red-plaid wool jacket and rubber boots. And although he could use any modern mechanism to gather oysters on his private beds, he is fishing, as islanders have done for more than a century, with tongs that resemble giant salad forks, scooping the molluscs off the ocean floor. As he rows in to shore, I take in his trim black beard salted with grey, his massive suntanned forearms and a handsome cherub face that manages to look happy and sad all at once. And then those Irish blue eyes, the very colour of the sun-splashed sea.

He's shaking my hand before he's out of the boat, inviting us into the house to meet his mom, who's suffering badly with arthritis. Soon the whole Souris clan is dropping by—Johnny's wife, Mary Jane, a smart and attractive redhead; his younger brother, Leo, who lives across the street; an assortment of Johnny's three children and Leo's two; neighbours and cousins from town. The gathering seems like a family reunion, but this is just watching six o'clock news with mom.

Oyster farming, Johnny tells me, has enabled him to bring his family even closer together. Back in 1998, when the business began showing "a glimmer of hope," Johnny, then forty-one, persuaded Leo, then thirty-eight, to leave his home renovation business and join Johnny fishing lobster and raising oysters. Last year, Mary Jane left her job as a nursing manager to keep the books and fill orders. A major goal, Mary Jane tells me, is to build a company that will enable their children to stay home and make a living. As Johnny says, "I get Darwin, but I'm also spiritual. I guess I believe that community-minded sorts are the fittest to survive."

Well, this is something I wasn't expecting—an oysterman with profound ideas. I feel a weird twinge. But maybe it's just Johnny's gentle ways—he kisses his mom goodbye before he leaves. Or maybe it's the soft salt air. Or maybe it's the oysters, for Johnny, bless the man, sends us to our rental cottage with three dozen.

Our home for the next week could not be more perfect for our mission to learn about Johnny's oyster operation. Situated on a high shore cliff, it has a wraparound deck with a hot tub and panoramic views of Colville Bay. At the southeast end, the bay opens onto the Northumberland Strait and dramatic sunrises. At the northwest end, it channels into the mouth of the Souris River—site of Johnny's farm and heart-swelling sunsets. Incoming and outgoing tides create a natural flush that funnels plankton-rich tidal waters right over Johnny's oyster beds. Not that we can see them, as it's high tide and whatever magical contraption he employs is underwater. Still, I sense what's lurking there will help the PEI oyster industry find its way back from nearly a century of hard times.

A bit of history is required at this point. Although Prince Edward Island is the oyster's most northerly home, the bivalves were once so plentiful in Malpeque Bay, which gives its name to the island variety, that early settlers—the Acadians—fished them out of the bay and spread them over the land as fertilizer. The completion of the Intercontinental Railway in 1876 connected Canada's eastern provinces to markets in Montreal and Toronto and beyond, and Prince Edward Island quickly became famous for its Malpeques—prized not only for their exquisite taste but also for their hardiness.

The island's harsh winters have much to do with both. The oyster feeds hard through the spring, summer and fall, packing on so-very-sweet-and-good-for-you glycogen-rich protein. Then, when the water plunges below freezing, the oyster seals its shell and hibernates until spring. While a limpid Florida cousin might last a week out of the water, Malpeques, with proper refrigeration, can survive up to four months (easily a month in your refrigerator—though so will the smell), making them easier to ship to distant markets. When the PEI oysters arrived at a 1900 Paris exhibition, judges declared them the best in the world. During that heady time, some five hundred boats hauled 4 million pounds a year out of Malpeque Bay alone.

Alas, the fishers virtually cleaned out the bay. Oystermen brought in stock from New England to replenish it—likely the source of a mysterious and contagious disease that, by 1915, nearly wiped out the fishery. Though it had no effect on humans, Malpeque disease killed 90 per cent of the oysters in the bay.

To restore its wild fishery, Prince Edward Island looked to cultivation techniques developed in France in 1857 under Napoleon III.

Surviving PEI stock had developed a resistance to the disease, so experts here set out collectors (anything from egg crates to drainage tile covered in a fresh thin-set coat of cement) to capture young oysters, called seed or spat. They redistributed the spat to shallow bays and estuaries, in the hopes of establishing new oyster beds. Easier said than done. As late as the 1980s, the entire island produced just 2 million pounds, half the haul of Malpeque Bay in its glory years.

In the early 1990s, a few large PEI mussel producers travelled to France to study oyster cultivation first-hand. Mussels—dubbed the poor man's oyster—grow in the same waters but are much easier to cultivate, and the producers had scored big, building a $24-million-a-year industry that produces 37 million pounds of the famous Island Blue. They intended to do the same with oysters. The mussel men and a number of commercial fishers, using a government aquaculture program that offered interest-free loans for five years, invested millions of dollars attempting to adapt the French technology to mass-producing the finicky oyster. They lost millions.

Johnny is telling me this story in the middle of the night. Why has he woken me up to tell me this? Oh, right. It's pitch-black and spitting rain, and Johnny, his brother, Leo, and I are on our way to fish lobster. My wake-up call came at 3:15 a.m. Leo still seems half-asleep, but, this time of the morning, Johnny's a regular chatterbox. He tells me that in 1993 he bought eight boxes of mature oysters and tossed them in a saltwater inlet up the coast, to see if they would survive the winter. Back then, he was fishing cod along with lobster, but, stung by the 1992 moratorium on cod, he was casting about for ways to make money and "keep busy" the ten months of the year he wasn't fishing lobster. He had tried other careers as a young man—worked on northern survey crews and western oil rigs, considered teaching history and spent a year studying at the University of Prince Edward Island, did a stint in the Coast Guard—but he was always drawn back to Souris. He grew up here on the mixed farm his father worked on as a labourer—lean support for Johnny and his three brothers. But the idea of combining his father's passion for farming with his own for fishing appealed to him. After ice breakup in spring, when Johnny discovered his experimental oysters had lived, he invested $3,000 in oyster seed and equipment and jumped into his new venture with both rubber boots.

The most critical choice an oyster farmer can make, he says, is selecting the water. Turns out, the best piece of ocean for raising oysters Johnny's way was right out front of the old Flynn homestead, on Colville Bay. As Johnny says, "The opportunity was looking me right in the eye."

As we motor out of East Point harbour in Johnny's boat, I ask him why we're heading out in the middle of the night to fish lobster. "After all, they're in the traps," I say. "No fear of them going any-where." I might ask why he's fishing lobster at all, with his oyster farm thriving.

"Well, there's tradition," Johnny hollers over the motor, "and the sea's usually calmer. And I guess if there's a breakdown, there's time to fix the boat and get back out there."

Well, that's the rational explanation. Then Johnny admits that he loves the ocean. He loves her fierce, calm, warm, cold. He loves her changeable ways. "Nothing wrong with a snowstorm in winter," he says. "Gives you a chance to stay in and read a book." But I suspect he loves the ocean most in the still, quiet dark, just before sunrise.

The sea wears a black silk dress. The air is a soft kiss, the moon a steady pull.

"Big spring tide at a full moon," Johnny says. "Old-timers called them bull tides."

"Really," I say. "That's kind of suggestive."

"Hmm," he says.

Although he was raised Catholic and takes his children to church—"more for the community" than anything—Johnny seems to worship a more elemental spirit. He's always saying things like, "Mother Nature will look after you." Or, "You have to work with Mother Nature." Or, "No matter what, she'll always give you a good kick or two in the arse."

Johnny and I have only a few minutes to chat before he locates the first set of traps with his Global Positioning System. Leo, slip-ping a hook into the water, catches the yellow buoy marker. Johnny winches up the first trap, hefts the 100-pound wooden cage the last couple of feet over the side of the boat by hand. He pushes it along the side to Leo, who shakes out the lobsters, baits the trap with herring, and pushes it to the back of the boat in time to catch the next one Johnny winches up. They work, steadily, without talking, until they've fished the six traps. Johnny wheels the boat in a circle while Leo pushes them back in the water, then Johnny speeds onto the next set—fifty in all; we will fish some three hundred traps over the next seven hours.

Leo gives me the easiest job, using a bander to slip elastic bands on the snapping claws of market-size lobsters. I work hard. I want to impress Johnny. I'm not sure why. Maybe it's the oysters we ate last night. The sea drips with sex. Leo flips over every lobster to check for females—males have larger and harder forelegs. Ovulating females have great grape clusters of black eggs bulging from the outside of their tails. Leo throws these back in the water along with large females between about 2 and 4 1/2 pounds (good breeders). As well as all the little ones, those under half a pound.

...

Leo uses a gauge to measure. Sometimes he'll size a lobster two or three times—not for the measure to go his way but the lobster's. With a 4 1/2-pound female, it's like tossing twenty bucks back into the sea. Leo will say, "That'll make Johnny cry." And Johnny will holler, "Nope, I don't care." It's not as though any authority onshore is going to measure as thoroughly. But the two brothers have made their pact with the ocean. They look after her, she'll look after them.

This spring, they're getting $4 to $6 a pound for lobster, some $100,000 for two months' work; their expenses take about half that. In the off-season, many lobster fishers go on unemployment—virtually an East Coast ritual that irks the brothers.

"This is easy compared with oyster farming," says Leo.

"This is a two-month paid holiday!" shouts Johnny.

Finally, the sun pushes light into the sky, and the sea changes into a smoky grey outfit, then a shimmering blue silk as the sun pops over the horizon. With that blast of orange comes warmth. And Rankin Family tunes from the stereo in Johnny's wheelhouse.

We were alone in the dark. Now the water is dancing with lobster boats, springing between traps and flinging about buoys to the tune of fiddles and flutes. At 8:30 a.m., when my hand is cramped from banding, we stop for sandwiches. At 10:30, when I'm about to flop face first into my bin of lobsters, we're finished and cracking open cold beers, soaking up the sun. "I think I could enjoy this," I say, "on a day like this."

"First nice day we've had since the start of the season," says Johnny. "But one nice day makes you forget all the rest."

On the way into harbour, Johnny tells me that he named his boat after an Irish king. "Well, after buying it, I guess I'm Owen Mor, too."

Then he sends me home with a dozen lobster.

I return to the cottage exhausted, famished, and somewhat perturbed, for when Johnny drops me off, he tells me that on top of oyster farming, on top of lobster fishing, he has been doing research on his family tree. He located his long-lost American cousins and invited them to Prince Edward Island and, lo and behold, they accepted immediately. He expects them to arrive any minute. His voice quivers with excitement. Mine does not. For they, rather than I, will get to hang with Johnny for the next two days.

Nancy and I turn our attention to eating. She has been up just long enough to fetch a pot of fresh sea water, to boil up the lobster I have brought home. We lunch on the front deck, with Johnny's oyster beds in constant view. The tender claws are full and bursting with sweet ocean flavour. We make a dessert of raw oysters, tarted up with a drop of fresh lemon juice or twist of pepper or a dollop of Tabasco and two of vodka.

There is just enough time for an afternoon nap and then, deliciously, it is supper. We shuck and slurp raw oysters while cooking up a pasta sauce of lobster and oysters in cream and tarragon. And then, after a hot tub, it is time for a bedtime snack—oysters sautéed in a dash of butter, garlic and wine and slathered on toast.

The next morning, we breakfast on oyster and lobster Benedict, then hurry our morning hot tub to make an oyster chowder for lunch, which goes very nicely with a lobster roll. But as we eat, dreamily looking over Johnny's oyster beds, we start to wonder about that other old saying—that you are what you eat. This is disconcerting, for oysters are shamelessly lascivious creatures. Juveniles born into the sea settle down quickly enough, secreting a gluey substance that cements them in one place for life, usually an old shell in an oyster bed. They then pass the rest of their days gorging on seafood and enjoying staggering amounts of group sex.

Not surprisingly, the lusty little molluscs have only a few lonely cells dangling in place of a brain. Yet, they possess prodigious sex glands that swell during spawning to obliterate all other organs. And what adaptable and potent gonads they are. Maybe male one season, perhaps female another—all the easier to seduce whoever lives next door—the transsexual trollop spews millions of eggs or billions of sperm into the water each season. A group of presumably excited mathematicians once calculated that if a single oyster's ova were fertilized through five generations, she could produce a brood of full-grown offspring equal to 250 times the volume of the earth. Such is the fecundity of a species that has staked its four-hundred-million-year existence almost entirely on passion. If Darwin had confined his studies to the oyster, he may well have coined a different theory: survival of the sexiest. Yet, an oyster has only a one in a million chance of surviving to adulthood, which is where the finicky work of the oyster farmer comes in.

After an afternoon snack of grilled oysters à la M.F.K. Fisher—pop open a shell, add a little butter, "some pepper, some bread-crumbs," close and set on the barbecue for a minute or two—we decide that we simply cannot stand it anymore.

"I can't wait until Tuesday to see Johnny Flynn," I confess.

"Neither can I," Nancy also admits.

This is odd. Worse, it's only Sunday.

We stroll to the end of Souris Beach for a closer look at Johnny Flynn's oyster beds. We flop cross-legged on the sand not far from an endangered piping plover nesting area. We crack open beers and contemplate our predicament: we are two gay women falling increasingly fond of a PEI oyster farmer.

"It's the oysters," I say.

I'm not sure if Nancy believes me. Her right eyebrow shoots up. "Would you turn straight to be with Johnny Flynn?" she asks.

"No," I say. "Absolutely not."

"But what if Johnny turned into a woman?"

"He'd have to shave his beard. . . ."

But we are not oysters. Unlike them, we cannot change our sex willy-nilly.

Nor do we want to.

"It's nothing," I say. "We're running out of oysters, that's all."

"Maybe," says Nancy. "When do you think we can get some more?"

After much debate, we decide finally, and to our great relief, that we have come to care for Johnny like a brother. Which makes us think instantly of a scheme to lure him to us—a family reunion, hosted by us. So what if we are not family? We will invite Johnny, Leo, their wives, their children and all their American Cousins—the whole damn clan of Flynns back in Ireland if they show up—for oysters at our cottage at happy hour.

I call Johnny, and he's thrilled with the invitation—and I know why. He's haunted, even inspired, by his father's struggle to forge a living on this tiny, remote end of Prince Edward Island, rather than leave as so many others have, as his cousins' mother did. Johnny's bursting with pride for this place, and he wants to show his American cousins the island's huge potential and even bigger heart.

But the man's not one for boasting, at least not about himself. The locals we rent the cottage from are stunned to find out his oysters sell in Toronto—let alone that we're here to write about Johnny. When we ask for Colville Bay oysters at a pub in Souris that overlooks the bay, the waitress says she'd never heard of such a thing. Johnny himself jokes about an elderly woman in town who always asks how his mussels are growing. He always says, "Great, they're doing just great."

So I will play the Food Writer from Toronto, and we will spread the glory of Johnny. The thought makes us giddy.

We drive an hour and a half to the island's lone winery at Little Sands, returning with a Rossignol Chardonnay, and also a fruit-cranberry wine, which goes surprisingly well with oysters. We set up a shucking bar in the kitchen. Nancy whips up her irresistible version of Oysters Rockefeller, which has very little to do with the classic recipe other than the oysters. At six o'clock, Johnny, Mary Jane, and Leo arrive with their American Cousins. They are three middle-aged sisters from Pennsylvania who have never shucked an oyster, reel at the thought of eating one raw and know nothing of Johnny's fame. They are putty in our hands.

As Johnny sits at our makeshift oyster bar, arms crossed, beaming, we teach the sisters to shuck. We tease and cajole them into trying raw oysters, to much shrieking and delight. Finally, we move the party to the deck for the pièce de résistance, a view of Johnny's oyster beds at sunset, served up with Nancy's Fellers—an oyster on the half shell, doused in garlic butter, topped with grated Gruyère cheese, then broiled for two minutes.

Mary Jane, who doesn't like raw oysters, loves Nancy's Fellers. Leo, who has never eaten a cooked oyster, laps them up. Johnny eats three in rapid succession, cheese dripping into his beard.

And the American Cousins?

They pounce on them and they do not stop eating, until there is only one. The oldest sister points out the conundrum. The middle sister suggests sharing it. The youngest sister says, "I will stab you with my fork if you so dare as touch it." And then, before the older sisters can take the dare, the youngest plunges her fork into the heart of the Feller and eats it. Nancy and I bask in our happy success, for the Cousins have fallen as hard for Johnny and his oysters as we have. Alas, Johnny departs, though not before leaving us with another bag of oysters.

We fill the next day by visiting other farms. There are some 750 private oyster leases in Prince Edward Island. The Department of Fisheries and Oceans charges only $10 an acre for oyster and mussel leases, but it isn't issuing many more, as new housing developments are getting dibs on the island's increasingly precious shoreline. Consequently, farmers can turn around and "sell" established, successful leases for anywhere from $5000 to $15,000 an acre.

But visiting other oyster farms makes us homesick for Johnny's. At one, run by a large mussel producer, employees do the actual fishing while the owner works a calculator back in the processing plant. At another, ten employees alight on the beds one day a week to harvest, grade, and ship. This operation seems more like banking than farming. Rather than raising oysters from seed, they purchase two- and three-year-old oysters, deposit them on the ocean bottom, then withdraw them two or three years later when the oysters have reached the minimum market size of 3 inches. Two partners show off the farm by driving us around in a state-of-the-art, $50,000 harvester boat that blows water onto the ocean bottom and stirs the oysters up a conveyor belt. The thing sounds like an industrial vacuum cleaner and would surely scare the life out of Johnny's endangered piping plover, not to mention any birds nesting along these shores.

Between visits to farms, we manage to sample the island's bounty of cooked-oyster dishes. Tyne Valley, near Malpeque Bay, is home to the Canadian Oyster Festival and The Landing Restaurant, where the specialty is an old family recipe—oysters coated in a light batter and deep-fried for one minute. The delectably tender morsel is perfect for an oyster virgin's first taste—the deep-frying mutes the commanding notes of sea and mineral.

At Carr's Oyster Bar at Stanley Bridge, we spend a sunny afternoon on the deck overlooking the harbour, sampling oysters steamed in a wine and garlic broth, an easy and delicious dish to whip up at home.

When it is time for dinner, we visit the gorgeous Dalvay by the Sea, a stand-in for the White Sands Inn in the movie *Road to Avonlea*. Here, we sample chef Andrew Morrison's latest specialty: six oysters seared with lemon, cilantro, and black truffle oil. The taste is otherworldly.

But the highlight of our tour is a sampling of PEI varieties with champion shucker John Bil.

But first, a few tasting notes. Like wines, oysters can be distinguished by their species (think Chardonnay), their region (say, Napa Valley), and the waters (like vineyards' soils) they grow in. Starting with species, three are widely available commercially.

The Crassostrea gigas, or Japanese oyster—such as the Kumamoto—is now cultivated in the Pacific coastal waters of the western United States and Canada. We suspect it migrated to Toronto oyster bars only because East Coast varieties are iced under in winter.

Connoisseurs with their sophisticated palates will wax on about the gigas possessing hints of melon, cucumber, grass, and metal. Which means they taste like seaweed and copper.

The Ostrea edulis, or European oyster, is the variety the French predominately cultivate and consume—some 143,000 tons a year. Call me a home girl, but I nearly gagged after tasting their notes of rusting metal. Our clear favourite is our own Crassostrea virginica, which grows along the east coast of North America from the Gulf of Mexico to their northernmost range in Prince Edward Island. The Florida Gulf, Maine Glidden Point, Cape Cod Cotuit, New Brunswick Caraquet, and PEI Malpeque are all from the same family, yet there's a reason why folks in New Orleans douse their regional oysters in Tabasco and hot salsas while islanders here chase theirs down with nothing more than a cold beer.

As M.F.K. Fisher suggests, a southern oyster is like a Southern belle—"listless and bland." But our PEI oyster—courted by four seasons, from sultry summer to frigid winter—is a tangy tart, bursting with flavour. And yet, as John Bil so aptly shows us, all island oysters are not the same. Malpeques can grow in waters just ten minutes apart and taste different, which is one of the reasons farmers like Johnny Flynn name their brands, usually after the water they harvest in. Water temperature, salinity, bottom soil, vegetation and even current conspire to make each unique. Tasting PEI brands side by side is rather like tasting Chardonnays from different vineyards in a region or even different slopes in the same vineyard.

So we sample, slurp, and chew. Trying each is still like the first raw one I ever had—there is that ritual, a hot-and-bothered buildup to that tiny explosion of salt tang on the tongue.

We find that the oysters from the south shore, which opens to Northumberland Strait—from Hillsborough River, Clyde River, and Bedeque Bay—have decidedly less salt. They're both milder and creamier, with a soft vegetable aftertaste. Oysters from the north shore and eastern tip, which opens to the Gulf of St. Lawrence and the vast Atlantic—Cascumpec Bay, Conway Narrows, Raspberry Point, Stanley River, South Lake, and Colville Bay—have that classic Malpeque flavour. They're saltier, with a sweet hit on the chew, and a clean-steel finish. We prefer the north shores, and still love Colville Bays the best.

Our loyalty may well explain why a pek (a box of 100 to 120 small-size choice oysters) wholesales for 10 per cent more than most Malpeques. As John Bil explains, oysters are still an esoteric product that requires a huge amount of trust. "A brand shows that the producer is taking care. And every time you open a box of Colville Bays, it's a great box of oysters."

But today we have none.

We awake, stirring to fantasies of gravel flying from the wheels of the American Cousins as they leave Prince Edward Island. Ciao bellas! Finally, we will have Johnny to ourselves. And today we are to see his oyster beds. But at noon, Johnny calls. Big tears in his voice. He spent the morning saying goodbye. It clearly got to him. It's his daughter's last day of school and, to cut his long story short, he's throwing over the Food Writer from Toronto for his kid's school-end concert.

"At least the guy's got his heart in the right place," Nancy says when I hang up the phone.

I hiss until I have released a good bit of steam. Then grin. For I have worked Johnny's guilt to secure two dates for the next day—one to see his oyster beds right after lobster fishing, the other for dinner with Johnny and Mary Jane at our cottage.

But the next day, he doesn't call at noon as we had agreed. Or at one o'clock, or two. At three, I call him on his home phone. I call him on his cellphone. Ring, ring, ring. Outside, big storm clouds gather over Colville Bay. As lightning cracks and thunder rumbles, the Food Writer from Toronto marches out to the shore cliff, stamps her foot and screams with the fury of Lear: "What the hell do we have to do to get into Johnny Flynn's oyster bed?"

Five o'clock arrives, but Johnny does not. At six, just as we're about to throw in the towel on our dinner date, Johnny and Mary Jane appear, right on island time, apparently. Johnny offers me ten lobsters, a bag of oysters, a loaf of his mom's homemade bread, and an apology. Johnny refuses to hand over the bread until I forgive him. The loaf lingers between us.

Family is only half his excuse this time. One of the giant mussel producers on the island who also cultivates oysters dropped by for a visit. Johnny says the two spent the afternoon as farmers do when it rains, "standing in the workshop talking about how to grow a better oyster and solve the world's problems."

I would have loved to hear that conversation. In clandestine cell-phone calls Johnny made to me during the Cousins' visit (he has an endearing habit of thinking deeply about my questions, then calling me later with his answers), he talked on and on about limiting production, keeping prices high so farmers can take the time and care to produce a quality product and still make a fair buck. He credits the big producers for helping rebuild the PEI oyster fishery into a $7.5-million concern, but also criticizes them for being secretive. "They don't share research that could help others get a start and be successful," Johnny told me. "I'd hate to see two or three monopolize the industry. I'd rather have competition from a hundred small producers like me." Indeed, he served as president of the island aquaculture association for six years, playing, as he says, "cheerleader" to other producers. He claims his door is open for anyone to come and see his operation. "I've got nothing to hide," he says now. "Anyone can come and see my oyster beds."

"Except the Food Writer from Toronto," I say.

Johnny whips back the loaf of bread and comes out with the other half of his excuse. After the oyster producer left, he says it started to storm. And his eighty-two-year-old mom gets nervous in a thunderstorm, so Johnny sat through it with her.

Damn it, I think. Family, again. Still, I remind him that I'm here to write about him, that we've flown 1,600 kilometres to see his oyster beds and that tomorrow is our last day and we really have to see them. He promises, right after lobster fishing. Crosses his heart even.

The next morning, I refuse to let Johnny out of my sight, which means I am back on the boat fishing lobster at 4 a.m. Today, the ocean swells with 8-foot rollers, and I nearly lose my week's oyster gorge. After emptying the traps, we must haul in all three hundred of them for the winter, which takes a few trips back and forth. Our day drags on, to three o'clock in the afternoon.

Then, finally, we are pushing off shore into Colville Bay—to see the Promised Land at last. We motor the few feet out to the rearing grounds on an aluminum barge, a platform Johnny and Leo use to work on the water. Sarah, Johnny's youngest, comes along with us. She's a bright sprite of a ten-year-old, but was just a glint in Johnny's eye when he started in the oyster business over a decade ago, so we call her Oyster Girl.

She has carrot-orange hair and her father's determined blue eyes, and she makes one thing clear to us: we are taking her dad away from his real responsibility on end-of-fishing day, which is helping her build a bonfire on their beach, where the Flynns will all gather the next night to watch Canada Day fireworks soar over Colville Bay.

Compared with the other farms we visited—some as large as 200 acres—Johnny's operation is tiny, comprising Johnny's 15 acres and Leo's 10. Rather than specializing in one aspect of oyster cultivation, they do everything—raising the seed from spat to finish, a seed-to-harvest cycle that takes a minimum of four to five years. "It's the farmer in us, I guess," says Johnny. "It takes patience and sometimes being stubborn, but we get real satisfaction from seeing an oyster grow up."

Johnny kills the motor and Oyster Girl hands him an oar—clunking me on the back of the head as she does. In a quiet hush, he poles us over three acres of oyster-rearing grounds. Here, Johnny's secret is finally revealed, though, as Johnny kept telling me all week, it's not much of a secret. While the big mussel producers tried to adapt the French Table method to grow oysters cheaper and faster, Johnny read up on the traditional approach and stayed true to it.

In August, about three weeks after the oysters spawn, Johnny and Leo put out some four hundred collectors at the mouths of two rivers at opposite ends of the island. In days, millions of wild spat—each the size of a grain of pepper—will cement themselves to the collectors. After the brothers retrieve the collectors, they knock off the minute flecks—a laborious process they perform by gloved hand. They then take the minuscule oysters out to the French Tables, which are foot-wide, wire-grate platforms that sit in long rows about a foot above the ocean floor. Attached to these by bungee cords are hundreds of Vexar bags made of a heavy plastic mesh. Johnny pulls a bag on board—it's slightly larger than a 10-pound potato sack. Inside are thousands of seeds the size of Oyster Girl's baby fingernail. They're exposed at low tide, covered at high. The "baring off," Johnny believes, makes the oysters "feed harder" when they are submerged. This is organic farming at its best—the oysters feed naturally on phytoplankton in the water while also filtering hundreds of gallons of water a day, which actually cleans the water. If all goes well, the spat will grow to the size of a dime before winter, add an inch over the next summer, reach two inches by their third summer, at which time they're ready to spread on the bottom of Colville Bay, to reach their full size over the next summer.

But as the oysters grow, Johnny and Leo have to thin each bag several times during the year—if overcrowded, an oyster won't feed well and can even suffocate. They bring the bags to shore and empty the oysters onto a grader—three wire grates with holes of varying sizes. When they shake them through, the grater knocks off irregular shell formations and sorts the oysters into like-sized piles. Over the years, Johnny has discovered that oysters grow better if returned to a bag with similar-sized mates. It's one of the tricks, as Mary Jane teased at dinner the night before, that Johnny has picked up from walking around his farm at low tide "thinking like an oyster."

Johnny's meticulous approach requires a huge amount of work. Each thinning takes up to three weeks. During their busiest season, fall leading up to Christmas, they can spend twelve hours a day tonging, grading, and packing oysters into plastic-coated cardboard boxes for shipping in refrigerated containers, by truck or plane. And each winter, to prevent freezing in the shallow waters, they must sink the bags in about 12 to 14 feet of water. From seed through packing, Johnny estimates they will handle each oyster at least a dozen times—that's a lot of contact when you consider Colville Bay ships about a half million a year.

"Most people find the French Table method too labour intensive," Johnny says, "but it works for us." So he holds true to it, using only the help of two university students during the summer. His philosophy is to be both his own boss and his own employee, responsible for getting things done and close to the action to know exactly what needs to be done. "You have to get your rubber boots and rubber gloves on and go out and work it yourself."

Johnny drops the bag back into the water. As he poles on, Oyster Girl scoops a starfish from the deck and places the creature in the palm of my hand.

"They eat baby oysters," she says.

"Hmm," agrees Johnny. "Suction cups on the legs pry open the shells just a crack, then it slides its stomach inside the shell and eats the oyster right there."

But the Vexar bag protects the oyster from the nasty starfish and other predators. The tables also keep the wee guys from sinking into the silt bottom of the ocean and suffocating.

We glide over to the maturing beds, covered at high tide by about 6 1/2 feet of water. The bottom is studded with thousands of oysters that glow an eerie grey under the surface. "They just sit there," says Johnny, "but we can't ever forget they're living creatures. We try not to step on them. We try to treat them with dignity."

Before Johnny can ask for them, Oyster Girl races for the set of tongs lying on the front of the deck. Nancy and I duck this time as she swings the 10-foot-long sticks over our heads, and hands them to her father. Johnny scolds her to be careful. She sulks but not for long, for, with one scoop, Johnny tongs up about fifty market-sized oysters, and Oyster Girl is at his side, begging him to shuck one for her. She's the only one of Johnny's children who likes raw oysters. As we contemplate the freshest ones we'll ever eat—right out of the water—she whips the half shell to her lips and her face breaks into a wide smile as she swallows the mouthful of summer ocean. For me, it is more like a mouth-puckering hit of warm salt that leaves me gasping for a cold beer.

As Johnny shucks us another round, I ask him about future plans. Will he get bigger? Expand into South Lake, where he also has a lease? He looks over his oyster beds and shakes his head. "Really," he says, "we're right where we want to be." There's always risk in working with Nature—say, a poor spat season, another Malpeque disease, a red-tide algae bloom that can close shellfish waters for a season, even years. But things are going his way now. After losing half his oysters through the first two winters, he has reduced mortality to about 10 per cent a year. About 80 per cent of the oysters he raises are choice, which commands top price. He's also starting to sell directly to restaurants, including Catch in Calgary, and he'd like to do more of that. "The trick now," he says, "is to just keep doing what we've been doing, keep consistent, keep in the rhythm of it all." And then, he says, he will consider expanding.

And if someone were to come along, I ask, and offer him a million bucks for it all? I regret the question as soon as I ask, for Johnny's sea-blue eyes water up.

"No," he says. "No, I couldn't ever. This is home."

He hands the tongs back to Oyster Girl, who dances them to the front of the barge. Johnny starts up the motor and steers us back to shore. As Nancy and I step onto the beach, Johnny nods to the pile of freshly fished oysters and asks if we want to take some back to Toronto.

Truthfully, we want to take everything home—Johnny Flynn, his family, his oyster farm, his sunrises and his sunsets. But we will settle for his oysters, if we must.

Geared Up: On the road to two-wheeled transcendence

Bill Reynolds

RIDE ALONG QUEEN, head west across Parliament. Too crowded. Hang a left, south on Ontario, one block. West on Richmond. One-way with synchronized traffic lights. Perfect. Dinner with Deanna at six. Ten minutes to go. Hug the curb. Guy behind me. Parked car. Get around it. Hey, he brushed me! Don't panic. Grip down on the handlebars. Steady, steady. Running me into the curb. Brake . . . not too hard. Don't throw yourself off. Brace for the shock. Watch your crotch. Watch the *Toronto Star* box . . .

Uh, where am I? How long have I been lying here? My hands. Can't close them, they're throbbing. Look up . . .

"I saw the whole thing," says the skateboard guy. "He ran you over."

My head. Can't think. Good thing Jim and Warren goaded me into wearing a helmet: "Bill, for Chrissake, you've got a three-year-old kid!" they said. Bucket's cracked like an eggshell.

Could've been my skull. Three-quarters of the riders who die in accidents don't wear helmets.

"The guy sideswiped you. Do you need help?"

"I-can, get-up, on-my own." In fact, I've been knocked a few rungs down the evolutionary scale, and, for the moment at least, I can't do anything.

"I've got a cell. Want me to call the cops?"

I'm shaking. "Guess so."

I look around, wild-eyed. An off-duty Toronto Transit Commission bus driver cordons off the accident site.

"I'll radio it in. Where's the driver?"

"Took off," says the skateboarder.

A motorcycle cop rolls up.

"You all right?"

"Don't know. It was a white van."

The Utilitarian

My friend Jeff used to wonder why I keep riding, why I couldn't out-grow biking as I settled into marriage, a career, house, family, and five kinds of insurance. The bike is for recreation. You want to go to a grocery store, take the car, he'd say.

But not everyone is wedded to the car. Some use it to drive out to the countryside in order to ride. Others are gearheads who fall in love with every latest bike innovation; or ecofreaks who detest cars; or those shredders of mountain terrain, the off-road recreationers; or samurai couriers; or sleek, Lycra-sheathed road racers; or hybrid aficionados; or advocates knocking on city hall doors, protesting the bike's lowly status in the transportation hierarchy; or those polyamorous swingers of sport, the triathletes. Or simply speed demons: on a bike, you feel the acceleration, not like in cars these days, which are smooth and quiet, and where the difference between fifty and eighty or, on the highway, between one hundred and one-forty, is observed on the dashboard rather than felt in the gut. I've often wondered where I fit in.

I ride to work, the DVD shop, the fruit-and-vegetable stand, the theatre, the mall, a gig, the bar, the bank machine. It seems the practical, economical thing to do. I'm not against cars. I own one—a beat-up 1991 Buick Regal my dad sold me at a price only a parent would set—but I prefer not to use it. I didn't bother learning to drive until I was twenty-three.

I started riding to school in grade two. While my high school classmates parked their rides in the lot, I locked my ten-speed to a post. After grade thirteen, I mailed my Chiorda to Banff. I rode it through an undergraduate degree in Calgary, weather permitting. Then, during my second year of graduate school at Waterloo, a woman driving a compact delivered a right hook. That's when a car zooms ahead of you, then slows down and hangs a right, unaware of your velocity. I bounced off her passenger door, and typed my master's thesis with a broken right hand. Now I pedal from my home near High Park to work at Ryerson University downtown. Except in snowstorms, it takes about twenty-five minutes.

Without the bike, maybe I'd be less ponderous, wouldn't have two degrees in philosophy, would've made good on my childhood fantasies of owning a hot car like Steve McQueen's green Mustang in *Bullitt*. But I didn't, and I'm happy with the level of freedom (and speed) my bike affords me. The novelist Henry Miller considered his bike his best friend. "I could rely on it," he wrote, "which is more than I could say about my buddies." Maybe I'm like him; maybe that's just pretentious, if not ponderous.

It turns out I'm not part of any visible biking subculture. Rather, I'm part of a culture hidden in broad daylight: a utilitarian rider, according to a recent academic taxonomy of Canadian cycling types. Unfortunately, even with new bike lanes coming on stream, Canadian cities aren't built for riders, utilitarian or otherwise. We manage by slipping through the cracks in the urban bustle, finding the seam, whether through a traffic jam or in a designated lane. Still, the act of riding encases us in a protective fantasy. With one push of the pedal, the rider is bombing around the neighbourhood—ignoring the dull parade of adult duties, full of youthful optimism, insulated from the stultifying conformity of public transportation, the headaches of car ownership, the myriad rules awaiting any adult who steps outside the front door. On a bike, each directional choice is active, not passive, and something forbidden nearly always lies beneath. Each decision creates the possibility of finding the next secret route, riding the wrong way, negotiating a sidewalk, or slithering between cars jammed in like sardines, waiting for the go signal. And there is danger. If Icarus's tragic flaw was flying too close to the sun, the rider's is brushing too close to a car.

For all the chances riding creates to break society's countless rules—and infuriate drivers—there is a sense of beauty and formalism to it. Even at high speed, riding is ruminative, allowing for brain activity not possible when hoofing around a track, flailing sweat from a running machine, or in the confines of a four-wheeled exoskeleton. Bikes don't fit into society's grand scheme of civility. They are everywhere and nowhere, attach themselves to fences and posts, don't pay taxes or obey the rules of the road. To ride is to transcend quotidian reality, but also to manage the fear of getting hit. On this, the rider's life depends.

The Thirteenth Rider

November 14, 1992, a sunny, brisk Saturday morning, around 10 a.m., and thirteen members of the London Centennial Wheelers (LCW) cycling club pass through Delaware, Ontario. They hang a right out of town and remain on Highway 2, falling once again into a tight double-file formation. The route is a club favourite. They'll most likely head to Mount Brydges, cutting north across Regional Road 81, and stop at the Korner Kafe family restaurant. They may wolf down eggs and coffee before passing through Komoka. Eventually, the 74-kilometre run will wind through Springbank Park in southwest London, where the club hosts its prestigious Springbank Road Races each May. The event has been won by Steve Bauer and Jocelyn Lovell, among other cycling luminaries.

The club congregates at Victoria Park in London every Saturday morning, usually at 8 a.m. (an hour later in the fall). Sometimes they ride in two groups. One of the riders, renowned artist Greg Curnoe, nicknames them "the Hammerheads" and "the Loquacious." Hammerheads are competitive, maintaining a touring speed of 35 kilometres an hour—not quite road-racing speed, but a tough pace nonetheless. The Loquacious group cruises at just under 30 kilometres an hour and indulges in lively debate, something the contrarian and opinionated Curnoe loves.

This time around, there is only one peloton, or platoon of riders. Even though the temperature struggles to attain the freezing mark, a few wear little more than their official club jerseys. Curnoe's chosen colour scheme—bright yellow with green, orange, and grey stripes—was inspired by his love of reggae. The back riders take advantage of the slipstream the peloton creates. Curnoe, who rode lead until Delaware, drops to the rear and takes a break.

About 300 metres beyond the Highway 402 overpass, the two-lane road cuts across a farm-country panorama. Ahead is an elongated incline that requires extra exertion. The landscape to the south gives way to pasture, but the grasslands are submerged in a metre of water and look like a small lake. The riders have never seen such massive flooding here before. The dilapidated, weather-beaten grey barn up ahead appears to be floating on a bright reflection.

As the Wheelers approach the barn, Roger Williams exits onto Highway 2 from Barrie and heads west in his pickup truck. He accelerates to a cruising speed of around 80 kilometres an hour and comes upon the Magritte-style vision of the floating barn. He can't take his eyes off it.

Thud! Something hits the truck. Smacks the windshield. Shatters the reinforced glass.

The windshield holds together but turns opaque, and Williams can't see.

Thud! Another smack on the windshield.

What the hell?

Thud! Another.

Williams is terrified.

Thud! Again.

He slams on the brakes, but he keeps hitting things.

Thud! Lorne Falkenstein lies on the hood.

Thud! John Thompson, a bruiser of a man, pushes Falkenstein through the windshield.

Williams receives Falkenstein and shattering glass.

Thompson slips off the hood, rolls onto the ground, and sees scattered bodies and bikes everywhere. It looks "like a war zone." He hears Williams say, "Oh my God, what have I done?"

The decisive moment—no more than several seconds—is over. The peloton, as seamless and fluid as a school of fish, and seemingly impervious to outside forces, lies wriggling on the asphalt, destroyed. Mike Lesko had been leading the pack. When he looked over his shoulder, he says, "all of a sudden, they just seemed to bunch up and fly everywhere."

Curnoe, Dale Nichol, Jorn Pedersen, and Bill Harper were the first four human dominoes. Falkenstein performed CPR on Curnoe. Green and yellow bile came out of the felled cyclist's mouth. It was gruesome, but the CPR worked. Curnoe was breathing. Then Falkenstein went off to help other riders. The ambulance arrived and whisked Curnoe 15 kilometres to the regional hospital. In all, six men and one woman required medical attention, but Curnoe, fifty-five years old and in great shape, was the only rider killed. Falkenstein's sense of guilt was profound. What if he hadn't left Greg's side, he kept asking himself. (Months later, the doctor who treated Curnoe ran into Harper. The medical opinion was that the injuries were so massive no one could have survived them. Harper asked the doctor to emphasize this point to Falkenstein.)

Harper, the fourth rider, remembered seeing the floating barn, and then waking up in the hospital two days later with a concussion and double vision. His ear had dangled by a thread of flesh but had been sewn back on. Gradually, he realized he'd be in a wheelchair the next day, Tuesday, attending his buddy Greg's funeral. He pictured his first ride with Curnoe two decades earlier, an 80-kilometre tour to St. Marys and back. Curnoe was riding a civilian bike, not a racer, but he completed the entire loop.

Curnoe's death was bitterly ironic. Biking had been central to his artwork for twenty years. He was first exposed to Dadaism, cubism, and Surrealism in 1954, when he enrolled in a special arts program at London's H.B. Beal Technical and Commercial High School. Three years later, drawn by the gravitational force of the larger city centre, he moved to Toronto to study at OCA, the Ontario College of Art. He didn't have much time for his professors, but one of them, Graham Coughtry, was knowledgeable about the art movements that so piqued his curiosity. Then, in 1958, he met Michel Sanouillet, owner of a French bookstore in Gerrard Street Village and the author of a book on Marcel Duchamp. The young artist couldn't believe it—stuck in a city where no one seemed to share his love of

Duchamp or, for that matter, the German expressionists, he'd found a Dada scholar in a modest shop in Little Bohemia!

Back in officialdom, OCA returned Curnoe's lack of respect by failing him in his final year. His response? Tear up the big-city script, vow never to return, and head back to London, where he hooked up with avant-garde artist and musician Michael Snow, filmmaker Jack Chambers, and poet James Reaney, and where regionalism quickly became a defining feature of his work. In 1961, Curnoe's first solo exhibition was mounted, and his magazine, *Region*, published its inaugural issue. His first gallery (also called Region) opened in 1962, and the next year he formed the Nihilist Party of London, Ontario, its first political campaign launching with a poster of then premier John Robarts, his eyes covered with the slogan VOTE NIHILIST— DESTROY YOUR BALLOT. In 1965, he formed the influential noise collective the Nihilist Spasm Band (which continues to this day), and the National Gallery of Canada bought its first Curnoes. From there, it was straight up: Canada Council and Ontario Arts Council grants; infamy for his anti–Vietnam War commentary, in a large mural at Dorval Airport in Montreal in 1968; representing Canada at the XXXVII Venice Biennale in 1976; and his large show, *Retrospective*, touring the Montreal Museum of Fine Arts, the National Gallery, and the London Regional Art and Historical Museum in 1981. Curnoe's mixture of regionalism—what critic Sarah Milroy described as "the notion of making art out of a passionate loyalty to one's immediate surroundings and community and not in slavish imitation of international styles"—and dadaist tendencies would remain potent throughout his career.

Ignited by that first road trip with Harper, Curnoe's art intersected with riding in 1971; after that, vocation and avocation became impossible to separate. Writer, poet, and Curnoe friend Christopher Dewdney says, "It was as if Greg had been made for cycling. His art, which had always been part of his life, became even more inextricably bound up with his physicality in an intense symbiosis. Bicycles represented the stripped-down relationship between form and function that so appealed to him."

I begin to get a sense of Curnoe's long shadow when Harper shows me around London on a gorgeous summer afternoon. Our first stop is

Harris Park, where a red maple tree was planted in Curnoe's memory in 1993. Sadly, we can't find it. (Hours earlier, Curnoe's widow, Sheila, had mentioned to Harper that the tree might not have survived.) Undeterred, we hustle up the hill. A University of Western Ontario philosophy of science professor, Harper is sixty-five (fourteen years my senior), but he maintains a three- or four-step jump on me. He tells me, "Greg and I were mystified when people said they rode to look fit. He used to say, 'I don't ride to look good. I ride to wear people out!'"

We reach Museum London. Three Curnoes are on display, including a radiant, life-sized Plexiglas painting of one of his cherished Mariposa bicycles. Then we head over to the Greg Curnoe Connection, a tunnel that links a bike path from Wharncliffe Road to Greenway Park. Completed in May 1995 and dedicated to Gregory Richard Curnoe: Artist, Writer, Musician, Athlete, November 19, 1936–November 14, 1992, the tunnel allows cyclists safe passage beneath the train tracks.

Finally, we drive out to the crash site. Just before Delaware, Harper catches a lump in his throat. A couple of kilometres past the village, out here on the gravel shoulder and trying to locate the precise impact zone, he regains his composure. It's me who's spooked. Vehicles whisk by. I feel the blowback of a half-ton pickup truck and see the lack of room on the road. There is no plaque to commemorate the tragedy. We stand there for a while looking out, and then silently drive back to London.

What caused Roger Williams to plow his truck into a formation of disciplined, experienced riders on a bright, sunny autumn morning? I wonder. I broach the subject with Sheila, suggesting that Williams's brief, appalling inattentiveness is the kind of blunder that can haunt a man for the rest of his life. She's obviously heard this kind of empathetic consolation before. "He can sit around, drink a few beers, and have people feel sorry for him. I mean, that's what he's going to do. I have no sympathy for him at all. You're a young guy, twenty-six years old, driving a truck. Pay attention to the road."

Curnoe loved everything about bikes—the wheels, gears, derailleurs, the riding, speed, testosterone, and camaraderie. I cross-wire this passion with his steadfast anti–U.S. imperialism, and suggest that biking must have been an enviro-political act for him. "*O-h n-o-o!*" Sheila says. "Greg never talked about the environmental aspect of bicycles at all. I don't think he ever thought about it. Greg loved cars. He wanted to get a Maserati. When I married him, my mom and dad loaned him their car. He gripped the steering wheel like a maniac, leaning forward with the thrill of it all. He got so many speeding tickets, I said, 'Greg, we can't afford this!'"

Curnoe transferred his love of speed to a love of bikes. He forever searched for the perfect flat roadway to better his time trial scores, sought out the best equipment, and never, ever, threw anything out. Spent inner tubes, broken derailleurs, a worn out sprocket could all be raw material for his art. Seven years ago, Sheila's office replaced the bike workshop on the main floor, but most of Greg's bikes and all of the various parts and paraphernalia still sit in the basement of the 107-year-old converted lithograph factory. They remain as if time stopped on November 14, 1992.

Sheila did sell a couple of the more famous bikes—ones used as models for Greg's paintings—to bike club friends, but everything else is still there. Everything, that is, except for his favourite, the bright yellow Mariposa road bike. Sheila didn't want to have anything to do with the mangled racer, and the red helmet with the missing chunk, when they were returned to her. She sorely wanted to throw them out, but was urged by friends to show caution. An opportunist might fish them from the garbage to claim as The Bike And Helmet Greg Curnoe Died Riding And Wearing, so she thought better of it.

Instead, Sheila looked towards the embankment that falls precipitously from the backyard perimeter. Her children used to call it "down the back." This was the place where, in 1981, below the fence, Greg discovered part of a litho stone—labels, letterheads, and all—jutting out of the cliff. He was fascinated with rubber stamps and lettering, and used them for his later art. This was the place where, in 1991, Greg undertook an archaeological dig and found a colour separation of the Union Jack, among many other artifacts. And this was the place where, opening still agape months after Greg's death, the chilly reminders were entombed in the hill, above the old Thames riverbed. Over time, the bike-and-helmet burial ground has been obscured by dense growth.

Two weeks after the accident, Williams was charged with one count of dangerous driving causing death, and five counts of dangerous driving causing bodily harm. The prosecutor measured the distance between the Highway 402 underpass and the point of impact on Highway 2. He was convinced he could show that Williams had taken his eyes off the road for as long as thirty seconds, which justified elevating the charge from careless to dangerous driving. A conviction on the lesser charge carried a maximum penalty of six months in jail, a thousand-dollar fine, and a two-year driving suspension. Dangerous driving carried a maximum prison term of fourteen years.

When the trial finally opened in January of 1994, however, evidence demonstrated that Williams was sober and in control of a mechanically sound vehicle, and that he bore no malice. He said he'd been distracted by the glare from the sun and the flooding. The prosecutor pointed out in his final address that the highway at that point was straight and flat, visibility was first rate, and the thirteen riders looked "like a 45-foot multicoloured snake wearing every colour of the rainbow moving down the road." Williams's lawyer said there was no doubt that his client was responsible, but not criminally responsible, which is what the charges claimed.

The trial took four days, and after five hours of deliberation the jury acquitted Williams of all six charges. Sheila Curnoe (along with riders Dale Nichol and Jorn Pedersen) pursued Williams in a civil trial suit, and won. The money was nice, but it merely papered over the hole in the family's life. "There's this empty space," Sheila said a year later.

Switching to Glide

The bicycle, according to scholar Donald Zaldin, revolutionized nineteenth-century culture. Its progenitor was the two-wheeled velocipede, invented in 1817 by Germany's Baron Karl von Drais. The velocipede looked like a bike, but it had no crankshaft or drive train. The rider was propelled along by foot power alone. Then, sometime in the mid-1860s, a French metalworker figured out how to add a crankshaft. Two decades later, in 1885, England's John Kemp Starley attached gears to the rear wheel instead of the front. Three years later, John Boyd Dunlop, a Scottish veterinarian, improved pneumatic tires and introduced the smooth ride. Suddenly, anyone, rich or poor, young or old, could travel beyond his or her immediate surroundings at no extra cost and with little wear on the body. The past century has seen numerous design upgrades and innovations—the three-speed Raleigh, the ten-speed derailleur, the mountain bike, the hybrid—but the concept remains the same.

And that concept's irreducible nut is the body defying gravity. Riding is governed by physics, specifically by torque-induced precession. Gravity causes a stationary bike to fall over, but applying torque—using the legs and feet to push down on two pedals attached to a crank—changes the equation. The drive train transfers the rider's energy directly into movement. The wheels turn and stay upright, and torque allows 182 pounds of human tissue to move on two flimsy pieces of rubber filled with air.

The thinner the bicycle's frame, the less wind resistance, and aerodynamics only increases efficiency; leaning over the handlebars, especially going downhill, reduces drag and boosts speed. Spoked wheels are almost as strong as solid ones, at a fraction of the weight. Using a derailleur, a transmission system invented by the French in the late nineteenth century, the rider easily switches the chain to a smaller sprocket and—voila!—more torque, more distance in less time. As the rider increases cadence—the number of revolutions per minute—he injects pure power, especially in higher gear ratios. The work is hard but satisfying.

Lawrence of Arabia, masochist that he was, reportedly searched for the steepest hills to climb, and once he reached the summit he'd walk the bike down. He was hardly alone in this apparent self-sacrifice. Asked why he put himself through gruelling punishment in preparation for races, 7-time Tour de France champion Lance Armstrong said, "I didn't do it for pleasure. I did it for pain." The Dutch novelist Tim Krabbé, known for his psychological thriller *The Vanishing* but also a one-time racer, elaborated on this embrace of physical misery. In his novel/memoir *The Rider*, he wrote: "Velvet pillows, safari parks, sunglasses: people have become woolly mice. They still have bodies that can walk for five days and four nights through a desert of snow, without food, but they accept praise for having taken a one-hour bicycle ride." An acquaintance of mine, Shauna Gillies-Smith, told me that when she was in labour she almost gave birth before leaving for the hospital. So inured to heightened pain from competitive riding, she hardly noticed her contractions.

Because of torque-induced precession, most riders don't have to go to these extremes. Generally, we lie back and enjoy the glide. Cycling is up to five times more efficient than walking. "Cycling is probably the most sustainable of all transport modes," say Rutgers researchers John Pucher and Ralph Buehler in their 2005 study of Canadian cycling patterns, "producing virtually no pollution of any kind and requiring no non-renewable energy resources at all." All very well, and there are more riders on Canadian roads than ever, but our numbers are puny compared to Europe's. In Copenhagen, city officials estimate that a solid and very respectable one-third of commuters use the bike. In Canada—with Victoria, British Columbia, in the lead at about 5 per cent and Toronto lagging way behind at 1 per cent—for every two-wheeled insect buzzing around on pedal power, there are sixty-one sleek, fast-moving, fuel-injected four-wheeled animals on the road.

There is some momentum in urban Canada for mass engagement with the freedom of cycling, but it has to be tempered by the law of the urban jungle. The four-wheeled beasts are stronger than the two-wheeled insects, and sometimes insects hit the windshield. In 1984, there were 126 cycling fatalities in Canada. Since then, despite the lack of mandatory laws for adults in all jurisdictions, increased helmet use appears to have reduced the number of head injuries, and government awareness campaigns have convinced many drivers to watch out for cyclists. By 2002, the number of deaths dwindled to sixty-three, and cycling injuries fell from 11,391 to 7,596. These encouraging results are borne out anecdotally by a neighbour. He tells me that in his twenty years of bike commuting, he's noticed a change in drivers. Intersections are still treacherous—riders never know when drivers will speed ahead and hang a right on them—but most drivers now understand that cyclists are part of the road.

Still, when you consider that vehicles cause nearly 90 per cent of fatal cycling accidents, riders must maintain a healthy respect for the beasts. Gillies-Smith, a Canadian landscape architect now working and raising a family in Boston, and until recently a competitive cyclist (she twice won the Canadian Cyclocross Championship and was ranked in the top ten on the much larger American circuit), says, "In a car, there's a real disassociation with the world. There is this belief—although almost every driver hits a cyclist by accident—that bicycles don't belong on the road." When drivers are protected inside a hull, invincibility is an illusion easily achieved. "When I ride in the city," Gillies-Smith says, "I'm extraordinarily cautious. I don't take risks. I really, really back off."

Drivers on the Storm

Drivers can be the victims of bad luck or bad driving as well, but for riders it's the lack of armour that counts. And once in a while, a story comes along to throw an icy shroud around every rider's heart.

On Canada Day 2000, Frank Groves set out on his usual early-morning ride. He headed southeast on Elliott Street in sleepy Brampton, a suburban enclave 30 kilometres northwest of Toronto. The recently retired Northern Telecom employee was an avid cyclist who liked to get going around 5 a.m. At sixty-five, he kept himself in good shape, either biking or swimming every day.

Elliott Street was without traffic, except for one car, a stolen Dodge Shadow. It was moving fast and, unbeknownst to the silently gliding Groves, bearing down on him. Just before Craig Street, the drunken driver spotted the bike, and aimed his vehicle for its skinny rear wheel. He plowed into Groves, propelling the rider's body over the Shadow's hood. Groves smacked the windshield, then fell away from the speeding vehicle. He was killed instantly. Police told reporters the bike remained trapped under the chassis and scraped the road for 700 metres. The car was found on Frederick Street, less than a kilometre from the hit and run. Stymied by construction equipment blocking his path, the driver had abandoned it.

The police appealed to the public for clues about the death, but nothing was revealed. Then, about ten months later, they caught up with twenty-two-year-old Jeffrey Campbell in a Niagara Falls motel room, planning a home invasion. At the trial, the court heard that the young man had smirked as he knocked Groves into the windshield, and laughed while watching television news reports of the homicide the following day. Campbell has displayed no remorse and has since been declared a dangerous offender, after achieving Bernardo/Olson–like numbers on clinical tests. His behaviour affirms every rider's instinct that in the urban jungle the car is king, and a heavy, four-wheeled object can—and sometimes will—eradicate a light, two-wheeled one.

The Right Hook

Mayhem involving vehicles and riders is typically more banal, the carnage mostly attributable to repetitive patterns that could easily be stopped. On October 31, 2005, Ryan Carriere, a thirty-one-year-old postal worker and budding cartoonist, was heading home early in the afternoon after finishing his route. He was planning a barbecue dinner before taking his two daughters out trick-or-treating. He never made it. At the intersection of Gladstone Avenue and Queen Street West in Toronto, Carriere caught the right hook. He was sucked underneath a truck's wheels and crushed to death. Apparently, that stretch of Queen around Dufferin Street—with a train overpass immediately east of the lights—is known to city officials. Apparently, it has been slated for improvement. Apparently, a discussion has been going on for a decade about making side guards mandatory for trucks.

I call Darren Stehr, spokesperson for Advocacy for Respect for Cyclists. He refers me to a document called "A Report of Cycling Fatalities in Toronto 1986–1998" by regional coroner W. J. Lucas. Under the heading "Large Vehicles and Bikes," recommendation fifteen asks Transport Canada to "investigate the feasibility of requiring 'side guards' for large trucks, trailers and buses operated in urban areas to prevent pedestrians and cyclists [from] being run over by the rear wheels in collisions with these large vehicles. . . ." Lucas's report was issued a decade ago, and riders like Carriere still aren't bouncing away from the right hook; they're being dragged under. In Europe, side guards on trucks are standard.

Cycle Paths and Psychopaths

Along Amsterdam's many one-way cobblestone canal paths, on dedicated bicycle highways, and sharing the roadway with cars, there are tens of thousands of cyclists. They get their very own traffic lights—with bicycle icons lighting up red or green—in the central core. Dutch city bikes tend to be clunky: hard to lift, uncomfortable to ride over long distances, and forcing riders to sit too far back. (No one in North America would dream of riding such a bike.) But they're solid, the tires are large, and they don't break down—in short, they're perfect for city riding. Couples lazily ride to dinner, formally dressed in suit and gown, he pedalling (usually) and she sitting on the baggage rack. Moms and dads transport kids the same way. No one wears a helmet. Down at Central Station, the confluence of lanes makes the Arc de Triomphe traffic circle in Paris look like the idyll of Manhattan's Central Park. Amsterdam is inner-city kinetic energy at its finest.

H-i-i-i-s-s-s-s . . . a middle-aged woman admonishes a walker for dallying on her bike highway. She's one of the ones who have taken up cycling later in life, the government's social engineering having successfully pushed bikes as a way for people, women in particular—Surinamese émigrés and Dutch citizens alike—to become more independent and mobile. She's learned the rules of the Amsterdam system to the letter, and her message is: Don't get in my way.

Bikes rule Amsterdam. If a car hits you, it's the driver's fault. Period. Down these crowded streets, walkers fight through designated traffic lanes—one for bikes, and one each for taxis, regular cars, and the tram. But nothing is perfect. When I tell Paul, our bed-and-breakfast host, about the supercilious, hissing woman and numerous speed-automaton men—like our slick-haired cab driver from the airport—he says, "Yes, here in Amsterdam we have our cycle paths, and we have our psychopaths." The system, no matter how ingeniously regulated, still induces stress. Car congestion has given way to a different anxiety: moving through public space that is on the verge of becoming a bike dystopia. I wonder if bikes here have become the new cars; if they are two-wheeled insects, they're sizable ones, like dragonflies. So what does that make walkers—mosquitoes? Maybe there is something in wheeled motion itself that induces aggressive behaviour.

Down at Central Station, buzzing car and bike traffic rattles Justine, my ten-year-old daughter. She scrapes her hand on my wife's left brake handle—her second minor bike accident in two days. It's intense out here for a young girl. The congestion can offer the worst of both worlds: scooter drivers and cyclists whiz by on bicycle highways, with little regard for pedestrians; meanwhile, car traffic is no less dense. Pedestrians are wary, too, and reserve their ire for tourists on bikes who don't know where they're going. Teenagers snicker and quack, "MacBike! MacBike!" as we parade by on a canal street. We're fat targets for derision. The MacBike rental company, which has three locations in central Amsterdam, bolts onto its bikes a round metal plate that says "MacBike" in large lettering—mainly to alert pedestrians that you're an idiot tourist. Around here, "MacBike" is a scarlet letter.

We flee this hornet's nest of traffic and find refuge in Vondelpark, Amsterdam's large, leafy inner-city sanctuary. In the days before the classifications *yuppie* and *boomer* were coined, hippies used to camp out here and protest the value systems of their parents. We lock up and meander about the park. It's blissful, but even here the tension winds up. Laura wanders onto the quiet roadway. Suddenly, a middle-aged woman, seated primly, her back straight on her practical machine, heads straight for her. Twenty metres. Should Laura get out of the way? Eighteen metres. What if she moves and the rider veers the same way? Fifteen metres. Better stay put and let the rider go around. Ten metres. This is not happening. Eight metres. It is the rider's road. Six metres. Rider is determined. Five metres. Rider better break. Four metres. Rider sputters, hisses—three metres—clucks like Mother Goose. Two metres. Guttural noises. One metre. Rider comes to full stop. A look of certain doom is etched on my wife's face. The rider says, imperiously, "*Thank* you!" as Laura moves. The rider resumes top cruising speed. Laura heads for the edge of the pond to calm down.

Paul, our B&B owner, says some riders "try to find the absolute shortest way between two points and go as fast as they can. The only thing they respect is the tram because it is heavy and takes time to stop." In 1987, the American satirist P. J. O'Rourke theorized that his nation was "afflicted with a plague of bicycles." Right theory, wrong country, perhaps? Then again, after two weeks any new rider will graduate from naiad to dragonfly and thrive in this cycling ecosystem. Amsterdam's good councillors organize their chaos with fine attention to detail. They have little space, and less choice. They don't have the luxury of the Danes in Copenhagen—where bike tracks are gloriously wide and neatly separated from vehicle roadways by shallow brick barriers or marked off with blue paint— but they have succeeded in making their town a bike town.

We head back to North America, to Canada and Toronto, with its enfeebled version of safety for cyclists.

Brushed

I'm reading participant diaries from Web archives of the 2003 inaugural Tour d'Afrique, a four-month-long, 11,900-kilometre course from Cairo to Cape Town. It was completed by thirty-two of thirty-three riders, over half of whom came from Canada. I notice a newspaper clipping on the long table in the middle of my workspace. The *Toronto Star* article is dated April 21, 2006. TWO CYCLISTS DIE IN SEPARATE ACCIDENTS, reads the headline. Both riders were on the receiving end of the right hook, inadvertently delivered by large trucks. One was a sixteen-year-old kid, "a jolly little girl," a neighbour told the reporter. My eyes water; I get up and reel around the room. I taught Justine how to ride, and now can't avoid the thought: it's only a matter of time.

Man-Machine

"How's your head?"

Start assessing the damage. Got seven minutes to meet Deanna at Peter Pan. Left knee's bruised and bleeding. Hey, what's that, a pain vector out of my left shoulder. Blood trickling down my leg.

Face scraped. Ouch. The cop is halfway through writing up his report.

"Where is the driver of the vehicle?"

"I don't know. He's probably gone."

The skateboarder offers his cell again, in case I want to phone Peter Pan. I don't know the number. He helps me lock the bike to a metal signpost. It looks better than I feel—salvageable.

The Good Samaritan bus driver shoves off. He protected the site, and me, until the cop arrived. Suddenly, the officer notices an older man across the street, half a block west. He's coming towards us. Now he's leaning the other way, thinking, I suspect, "Hey, did I hit something? Better go back and check. Uh-oh, you know what, maybe I'll just get back in my van . . ."

"Just a minute," the officer says, striding towards the man. "Sir, are you the driver of the vehicle involved in the collision?"

A conversation ensues. The white van is parked one block west. The driver is in his late fifties, with grey, matted hair and jagged yellow teeth. He doesn't have his driver's licence with him, or his vehicle registration, or his car insurance. He's written up. Four violations, with failure to negotiate a left turn the most critical. Later, when I appear in court to testify against him, he doesn't show. Failure to appear means the charges will stand and he'll be fined several hundred dollars. I sue his insurance company, settling two years later for an amount my lawyer tells me is too low.

That fateful evening, though, I scrape myself off the curb, get into a cab, and make my Peter Pan dinner date. May 27, 2002, is immediately filed in my memory bank as the day I almost bought the farm. I order risotto—no need to cut anything, right?—and drink a martini. Deanna looks at me looking at the waiter. "Bill, you have to go to the hospital," she says. A command.

At St. Michael's, X-rays show a nasty spiral fracture of the ulna. The emergency doctor places a cast on my broken right arm. Six weeks later, it's still there and I'm in my GP's office. No break was discovered in my left hand, but an acute pain persists. The doctor feels my left hand for a minute, digging around, pinpointing the ache. She orders me across the street and calls radiology, requesting a specific shot. At last, magnified X-rays show the shattered, kidney-shaped scaphoid. This peanut-sized marvel just above the thumb and ahead of the wrist has a notorious ability to break and evade detection. The stealth fracture only shows itself through time and further damage. The doctor phones from her office. "William, you have to get a cast on that left hand. Now."

I walk out of St. Mike's five hours later with a fresh plaster cast on my left arm and hand, to complement the scuffed fibreglass model on my right. They want the old cast to stay on for eight weeks instead of six, just to be sure. This means two weeks of double casting. I tell the emergency doctor I'm going to the cottage. "Oh okay," he says. "I know *your* type." Moulding a beautiful plaster cast around not only my left arm, not only my left hand, but also my left thumb, he tells me to position my left hand as if I'm holding a bottle of beer. "That's the only thing you're going to be doing next week," he says.

Now comes the big dilemma: Do I leave the hospital in a cab or on a bike? I'd ridden down to the doctor's office with my damaged left hand and right cast. Truth is, I've been back on the bike for a couple of weeks already. The first time, I experienced involuntary tremors in both hands and couldn't grip the handlebars. The thought—"Maybe I can't ride again"—shot like a flaming arrow through my mind. My heart pumped madly with the negative energy of failure, but the shakes eventually subsided.

After staring into the brilliant azure of the early-evening sky, I straddle and push off. Sidewalks only. Slow. Victoria and Shuter to Logan and Dundas . . . what, three klicks? I worry that I could become the target of a *Toronto Star* slice-of-life photo takeout: "Man with two casts rides bike—what an idiot!" But I carry on. Two blocks short of home, I dismount gingerly. I do not want my neighbours to see me riding with two casts.

I start to see myself in a different light and search for evidence of compulsive behaviour. In his novel *The Third Policeman*, Flann O'Brien writes: "The gross and net result of it is that people who spent most of their natural lives riding iron bicycles over the rocky roadsteads of this parish get their personalities mixed up with the personalities of their bicycles as a result of the interchanging of the atoms of each of them and you would be surprised at the number of people in these parts who nearly are half people and half bicycles."

Is that it?

But Flann, it's not just the rocky roadsteads—you forgot the rocky road falls. Not long after the casts came off, I wiped out. I went flying over the handlebars at 9 a.m. on a Sunday morning, surging down empty Gerrard Street to my university office. The road was empty except for a student driver, who managed to swing widely left to make a hard right turn, and nearly took me out. To avoid impact, I slammed on the brakes and landed exactly as I had nine weeks before—right hand outstretched, then left. This time, there was no damage. Miraculous. The following winter, I received my first-ever door prize. I'd just delivered a guest lecture for a friend at night school, and luckily was too tired to ride fast. Still, the driver's-side door nearly cleaved me in two, and cracked a rib. I didn't pursue legal action—I had no front light. Then, this summer, as my daughter and I charged up a steep bike and pedestrian path, Justine in the lead, she faltered. I hit the brakes, flew over the handlebars, and crashed my left shoulder onto asphalt to avoid landing on top of her. *Maybe that white van sideswiped my ability to avoid crashing*, I thought. *Maybe I'm a menace. Maybe I shouldn't be on the road at all . . .*

Or maybe these skirmishes along the road to man-machine transcendence were anticipated by proto-Dadaist playwright Alfred Jarry, if not by Greg Curnoe. The self-styled pataphysician—a "doctor" of the science of imaginary solutions—fantasized in writing about the power inherent in bike transportation, appending it to his theories of "the supermale." My friend Siobhan once advised, "Ride more slowly, and your chances of getting hit are reduced significantly." I took her advice, not the pataphysician's, but maybe too much so. I went indoors.

Hammerhead

On a July afternoon thick with humidity, Scott Robinson barks out commands to a dozen men and women sweating it out on exercise bicycles at the Yorkville Club in Toronto. Scotty, as he is known, is fifty years' worth of wiry, goateed, Hawaiian-shirt-clad guyness. I'd never taken a spinning class before, but was glad we were each free to establish our own cadences. Soon enough, however, Scotty ordered us to give the tension knobs on our machines a couple of twists, reducing our collective consciousness to fighting through the pain in our legs.

Scotty looks as if he'd rather kick back with a margarita, but by the end of our session he'll have us believing we've climbed all 1,567 metres of Mont Aigoual in the Cévennes and finished the day's leg on the Tour de France. Later, he tells me he doesn't think much of fancy-pants racers and their protective pelotons. "I find road riders a little bit girly. They want everything perfect. They want their massages at the end of the day, their nice food, and they want to be able to sleep in a good bed," he says. Mainly, though, he objects to looking at "ass and rear wheel" for a hundred kilometres. Riding involves taking in all the sights, sounds, and smells around you.

We're sweating profusely, but for the man who finished fourth in the 2003 Cairo–to–Cape Town Tour d'Afrique, it's "all a matter of putting in the saddle time." I can almost see the red blips as Scotty's cycling radar finds my lack of technique. He bellows over ear-splitting music: "You're not sitting right! You look awkward! You look like you're in pain!" If *Full Metal Jacket* had featured a hippie sergeant, his name would've been Scotty. "Your arms are stretched out too far! Your seat is too high!" He readjusts my bike on the fly. Suddenly, I'm more balanced and emphasizing the crank and pedals.

Scotty's not finished his gonzo act: "Use your power! Your arms shouldn't be doing anything! They're only for balance!" I've been riding for forty-two years and always used my arms. (Later, my wife, Laura, gently suggests that this is why my left shoulder has been such a wreck for years.) Scotty insists that the middle third of the human body is where the power resides, and, sure enough, I'm feeling a power surge through my midsection. I consciously pump—left-right, left-right—searching for binary precision. I came here to interview Scotty about being a competitive rider, and instead, four years to the week after getting hit, I'm relearning how to ride a bike.

Inside is inside, however, and I need to move. I need the freedom of wind in my face, of feeling speed and a certain recklessness. Scotty is an amusing modern archetype, but I'm done with his indoor biking emporium, if not his instructional advice.

Two mornings later, I ride to school. It's around nine-thirty, just after rush hour. Not much traffic along Dundas West, so I test Scotty's theory. Using thighs and midsection—and an assist from a strong westerly—I hunker down and pump the crank of my commuter Miele. All of a sudden, I start moving fast. I hit most of the greens and pop a couple of ambers. I jump streetcar tracks. I anticipate car doors. I fly. One wrong move, and I'm another novice trapeze artist falling, sans net. Acts of everyday transcendence are risky, but the speed is intoxicating, and like the hissing middle-aged woman in Amsterdam, I know the rules of the road.

Suddenly, behind me, two guys half my age blast by me on heavy-duty mountain bikes. As they fly past, one of them looks over and hollers the rider's rebel yell: "Hammmmerrrrrrr!!!" He flashes an ear-to-ear grin before they veer off to invade the north side of Trinity Bellwoods Park. We share the instant endorphin buzz, but their point is made: cycling is all about pure movement, propelled by something I'm still trying to get a grip on.

What Is It Like to Be a Whale OR The March of Perspective

Jeff
Warren

Light breaks on secret lots.
When logics die,
Truth jumps through the eye.
— DYLAN THOMAS, paraphrased

Imagine you are a whale.

Start by picturing the ocean. Picture yourself slipping into the water, naked. Hold your breath. Sink down. Imagine your body expanding with a comforting layer of fat. Imagine it lengthening, feel each vertebra click as your spine draws up and back, a little shiver as you shimmy out of your pelvic girdle, legs and hips set adrift. In their place you sprout a broad triangular fluke, which you force down now in a long, muscular undulation that drives you forward through the water. Your neck thickens, the back of your skull rolls forward and your face moves out to meet the sea—pushing so hard your nose folds up and flattens along the top of your forehead, just in time to take a breath as you breach the surface and fill your lungs with air. You dive again, plunging towards the sea floor, moving faster, long grin tucked in below your jaw. Your smile extends back almost to your arms, which have retracted into your barrel chest, leaving four long fingers stiffened with webbing which you use to direct the massive energy of your surging body. They direct you down, into the dark, the light from the surface fading quickly. But new lights gutter in your head; soon the hunt will start, and the lights will turn to sound, and the sound will light the dark, and these are some of the things you feel, some of the things you know. The wa-ters close around you.

That was a sperm whale you imagined yourself into, member of the largest of the toothed whales or *odontocetis*.

I had sperm whales on the mind, so to speak, because they were supposed to be nearby, though neither Shane nor I were having any luck spotting them. We scanned the horizon: nothing but whitecaps as far as the eye could see.

I struggled to keep my balance as our little single-engine skiff skipped across the big waves. Looming 2 kilometres in the distance was Dominica, my home for ten days, a small Caribbean island in the far southern reaches of the Antilles.

My host and companion was Shane Gero, a skinny fast-talking Dalhousie Ph.D. candidate from Ottawa with tousled brown hair and an ubiquitous tattered baseball cap. Shane told me he never used to be the seafaring type, but three years of marine biology fieldwork had transformed him. One hand on his cap, the other on the throttle, he gunned the engine in synch with the swells, so that we seemed continuously on the verge of lifting off from the ocean. I squinted into the wind and spray. Still nothing.

"What's the GPS say?"

I fumbled with the unit and read off the coordinates. Shane stopped the boat and we began to drift in the direction of the waves.

"OK. Let's do another station."

He picked up a coil of black cable, secured one end to the ampli-fier, and slowly lowered the line into the ocean. At the far end of the 10-metre length was a weighted hydrophone, which hung like a tiny electronic ear over the vast stadium of the sea. Shane put on the head-phones and flipped on the amp. His eyes went distant as he listened to the ocean. He handed me the earphones. "Tell me what you hear."

Nothing at first, and then, very faintly, a series of high notes, like sonic scratches. "Dolphins," said Shane. "Their high-frequency whistles don't travel far in the water, so they're probably pretty close." He shook his head and pulled in the line. "We'll go another 2 or 3 miles, which is about the range of our hydrophone. Do another test there."

We wanted clicks, not whistles, "the sound of bacon frying," said Shane, the rolling crackle of echolocation pings created by one of the toughest animals in the world to study. Adult male sperm whales grow up to 20 metres in length, though even at that size they're exceedingly difficult to find. In part this is because sperm whales spend 80 per cent of their lives hunting far from shore, kilometres below the surface, their lungs and intestines collapsed so that they surge through the pressurized dark like sleekly efficient torpedoes. Their prey, as every school kid knows, are squid, including the giant squid, whom they illuminate—and some scientists think stun—with powerful high-frequency pulses of sonar. Water is an excellent conductor of sound. Shane can hear these pulses on his hydrophone from as far as 7 kilometres away; he uses the GPS to conduct tests at multiple locations and thus triangulate in on their position.

This was our third outing in as many days and we had yet to see a single fluke. I thought I knew what to expect; Shane's doctoral adviser, the behavioural ecologist Hal Whitehead, had prepared me. In the first chapter of his scholarly monograph on sperm whales, he writes: "The cetaceans include some lovely creatures. The finback whale and right whale dolphins are as well-proportioned, beautifully coloured and graceful as anything in the animal kingdom." You can almost hear the authorial pause. "And then there is the sperm whale."

Viewed face-on, something very few people have had occasion to do, the sperm whale looks like a bruised upside-down pear. The jaw is surprisingly slight and narrow, outlined in white. Flaring above it is their bulbous dome ("this high and mighty God-like dignity inherent in the brow," wrote Melville), which consists, primarily, of the spermaceti organ, stacked like two barrels of a shotgun and filled with junk and, er, spunk—at least that's how the whalers classified all that white gooey matter. In fact it is oil, used to amplify and directionalize the world's most formidable biological sonar system. Behind the massive head are two small eyes and a long creased cylindrical trunk.

We steered a course south-southwest, away from Dominica's brooding skyline. Dominica has escaped the big tourist resorts because it has no beaches—instead, the lush green island surges vertically from the deep, a former volcano with a mountainous jungle interior that's become a destination for eco-adventurers. The island's high sheltering ground and steep sea banks combine to create perfect ocean conditions for a local group of sperm whales that are quite famous in the small world of cetacean research.

They're known as the "Group of Seven" because, Shane tells me, there were seven when he began studying them back in 2005, and besides, "a little Canadian art history never hurt anybody."

Ordinarily sperm whales are more far-flung and itinerant—nomads. But the Group of Seven are special—they like Dominica, the feeding is good, and they don't seem to mind the whale-watch boats. For Shane, they represent a rare opportunity to observe how specific sperm whales interact with one another over time, and thus to gain insight into their individual personalities and their mysterious social worlds. For me they represent something else. The fulfillment of a peculiar longing. An opportunity to enter into a consciousness radically different than my own. I was in Dominica because I wanted to know what it was like to be a whale.

You are a hunting whale.

Far from the shelf, deep under the water, you move heavily across the silted sea floor. You are in a trance of pressure, hypnotized, contained, directed. All around you the dark flickers with krill, squid, and the occasional fish, caught in crossbeams of directed sound. They sparkle like stars, like blood vessels on the retina. You feel the water course across your barred teeth, the pressure on your eyes, the weight of the sea above you. Down here is a kind of dream, always the same dream, a recurring sequence of appetite, and movement and struggle. And yet, it is a shared dream. You share it with your family, whose comforting presence you feel though you cannot see. As one, you and your family turn and move towards the island.

Over the next few hours Shane and I did four more stations, without luck. The Group of Seven were hidden to us, their bodies somewhere out of range. As we headed back to port I felt an almost childish disappointment. The animals. Shane reassured me.

"They're out there, trust me. It's weird we haven't seen them yet. They must be out in the channel somewhere, feeding. I'm sure they'll be back tomorrow."

"Yeah."

The sea was calmer. The gentle rise and fall of the boat, the smell of diesel, the sun low in the sky. It put me in a mood. I wanted to talk. I wanted to talk about why I was there, though Shane had heard it before.

"It's the animals, Shane. Something important is about to happen with the animals. I'm telling you."

"Right. Whale consciousness. I get it." Shane humoured me.

I could have focused on another animal, but whales have that oft-noted iconic quality, they excite the imagination. And imagination is important. Plus: complicated brains, mysterious societies, alien environment. Whales—especially sperm whales—are dramatic. Melville knew it. He wondered at their physiognomy, at their behaviour. He even wondered at their minds—at what it would be like to see with two eyes on either side of the head ("one distinct picture on this side, and another distinct picture on that side; while all between must be profound darkness and nothingness to him."). Melville tried to go in, through the eye.

"Genius in the Sperm Whale?" he asked, skeptically, halfway through *Moby Dick*. Maybe not. But there's a reason the white whale is one of the most interpreted symbols in American literature. He represents fate, or "Man's Hubris," or God. To me he represents something else: nature looking back.

"Look, this is my take on it," I said to Shane. "It's no longer about proving animals possess consciousness. That's the old game. It didn't lead anywhere. Animal defenders come up with newer and better standards of evidence—tool use, behavioral flexibility, symbolic communication, whatever. It's the wrong tack. You have to just accept that animals are conscious and take it from there."

Shane leaned on the throttle. "Sure," he said. "And pointing out similarities between humans and animals can help with this. It gives people a way to connect. Did you read about the crow that fashioned a hook out of wire to get at a piece of food?" He shook his head. "Crazy."

"But it's not enough to convince your hard-core behaviourist critic. To them all these anecdotes prove is that some animals are really flexible information processors, programmed by natural selection. Wet machines. They argue intelligence doesn't equal consciousness.

What
Is It
Like to
Be a
Whale

303

Animals could just be blindly responsive with nobody home upstairs."

"Scientists can't still believe that."

Some do, but for the first time they may be in the minority. This in itself is revolutionary, though hardly anyone has commented on it. Thirty years ago when the pioneering American zoologist Donald Griffin argued that animals had some kind of inner experience, he was mocked and derided. But science seems surreptitiously to be catching up with common sense. The University of Colorado ecologist Mark Bekoff, one of Griffin's proteges and a vocal proponent of animal emotions and mind, told me he now meets very few true skeptics. "Things have really changed in the last ten years or so. Most research biologists these days accept that animals have some kind of inner awareness. Yes, there may be different degrees of consciousness and there may be different layers involved, but no serious scientist that I know would deny basic sentience to mammals and birds—even fish. The paradigm has changed."

Spurred by the resurgence of interest in the study of human consciousness, some prominent neurobiologists and thinkers from outside the field have even begun to weigh in. So in a recent special issue of *Consciousness and Cognition*, the journal's editor Bernard Baars— a luminary in the world of consciousness studies—concludes that consciousness is "a fundamental biological adaptation" that likely goes back millions of years. "We have reached a point in our intellectual history," writes another contributor, the neuroscientist Jaak Panksepp, "where the denial of consciousness in animals is as improbable as the pre-scientific anthrocentric view that the sun revolves around the earth."

"This idea that there is a universe of creatures out there with subjectivities of their own," Baars told me, "it changes your view of the world. From a purely scientific view it's like being able to see the colour spectrum of the stars. Suddenly you see a whole new dimension of reality."

This is the second part of the revolution, one that is trickier to get at but may be more important. Once you accept that animals are conscious, the next question is: What might that consciousness be like? Very few scientists talk about this, at least not publicly. In a sense, they are locked outside their real subject matter. They measure and quantify in the reflection of the animal's eye but they almost never go in. Perhaps because they believe the philosopher Thomas Nagel, who in his influential 1974 paper "What is it like to be a bat?" argues that an animal's subjective interior world is something we can never know—at least not with the "objective" tools of science.

Nagel's is a lonely vision. I felt it out there on the boat with Shane, the near-deserted expanse of ocean yawning below us. Who hasn't felt the need to connect to another animal, to enter empathetically into a world different from our own? The great naturalist Loren Eiseley certainly did. "There is nothing more alone in the universe than man," he wrote back in 1960, in a famous essay called "The Long Loneliness." "When we were children we wanted to talk to animals and struggled to understand why this was impossible. Slowly we gave up the attempt as we grew into the solitary world of human adulthood."

By now it was almost dark as Shane steered the boat carefully through the clusters of moored sailboats, towards one of the long piers. Although Dominica's main town—Roseau—contains a few larger civic structures, the majority of the coastline is pretty spare— just the odd brightly painted building interspersed with smooth black boulders and nodding palm trees. This particular bit of waterfront property belongs to the Anchorage Hotel and Dive Centre. In exchange for Shane's services on thrice-weekly whale-watch expeditions, the Anchorage gives Shane use of the skiff and free accommodation. We tied up to the dock.

You are a breaching whale.

The feeding trance lasts an hour before something turns inside you. As one, you and your family begin to rise. The dream recedes as the pressure eases. At first there is only the darkness, but soon a faint radiance enters the water. It catches each suspended particle, and gently traces the outlines of your family, who move steadily upward, silent except for the sound of their beating hearts, which drum into your skin and form a rhythmic counterpoint to the muffled swish of your tail. As you approach the surface you feel lighter, faster, more expressive. Your sinuses clear, chambers in your chest crack and pop, your ribs curve back and out, all in anticipation of that other, longed-for medium. Now you are racing, you chase your own buoyancy, and

pierce the meniscus which divides your world. An explosion of mist an-
nounces your release. For a moment there is no resistance as your long body
twists in the nighttime sky. You breathe the air; you are in the thing you
breathe. You see everything: the first stars bright on the sea, the dark out-
line of the island, the blinking lights on the distant shore. You even see the
shadow of your own body on the slate water below you. And then grav-
ity—that novel force, so like a judgment—pulls you down. You meet your
reflected image with a final head-clearing slap and the ocean reclaims you.

We made our way to the hotel bar, where Shane spread out his various notes and logbooks and began to enter data from the day's expedition into his laptop. It was obvious Shane loved what he did. His
adviser, Hal Whitehead, told me Shane had an uncanny sense for the
whales. He noticed the body language, the social drama, the individual personalities. When I asked Shane about this, he said: "It's like
describing how you know it's your friend walking down the street
when you can't make out their face because they're too far away. But
the way they move and hold themselves make you certain it's that
person. Having watched the Group of Seven in the same social situation over and over, you start to recognize them, and eventually you
make out some of the nuances of how they relate to one another."

Nagel may be right that we cannot know everything about the
private minds of animals, but this doesn't mean there aren't ways of
gaining genuine insight into their preserve. Shane has one approach.
Call it the higher stratum of behavioural ecology—after rising
through all the data about feeding strategies and reproductive rates
you arrive at something ineffable: the nature of an animal, its character and way of being in the world.

This character forms the backdrop to all an animal's experience—it is the shape that contains the mind. And for the whale, there
is another, larger container: the sea itself.

"The way to enter the mind of a whale is to enter the water." The
writer Joanna McIntyre wrote that thirty-five years ago, in a book
published at the height of the Save the Whales movement, which
was probably the last time you could talk openly about whale consciousness without provoking a storm of giggles. Yet her instincts

were sound. Minds don't evolve in voids. They're shaped by particular habitats and conditions. How might ocean shape mind? As an inveterate swimmer, I was captivated by this question, in fact it was another reason I had come to Dominica: to think about the ocean, to imagine how sentience might have evolved within it.

Minds, of course, are yoked to brains, and here is another rich domain to till for clues. Ninety-five million years ago whales and humans shared a common ancestor. We stayed on land; they returned to the sea. Thirty-five million years ago they had the biggest brains on the planet—by comparison our brains didn't get big until two million years ago. And yet, for all the morphological weirdness of the whale brain—something I will return to—it is also true that all mammalian brains share basic features. Think of a painter's palette. Each blob of colour represents a different brain module. From these raw ingredients any number of "mind paintings" can be created. More red will change the picture, as will an absence of blue. Combinations of colours give rise to new hues or properties. We know some of how this works by examining human subjects. The same basic principles apply, at least in theory, to other mammals. By looking at the allocation of colour on their palettes, we can begin to make educated guesses about the composition of their minds.

To pull all this information together we have a tool—a magical perspective-generating tool that is the perfect fusion of literary imagination and scientific observation, and something I predict we will hear more about in the years to come. It's called the *Umwelt*.

The guiding text here is a famous—and famously eclectic—1936 natural history monograph called *A Stroll Through the Worlds of Animals and Men*. The author, a romantic German biologist named Jacob von Uexkull, was fed up with the reductions of American behaviourist learning theory, and decided to write a popular book that would present an alternative view of animals not as, in his words, "mere objects," but rather, as experiencing subjects. It begins:

> The best time to set out on an adventure is a sunny day. The place, a flower-strewn meadow. Here we may glimpse the worlds of the lowly dwellers of the meadow. To do so, we must first

blow, in fancy, a soap bubble around each creature to represent its own world, filled with the perceptions which it alone knows. When we ourselves then step into one of these bubbles, the familiar meadow is transformed. Many of its colorful features disappear, others no longer belong together but appear in new relationships. A new world comes into being.

Each new world Uexkull called an Umwelt, a private richly detailed "self-world" which corresponded to the unique sensory capacities and external triggers of each animal. So, for the eyeless tick, Uexkull's first subject, her Umwelt consists of the smell of butyric acid, which rolls off the skin of passing mammals and causes her to drop down to feed on the warm surface. The tick's world, then, is a simple one of temperature and smell, perhaps similar to the view through an infrared camera. By using our powers both of rational investigation and creative imagination, Uexkull argued convincingly that it was possible, at least to some degree, to enter into an animal's experience.

You are a young whale.

It's night. Your belly is full, though it's not yet time to sleep; time instead to play. In the dark you are invisible. You set out above the lip of the sea shelf, closely flanked by two members of your family. You do not need to see each other to synchronize your movements—you feel the alignment in your chest. You carve the waves with your dorsal ridge, and roll back down under the water, where you fall into a slipstream, a racing channel that pulls you forward. The ocean moves backwards, it curls away from your powerful body and tapers into beaten froth. You torque your body in time with the others and turn back, creating a small standing wave with the momentum. You roll into your family, and scrape your belly along the serrated column of their spines. You can't get close enough, you sound a stream of clicks into their sides, seeking, probing, caressing. And then your mother's voice passes through you, calling you back.

The first person to try to get inside the cetacean Umwelt was a brilliant medical doctor–cum–neurophysiologist named John Lilly. It happened by accident. In the late 1950s Lilly, curious about the relationship between external stimulation and brain activity, built the world's first sensory isolation tank. For hours he would float in a dark pod of water, his mind untethered, his body seeming to dissolve in the warm saline solution so he couldn't tell where his skin ended and the water began. He wondered what big-brained creature he could study that might give him insights into this exotic buoyant world. A friend suggested the dolphin, and thus began an infamous chapter in psychedelic history.

It started well enough. Throughout the sixties, Lilly provided some of the first descriptions of dolphin neuroanatomy and problem-solving abilities. He examined their vocalizations and found they had their own complex system of communication. This later began to obsess Lilly—he was determined to crack the "language barrier," both looking for patterns in the whistles (which he called "Delphinese"), and teaching the dolphins themselves to mimic English sounds. He flooded a house in the Virgin Islands and got a young woman named Margaret Howe to live full-time with a dolphin named Peter. "Heel-ooo Mee-geee-reeet" Peter would keen, when prompted.

What
Is It
Like to
Be a
Whale

309

The media went nuts. Lilly's popular books sold by the tens of thousands—he inspired the TV show *Flipper* and later a Hollywood movie, *Day of the Dolphin*. At first the scientific community was sympathetic—he published thoughtful papers in *Science*, received funding from federal agencies like the National Science Foundation and the Air Force Office for Scientific Research, and became a celebrated authority on inter-species transmission.

But at some point things started to shift. Lilly's genius moved outward, or perhaps it was flung outward, for by the late sixties he was heavily into psychedelic drugs and in fact had become close friends with many of the countercultural fixtures of the era: Timothy Leary, Ram Das, and others. On massive doses of ketamine, Lilly took to his pod, where his mind wheeled through multiple dimensions of hyperspace. Ideas proliferated. Like an inspired weaver, Lilly spun the threads of Eastern mysticism, computer programming, quantum mechanics, and neurophysiology into a bright and singular tapestry, a world view that still has its underground adherents today.

Into this heady mix he found a place for the dolphins: they were models of spiritual health, chirpy meditators who possessed an enviable cosmic perspective. Lilly's scientific "investigations" began to reflect his expanded outlook. He gave his subjects LSD and practised ornate communication strategies with them over the intercom. He spoke about compiling a human/dolphin dictionary. His experiments got increasingly bizarre—some said inhumane—funding dried up, and the flooded home degenerated into squalor. Margaret wrote about giving Peter hand jobs.

The result, predictably, was a backlash. At the very moment dolphins were being celebrated as the ultimate New Age animal, serious scientists went on the attack. "Lilly's writing," wrote the sociobiologist E.O. Wilson, is "quite unjustified in [its] claim to be a valid scientific report." And as far as dolphins went, pronounced Wilson, "all the evidence suggests they are about as smart as dogs."

Talk of whale and dolphin consciousness became another embarrassing excess of the Age of Aquarius, like joss sticks and humpback music. By the early eighties Lilly had become a fringe figure, one with a decidedly negative effect on the study of cetacean cognition. Whale and dolphin researchers were now viewed with suspicion by other scientists. One researcher told me he couldn't say he was interested in studying cetacean intelligence without provoking eye rolls and derision. It was, in some sense, the revenge of the behaviourists, who could now reclaim the moral high ground. The taboo against animal consciousness was reinforced.

You are a young whale, a tired whale.

Outside, on the dark water, you allow your body to tip back, so that only the top of your head protrudes from the surface. You and your family now hang vertically, several feet apart, like a forest of huge cylindrical kelp. The breath you draw in now through your exposed blowhole is close and damp. You body rocks with the waves, they massage your temples and tilt your body along its axis, back and forth, the rhythm of the sea now inside. You drift into a strange somnolence, at once murky and vigilant. For you, breathing is voluntary; there is no automatic mechanism to do the work. So the brain sleeps one hemisphere at a time, one part of you always aware of the need to connect to the surface. Air fills your dreams. Water encases them. And through it all move the members of your family. They pass among the shapes of the underwater world, the shadows on the surface, the roar of currents, the grinding of tectonic plates. The whales—your family, other members of your clan, strangers—they tell you things, which in the half-dream you struggle to understand. And then you take another breath, the waves tilt you gently back and forth, and your mind slips between worlds.

I admire Lilly, for all his excesses. He was ahead of his time. He didn't treat his cetacean subjects as chunks of meat—he fought hard to defend them. And his intuitions about their intelligence and sophistication turned out to be correct.

What
Is It
Like to
Be a
Whale

311

Today, the most vocal sperm whale champion—and the man who has shed the most light on their complex nature—is Shane's supervisor Hal Whitehead, whom I visited in a book-lined office at Dalhousie University in Halifax several months before going to Dominica. It was a brisk fall day, but in his shorts, wool socks, and sandals Whitehead seemed indifferent to the cold. In fact, he positively radiated maritime vigor: rough hands, calves like cannonballs, and a thicket of red hair that merged seamlessly with his bushy red beard so it looked as if he were peering out from the cinched hood of an Arctic parka.

Originally from England, Whitehead's first degree was in mathematics. After graduating, he wasn't sure what to do, and ended up travelling around North America, soon landing a job as a labourer in New England. He was drawn to the ocean, and bought a small sailing boat, eventually charting a course north to Nova Scotia. One afternoon a small minke whale surfaced next to the ship. For a time they moved together along the waves. Whitehead couldn't take his eyes off the animal—its dark matte skin, its humid exhalations. Later that same trip he met a whale scientist out of Halifax. They got to talking.

If the state of scientific knowledge around whales in general is paltry—and it is (not surprising given that a few hundred years ago cartographers were still drawing whales with fangs, claws and dragon wings)—then, despite Melville's best attempts, sperm whales have remained the proverbial enigma wrapped in a mystery.

"When I began studying sperm whales in the early eighties very little was known about their social structure," Whitehead told me in his gentle voice. "The dominant idea came from the whalers, who seem to have inadvertently projected their lonely fantasies onto the animals." Male sperms whales, the whalers decided, were "harem masters"—one male controlled a large group of females, and fought off other male challengers in fierce sea battles.

Whitehead wanted to know how accurate this was, but to do so meant spending long periods of time with the animals, a near-impossible task for a subject that passes its life far from shore and kilometres below the surface. What's more, unlike land animals, sperm whales don't leave tracks, or nests, or any evidence at all of their lifestyle.

Eventually he got a grant to study sperm whales in the Indian Ocean, and later in the Galapagos. On a 10-metre ocean-going sloop called the *Tulip*, Whitehead and a colleague named Jonathan Gordon developed an elaborate set of techniques for studying the animals, tracking them twenty-four hours a day with their hydrophone, sleeping in shifts, often ranging hundreds of kilometres from shore.

"Were they ever aggressive with you?" I asked. I was a bit nervous about my own upcoming trip to Dominica and had Melville's Old Testament scourge-of-the sea on my mind.

"Never. These are timid animals—easily startled."

They were also, Whitehead soon learned, far from male dominated. Sperm whale society, like elephant society (the two animals have much in common), is actually matrilineal. Females run the show; they live in extended familial units of mothers, daughters, aunts and immature males. They suckle each other's young, and alternate babysitting duty when the group dives to feed.

As for the males, when they reach seven or eight years of age they leave the group, sometimes meeting up with other males, more often making their way alone. While the female family units stay mostly in the warmer tropical waters, the big males venture all the way to the Antarctic and Arctic pack ice. In this manner they circumnavigate the globe, not returning to the females until thirty years of age, and then only to mate, announcing their presence with loud clangs that can be heard as far as 60 kilometres away. Their effect on females seems to vary—sometimes they are warmly received, other times the females are indifferent. Thus the life of the sperm whale plays out, anywhere from sixty to a hundred years of age.

The longer Whitehead studied them, the more he had the sense of being in the company of an ancient living culture. "You have to understand," he said, stroking his beard, "until a few hundred thousand years ago—and I think the evidence is fairly clear on this—most of the culture on earth was in the ocean. Certainly the most sophisticated cultures on earth were in the whales and dolphins, until the strange bipedal hominid evolved."

The idea gave me vertigo. While we were screeching and sticking berries up our noses somewhere on the savannah, whales were . . . well, what were they doing? They have no hands to manipulate their environment, and besides, what built technology could resist the boundless eroding excursions of the sea?

"What kind of culture are we talking about exactly?"

"Different dialects, different feeding and child-care preferences, different movement patterns. Even different rates of reproduction. These aren't genetic differences," Whitehead said, "they're learned."

Shane explained it to me this way: "Some Christians eat fish on Fridays, that's a social norm in their group. Some Jews don't eat pork. These aren't things that are genetically coded in Jews and Christians. It's a tradition learned from their parents."

The findings on sperm whale culture emerged out of work done by one of Whitehead's students, Luke Rendell. When Whitehead and Rendell began studying the patterns of clicks that sperm whales make when socializing—known as "codas"—they found strong differences between groups. Different acoustic "clans" had different patterns of identifying clicks. So there was a Galapagos clan, a Caribbean clan, a Chilean clan—half-a-dozen or so clans identified to date, each with their own "dialect" that turned out to be an accurate predictor of a whole set of defining clan characteristics.

Whitehead suspects that in sperm whale societies knowledge is passed from older females to younger members of the group. This allows the clan to survive things like El Nino, that sudden infusion of warm water that wipes out other marine populations. For the long-lived matriarch, knowledge of other feeding grounds—north to California, south to central Chile—can make the difference between life and death.

A wise elder. A babysitter. A social broker. The focus of Shane's research in Dominica was investigating the nature of some of these roles. What other roles might the culture support? A leader? A defender?

None of this says anything definitive about the sperm-whale mind, but it is suggestive. As Shane pointed out to me, a certain amount of intelligence is required to manage a large number of social relationships. It also hints at a level of individuation between members of the group—they have some sense of a role to play, one dictated by culture, not genes (to give one example, genetically similar sperm whales in different clans select different babysitters—in one clan the great-aunt seems to be the preferred babysitter, in another, babysitting duty is shared more equally among the group). This suggests a pooling of concerns, that they care for one another, and they change the way they do that caring.

It also hints at something else. Most scientists would echo Loren Eiseley in believing that for an animal, "there is no past and no future. There is only the everlasting present of a single generation—its trails in the forest, its hidden pathways in the air and in the sea." The findings on sperm whale culture suggest that whales may not be trapped in a single generation—their minds are stretched through time, with a sense both of past lessons and future strategies.

You are the matriarch.

It's early morning—the light is just coming up over the water. You rest in your ocean cradle, breathing with your family, and sometimes, it seems, with the tides. These days you are more conscious of the force of water against your skin. This negative space. It cups your torso with pressure. You have no fingers to seek out objects, niches, but you need none—the important texture is in the liquid itself. One sinus click can electrify the cloudlike swirls of heat and salinity and pressure. You wash your voice over your sleeping children, reassuring yourself that everyone is healthy. You remember their bodies. You remember all the waters, the paths and patterns through which you have guided them. You are tired now, always tired; you've been swimming for a long time. The sea, too, erodes.

In the distance you feel a disturbance in the water column. Something is coming. A current of fear shoots through your chest. It wakes your family. The water is alive suddenly with electricity.

The next morning we prepared for another outing. This one would be different. It would be a whale-watch expedition, with Shane as biologist-in-residence. Shane could still compile data; he just had to do so while fielding questions from throngs of camera-toting tourists. The tour began in an open-air "educational" atrium at the back of the dive centre. There, hanging 2 feet above the ground on thin guide wires, was the bleached and perfectly assembled skeleton of an adult sperm whale.

Without the bulging cartilage of the sperm whale's forehead, the skeleton looked like an enormous crocodile, with a snaking spinal cord, surprisingly handlike flippers, and a long tapered skull bristling with sharp teeth. Behind the jaw, a flat wedge of bone rose up perpendicular to the rest of the skull, which shielded the large brain cavity.

"Right in here," said Shane, as he strained to reach around the bony protrusion, "is where we'd find the brain. Biggest in the animal kingdom."

There is a debate in the world of comparative neuroanatomy about the relationship between brain size and intelligence. On the one hand, a lot of scientists think that a big brain is a big brain: more computational power = more smarts. This puts sperm whales, killer whales, and elephants at the top of the brain chain, with humans down somewhere below dolphins. Others point to the human "world-domination-we-know-quantum-mechanics" thing, and argue relative brain size is a better indicator, which puts humans near the top, though not so high as the shrew, who drags around a proportionally massive 2-gram brain, presumably weighted down with frustrated will-to-power scenarios ("If only we had more time!").

Emory University neurobiologist Lori Marino specializes in the whale brain, and for the past several years has defended it from various detractors, who pop up now and again to argue that the

What
Is It
Like to
Be a
Whale

315

whale encephalon is, in essence, a big ball of thermoregulating fat.

"This view has no credence," Marino told me. "It's true cetacean brains have more fatty glial cells than neurons, but then so do ours. Glial cells are known to boost connectivity in the brain, and may be one reason why they process certain kinds of information much more quickly than we do." In fact, these days glial cells are considered the dark matter of the brain—no one knows exactly what role they play in information processing, but there are hints that it could be significant.

If the pleasures of an Oliver Sacks book are those profound skeleton-key moments that magically connect some modular bit of brain activation with a function or hue of consciousness, then talking to Marino is like having the same experience art-directed by the Wachowski Brothers. Now the subject is the most exotic brain in the animal kingdom. As Marino puts it, "The way the cetacean neocortex differs from other mammal brains is more different than the way any other mammals' brains differ. There's no mistaking it for anything else."

So: it's big, with a wraparound folded cortex that makes each whale brain look like a massive soccer ball. Although the cetacean cortex looks quite different from the human cortex—cetaceans don't have our expanded frontal lobes, for example, though they do have a paralimbic lobe that is missing in humans—it seems to support many of the same high-level functions. "We have a lot of behavioural data to support complex cognition," she told me. "Everything from innovative problem solving to sophisticated memory to self-awareness to findings on the cultural transmission of knowledge." The conclusion Marino draws from this is that cetacean and primate brains represent "alternative evolutionary routes to complex intelligence." The brains may look different, but they do a lot of the same things.

And yet, in other ways the differences are revealing. Underneath the cetacean cortex, for example, is a highly elaborated limbic system, the seat of mammalian emotionality. "If you translate that into function," says Marino, "it could be that they have a level of emotional sophistication that we or other primates may not have. Certainly when it comes to self-control and self-regulation . . . you do see this very strongly with dolphins and killer whales."

The biggest differences have to do with the arrangement of their sensory cortices. The human visual cortex is at the back of the brain, with a separate auditory cortex at the sides. In the whale these two regions are jammed together into a densely interconnected area at the top of the head. "Something really unique is going on here," Marino told me.

That something almost certainly has to do with echolocation, more powerful than vision in water, a way of navigating through space and retrieving information about surrounding objects. Returning echoes are refined and processed by the large association areas in the whale's cortex. How is this information organized and presented in the whale's mind? A few speculative scientists hypothesize that whales may move through a kind of audio-space matrix, an immersive three-dimensional topographical "map" whose boundaries extend far beyond human sightlines. Of all the whales, the huge baleens may have the largest maps—there is some suggestion that their low-frequency songs have an echolocation function; they roll out across the entire expanse of an ocean basin, ricocheting off seamounts and ridges, illuminating the underwater world like strobe lights in a vast cathedral. Thus, in a sense, the map of the sea through which the whale floats may also be a map of time. The past constructed from memory, the future from sonar's predictive reach.

Each returning echo is further seeded with a dizzying range of possible data. Sound behaves differently in contrasting properties of liquid, so in addition to details about undersea and surface objects, the whale's map may include particulars about the water itself—its temperature, density and direction. What's more, because echolocation pulses, like ultrasound waves, may be able to pass directly through skin, the whale's map may include information about their *internal* worlds as well as their external ones. Sperm whales and dolphins and killer whales, in other words, may be able to *see inside* one another.

This idea absolutely blew my mind the first time Whitehead explained it to me. "The sonar system may see," he said, "in great detail, the internal organs of all the other members of the group. So there's no hiding what one has eaten, whether one's sexually receptive, whether one's pregnant, whether one's sick, it's all there laid out. Presumably, this changes social life a lot."

It doesn't stop there. Think of how much information is contained in the body—accelerated beating of the heart, tightness in the diaphragm, tension in the muscles. If it's a real capacity then it hints at a remarkable potential for interpersonal sensitivity. And while the theory has yet to be tested experimentally, it would account for the unusual reaction of dolphins to pregnant women. Dolphins get excited when a pregnant woman enters the water with them; they get distressed, however, if the woman is carrying twins, effectively a death sentence in the dolphin's world (dolphin mothers can only nurse one offspring at a time).

Water, texture, shape, movement, direction, contour, gut, emotion, skin—all these registers of information, washing over the whale, processed at lightning-fast speed. And not in isolation. For most astounding of all is the possibility that all of this may be shared. There is experimental evidence to suggest that dolphins can "eavesdrop" on another dolphin's returning echoes, an ability that may be akin to seeing through another's eyes. And sperm whales, too, may do this. Thus a group of widely dispersed whales may in some sense be part of a single sensory loop, sensitive to every twitch and shudder in the wide phenomenal world.

You, the matriarch, sound the clan call, and your family's voices unite to yours: "we are here, we are seven, we live in the shadow of the mount." Your urgency focuses the group's attention. A second ring of sound pulses outward, it ripples hundreds of metres until it connects with the threat: a pod of false killer whales, moving rapidly north of the family. Everyone knows what to do. You join ranks, forming a protective ring around the calf, heads inside, flukes out, like spokes of a huge wheel. You feel temporarily young, and prepare to drive your tail through the water in short powerful strikes. Silence. No predatory screams cut through you. Just the rapid beating of seven hearts. Tentatively, you send out a third ring of sound. The echoes wash over the retreating backs of your enemy, who, for whatever private reason, have chosen to ignore your family. You hold the formation for a time, but now it is without anxiety. You feel, in your stomach, the family's tension release into the water. You reassure the calf, rubbing across her flank with the rough edge of your mouth. The air is clean and pure in your lungs. You breathe deeply. Everyone dives, even the calf.

As Shane chatted amicably with the tourists I was lost in a daze, fantasizing about the whales, drunk on tantalizing scraps of science. The whales! No wonder people got obsessed with the subject. They were out there somewhere, bobbing around under the sea, maybe even hived into some kind of group mind, a "communal Umwelt" in the words of one brain researcher. This was huge! John Lilly knew it, bless him. Of course he was also crazy.

I blinked and looked around the dive centre. Just the skeleton, floating there. I wondered if whales saw the same view, if their searching echoes penetrated right to the bone. I heard the catamaran engines start up, and rushed down to join the others on the dock. It was time to see some live sperm whales.

We roared out to sea under sunny skies. One of the ship's crew served rum punch at a makeshift bar. Soon everyone was laughing and swigging from their plastic cups. The first marine attraction presented itself almost immediately: a pod of false killer whales. Shane was ecstatic. "Very rare sighting people!" The animals streamed towards the boat, glossy and purposeful. They passed under the bow—shadows like dark oil slicks—before disappearing into the depths.

"False killer whales are one of the sperm whale's few natural predators," Shane said. "If the Group of Seven are around they're probably deep underwater." We decided to do our first test. Shane positioned the directional hydrophone, which looked like a flowerpot on a stick with a microphone inside. Over the speakers came the groan and static of the undersea world.

This time contact was immediate. A distant crackle, like the clipped Morse-code taps of a telegraph machine. "OK, that's about a Force two—I'm hearing three, maybe four animals," Shane told the crowd. He slowly rotated the hydrophone, pinpointing the direction of the clicks. We set a southeast course, did one more test—"Force three," said Shane, "they could be right beneath us"—and turned off the engine. As the catamaran bobbed on the waves and the tourists

What
Is It
Like to
Be a
Whale

319

scanned the horizon, Shane pulled out his field camera and began scribbling notes on the data sheets.

About a half-hour passed, and then, from one of the crew high in the rigging: "Thar she blows!"

A stampede to the side of the catamaran, rum punch splashing onto the deck and a dozen cameras firing. Off in the distance, a squat grey plume. The boat lurched forward again in a roar of exhaust. Two kids began squealing as a trim middle-aged man in a Hawaiian T pulled out his military-grade Centurion tactical binoculars and shouted navigation coordinates. I wasn't sure which animal to watch.

The engines sputtered, then went silent. We held our breath. All eyes to starboard as we drifted, slowly, past what must be one of the more underwhelming wonders of the wild kingdom. "It looks like a plank," one of the kids deadpanned. As if on cue, the sperm whale snorted a briny cloud of mist.

This whale actually looked more like a log than a plank. A smooth grey log, perhaps 12 feet long, bookended with a labile blowhole and a blunt dorsal fin. A female, said Shane, who recognized the markings on her back, and thus only half the size of a mature male. Only the top of her head breached the surface; the bulk of her body hung below.

But if the animal appeared unremarkable, its movements under the water are anything but. Hal Whitehead showed me this on another occasion, when we watched some undersea footage sent to him by a tour-boat videographer working in the Sea of Cortez. On the screen, in clear blue waters, a dozen or so sperm whales roll over one another with exquisite delicacy. Different animals take their turn at the centre of the action, pivoting slowly on a vertical axis while others slide obliquely across their trunk, spinning, nuzzling, twisting back on one another with their open jaws, their eyes closed, seeming almost drugged by each other's presence. Although I recognized my own anthropomorphizing, it was hard not to read something deliberate in the movements. They seemed . . . ritualized. When I asked Whitehead what we were seeing he shook his head. "I have no idea. Some kind of social bonding, perhaps, but no one really knows." He paused. "There is only one young male and most of the interactions are between females, so it doesn't seem to be about sex." Codas and clicks purred on the sound track. We watched it three times. "It does seem possible," said Whitehead, "that there is a completely different consciousness present."

You are a young male whale.

You hear it coming, a familiar thrum, you feel the wide shape approach before you see its imprint pressed into the surface above you. You've seen this shape before—it roars and idles, appears mysteriously by your side, as if summoned by your presence. There seem to be more of these dark shapes every day, these dead things, so like a whale in size but filled with a cargo of small soft bodies who communicate in high squeaks. The matriarch dislikes them; she tells of burning spears and water thick with blood. She stays away and calls to the others to do the same. But you are old enough to make up your own mind. There is a mystery here, it pulls you in. You move towards the dead thing, which is silent now. It glitters above the water like a school of fish.

**What
Is It
Like to
Be a
Whale**

321

The writer Joanna McIntyre believes that water changes the relationship between the mind and the body, it forces a kind of unity: "When a human enters the water, what becomes apparent is the integral connection between mind and body that the sea forces on her creatures. Without the alienating presence of objects and equipment, with only the naked body encasing the floating mind, the two, split by technological culture, are one again. The mind enters a different modality, where time, weight and one's self are experienced holistically." Echoes of a different Umwelt.

Whitehead, a scientist, is more cautious. Like many behavioural ecologists, he believes that complex mind evolved directly out of co-operative social relationships. So the question for him is not how the sea shapes mind, but rather, how the sea shapes relationships. "All animal social structures are shaped by their habitats. Most terrestrial animals—humans, chimps, dogs—are territorial, they live in two-dimensional habitats filled with places to hide that are quite costly to move around in. Now the ocean, where the sperm whale evolved and lives, has none of these. The ocean is three-dimensional, it has nowhere to hide, it is relatively cheap to move around in. There are few, if any, barriers. And this really changes the constraints on social life and I think the evolution and nature of social life."

Most land animals depend on territory—they defend it, and a large portion of their cognitive resources are directed towards figuring out who is an enemy and who is a compatriot. This is a hugely defined structure of their social life. It presumably gives an us-and-them character to their cognitive processes, one that is informed by an underlying aggression. Nonterritorial animals like sperm whales, who roam over the whole ocean, don't have that looming structure in their social lives. They may also think in terms of us-and-them, but in Whitehead's words, "It isn't 'Are you in my territory or out of it?' It's 'Are you someone I socialize with and depend on or are you not?'" For nonterritorial animals in unfamiliar surroundings, he says, "the most important thing is each other."

The intense communality of the whale may shed light on one of the great mysteries of whale behaviour: the strandings. An entire community of whales will often beach together. There is excellent evidence that some of these strandings are caused by disorientation due to human noise pollution—large ships, Navy sonar testing, seismic oil surveys. But something more may also be going on. In one intriguing anecdote, a group of pilot whales pushed themselves onto a shallow Florida beach, where for three days their backs were blistered by the sun. When well-meaning humans tried to push them back into deeper waters the whales would return to the beached pod. One whale was sick—blood trickled from his ears. When this whale finally died, the others wiggled off the sand and left. It's hard not to interpret this as an extreme form of solidarity.

Back on the catamaran, the action had upped a notch. The log kept snorting, but now it was accompanied by a new performer: a distant fluke that cracked up and down on the surface of the water. "Tail lobbing," said Shane, breathlessly. The whale in question, he explained, could be a calf calling for its mother. We changed course for the young animal, and soon found ourselves floating between a group of four whales. One of them hunched her muscular back, and began to squirm in the water, like a massive ferret.

"Oh man," said Shane, in a whisper. We all leaned in to hear. "Prepare your cameras. Things are about to go social."

The water started to churn. The three closest whales began rolling over one another, their orgiastic clicks sending the tourists into a fever of rum swilling and speculation. OK, they sent me into a fever of rum swilling and speculation. I turned to Shane. "What do you think they're saying?"

He shrugged. "No one knows. Females produce most of the codas. The thinking is that they're used for group cohesion, but they could easily be communicating other things. You can store a lot of information in the timing and patterning of different click trains. Plus, we hear sounds we've never heard before all the time."

I tried to imagine what kind of language a whale would have. An exciting new paradigm in cognitive neuroscience and linguistics is well positioned to shed a bit of hypothetical—and metaphorical— light on the subject. It's called "embodied cognition," and it argues that our thoughts are the way they are because of the particular details of our bodies and environments. This is especially true of the language we use to express our thoughts, which is, the experts argue, entirely shaped by physical metaphors. So, to draw from a list of "primary metaphors," we view affection as warmth ("she had a warm demeanor"), importance as big ("this is a huge point"), help as support ("lean on me"), knowing as seeing ("I see what you mean"), and so on. The way our bodies interact with one another and our environment forms the substrate of our thinking—there is nothing abstract or computational about it.

This suggests that if whales do have a species of thought, it would likely be based on a different-but-overlapping set of metaphors, one that would draw on their unique bodies and environments. When I told Hal Whitehead about primary metaphors he saw the possibilities. "For sperm whales, resources are deep, so perhaps concepts of food and plenty and weaning may be linked to pressure and darkness and cold. Conversely, socializing is at shallow depths, so social bonds, motherhood and physical affection are linked with lack of pressure, with warmth and light. And, of course, Knowing is Hearing."

"So if you were a whale, you'd be more likely to say 'I *hear* what you mean,' than 'I *see* what you mean,'" I explained helpfully to an old lady I had trapped next to the bar. "Of course, we don't even know whether whales have any kind of directed thinking, much less a language. Still—they may not need to. These concepts may permeate their interior worlds as feelings or moods. You know what I mean? There are any number of different ways these ideas may be expressed." She blinked at me and said, flatly, "You're blocking my view of the whales."

As my audience pushed past me, one hand gripping her purse, a new drama erupted at the side of the boat. One of the tourists had spotted another whale in the distance, doing something completely weird. "That's called a 'spy hop,'" said Shane. The whale was poking its head vertically out of the water, rising and falling like a shiny dark tube. "Sometimes they like to see what's happening at the surface."

The same whale disappeared for a few minutes, then resurfaced, much closer to the boat. Shane recognized him. "The locals call him Scar. He's a juvenile male, somewhere between six and eight years old. He'll probably leave the social unit soon, migrate up to the Pole. This animal in particular is very curious. He likes to approach boats. The whale-watch operators here love him because he always puts on a good show."

A tourist asked if he was dangerous. "Not at all," said Shane. "Although one time when I was in the water he echolocated me. You can really feel the clicks in your chest—like a repeated bass drum. I don't think I swam so fast in my life. At that point I wasn't habituated to being in the water with these animals. Don't forget—they physically experience the world through their mouth. Without hands to manipulate objects, first contact is often with their teeth. That was the last thing I wanted to deal with."

We all looked over at Scar, who seemed aware of the attention. He snorted and shook his huge head. "So what do you think he wants?" I asked. Shane shrugged. "Beats me. He may just enjoy the novelty of having us around. It's hard to say—it's hard to get into the head of these animals. We just don't have enough time with them."

Suddenly, Scar surged forward, pushing a small wave into the boat as people leapt for their tripods and valuables. I stood unsteadily at the front of the catamaran, on the netting, and watched as he appeared below me. He drifted beneath my feet and turned onto his back, so that I could see the long white gash of his jaw, his wrinkled grey skin, and then, a single eye.

It was slightly larger than a human eye, oval and pinched at each end. It looked like a small pinhole in a smooth wall of grey, and it was bordered above and below with two convex ridges of flesh, like eyelids. I held my breath, and felt the hair rise on the back of my neck. *He sees me.* Time paused, and I dropped, for one vertiginous moment, into his Umwelt.

What
Is It
Like to
Be a
Whale

325

You are Scar.

At the centre of your focus is the silhouette of a small figure pinned to a crumpled sheet of light. He looks down at you—you recognize the seeing, the knowing. What does he want? Something obscure wells up in your chest, a sense both of foreboding and excitement. The shadow of the dead thing is long; the others don't like to play beneath it. But you like the way it blocks the light, the way it resists your calls, the way it catches at the periphery of your mind. You sink down and away. The upper world begins to blur, it loses resolution. A new world flickers before you: a world illuminated by your voice, which you send out in the form of pulses. Each pulse is like a line, it parts the space, and carries you through a three-dimensional matrix of form and movement and texture. You can follow the lines in any direction: out, to the surface, with its strange inviting shapes; or down, to schools of fish, to squid undulating in the depths, to the plunging contours of the ocean floor. But mostly you follow them back, to the six warm, lit bodies of your family, whom you approach now, the dark shape forgotten. Your family turns to meet you, to receive your signal, which curves through them, through their soft interior dispositions to each beating heart. On your skin you feel your matriarch's movements too, a reassuring transmission of pressure that connects your whole family through the water column. It draws you in, you "heave-to," and slide roughly past each familiar form. You click and purr and repeat the name of your clan. And then, as one, you dive, saluting the air with your chiselled flukes. These are some of the things you experience, some of the things you know. The waters close around you.

We engage in a kind of shorthand when we talk about animals. When we try to represent their experience. Even our best thinkers do this—like the German poet Rainer Maria Rilke, who in his famous *Eighth Duino Elegy* placed all animals into a single unperverted flow:

> With all its eyes the natural world looks out
> into the Open. Only *our* eyes are turned
> backward, and surround plant, animal, child
> like traps, as they emerge into their freedom.

It may be true that humans possess agonized self-consciousness. But nature—that Other—is not monolithic. It's multi-personality. This is Uexkull's great lesson. Nature is a series of different perspectives, each with its own integrity of knowledge.

As I watched Scar swim away from the boat I thought about imagination and the human Umwelt, which is conceptual as well as perceptual. This is our genius, though perhaps not ours alone. Imagination is like another sense—indeed, it is the ultimate sense, for it helps us move beyond lived experience into other worlds.

At the end of his monograph Uexkull considers the Umwelten of different scientists. The astronomer, he writes, looks out and up, to where "suns and planets circle in festive procession." The ocean researcher looks below, to the "deep sea fish [who] wheel around his sphere with their uncanny mouths." The chemist sees primarily the elements, the nuclear physicist "the mad rush of infinitesimal particles," and on through the physiologist, the psychologist and the behaviourist, all of whom are entranced by a domain "which constitutes but a small part of nature."

I think there is a lesson here for the study of consciousness in general. For too long, discussions of animal consciousness have been trapped in an outmoded Umwelt, one that seeks to find definitive "proof" of animal awareness. But whether it's culture, or intelligence, or social complexity, no amount of "proof" will ever satisfy the old-guard critics. That's because, finally, consciousness is not something you can prove or measure. It's not a quantity—it's a quality, a basic feature of life. You need only look in an animal's eyes to see this.

So, can we get behind the eye?

In his famous paper, Nagel argues that empathy and imagination can only tell what it would be like for *us* to be a bat, not "what it is like for a *bat* to be a bat." Others have questioned Nagel's conclusion. The philosopher Kathleen Akins, for example, thinks that science may one day be able to shed real light on the problem. "We do not know *a priori* what insights or even what *kinds* of insights will result from empirical investigation," she writes in a review of Nagel's argument.

Our models will improve as the science improves—the neurobiology, the behavioural ecology, and all the rest. Yet in other ways we are already behind the eye. Because science is only one line of inquiry—there are others, ones that make creative use of the Umwelt. At the end of his book on sperm whales, Whitehead writes admiringly of two Canadian novels: Barbara Gowdy's *The White Bone* and Alison Baird's *White as the Waves*, told, respectively, from the point of view of a family of elephants and a family of whales. These portraits, writes Whitehead, "ring true, and may come closer to the nature of these animals than the coarse numerical abstractions that come from my own scientific observations . . . We need to take these constructions, note the large parts that are consistent with what we now know, and use them as hypotheses to guide our work."

What
Is It
Like to
Be a
Whale

327

To enter into the lives of animals we need both science and art, the greatest two expressions of human understanding.

For my part, I have an intuition. I feel it in my belly, I see it in my mind's eye: the Umwelts are coming. They're on the march. This is where the arrow of consciousness studies is pointing: out, to the next concentric ring, in what one hopes is an ever-expanding circle of empathy and understanding. We can only imagine what new insights we may discover on the other side. And, right now, that's exactly the point.

The sun was low in the sky as we headed back to port. Someone yelled: "Look, look there!" I turned my head and saw the horizon filled with leaping bodies. We had intersected a pod of Fraser dolphins, hundreds of them. They swept up to the boat and surged around the bow, jockeying for position, flashing us their sexy pink bellies. Soon a group of pantropical dolphins joined them, jumping even higher, so that it felt as if we were moving through a cloud of enormous silent birds.

Each of those dolphins was looking—looking out, looking over at us, looking down at the sea, which rushed up suddenly and then parted, pressing and surging, directing each of them down and then up again, into the air—with the boat, the noise from the engine, the magnificent surging boat pushing the sea forward, cleaving the water as they cleaved the water. The dolphins joined with the boat, jumped and looked over at us, and you could see the sun's reflection in their eyes.

Contributors

Jonathan Garfinkel is the author of several plays, including *House of Many Tongues*, about a divided house in Jerusalem (Tarragon Theatre, Toronto, 2009). He is also the author of a book of poetry, *Glass Psalms* (2005, Turnstone Press), and a book of literary non-fiction, *Ambivalence: Crossing the Israel/Palestine Divide* (2007, Penguin Canada and Norton USA) that grew out of his article at the Banff Literary Journalism Program. He is a frequent contributor to *The Globe and Mail* and *The Walrus*. Jonathan is currently living in a castle near the Black Forest, watching for fleet foxes.

Charlotte Gill was born in London, England, and raised in the United States and Canada. Her work has appeared in many Canadian magazines, *Best Canadian Stories*, and *The Journey Prize Stories*, and has been broadcast on CBC Radio. Her literary non-fiction has been nominated for Western and National Magazine Awards. Her debut story collection, *Ladykiller* (Thomas Allen), was a finalist for a Governor General's Literary Award. It received the Danuta Gleed Award and the B.C. Book Prize for fiction. She has planted nearly two million trees across Canada.

Taras Grescoe is the author of the national bestseller *Bottomfeeder*, which won the Rogers Writers' Trust Award for Non-Fiction. His other books include *The Devil's Picnic*; *The End of Elsewhere*, a book about the horrors of travelling; and *Sacré Blues*, winner of the Edna

Staebler Award, the Quebec Writers' Federation Book Award, and the Mavis Gallant Prize for Non-Fiction. He is a Montreal-based journalist whose work appears in such publications as *The New York Times* and *National Geographic*.

Marni Jackson is currently Chair of the Literary Journalism program at the Banff Centre, as well as on the faculty of the Mountain Writing program. Former senior editor at the *Walrus* magazine and the author of *Pain: The Science and Culture of Why We Hurt* (nominated for the Pearson Non-Fiction Prize) and *The Mother Zone* (nominated for the Stephen Leacock Award). Marni's work has been published in various anthologies, including the upcoming *The Heart Must Break*, an anthology of writings on grief, edited by Jean Baird, from Random House in late 2009.

Jeremy Klaszus is an Alberta-based writer who grew up in small towns near Edmonton. A graduate of Mount Royal College's journalism program, he has written for *The Globe and Mail*, *Alberta Views* magazine, and *Fast Forward Weekly*, Calgary's alternative weekly paper. He has also reported for CBC Radio. In 2007, he won the National Magazine Award for best new writer. He lives in Calgary.

Penney Kome is an award-winning journalist and author. She has published six books and hundreds of newspaper and magazine articles and spent twelve years as a national columnist. Her books include *The Taking of Twenty-Eight: Women Challenge the Constitution* (Women's Press) and *Peace: A Dream Unfolding* (Sierra Club Books, co-edited with Patrick Crean). She was named a Toronto YWCA Woman of Distinction in 1987 and awarded a Canada 125 medal in 1992. A former Chair of The Writers' Union of Canada, she is currently editor of Straightgoods.ca, Canada's leading independent online newsmagazine.

Deborah Ostrovsky is a freelance editor and writer. Her non-fiction has appeared in *Geist*, *Maisonneuve*, *The Globe and Mail*, and *Lilith* magazine. She has also been a finalist in the CBC Quebec Short Story Competition. After completing a Master's in History, she worked and studied in Poland before settling in Montreal, where she now lives. She is currently writing about the life and times of

Molly Picon, an American-Yiddish singer and actress who was also a distant family relative.

Bill Reynolds is head of the magazine stream at Ryerson University's School of Journalism. He teaches the courses "Journalism and Ideas" and "Visions of Literary Journalism" and is writing a book about a man who earned $150 million on the Internet and then gave it all away. He's also studying the link between Canadian and American New Journalism (and similar topics) and hopes to crystallize his research into a book about Canadian literary journalism.

Jaspreet Singh's debut fiction collection, *Seventeen Tomatoes: Tales from Kashmir*, won the 2004 McAuslan First Book Prize and has been translated into Spanish and Punjabi. *Chef*, his first novel, was shortlisted for four awards, including the 2009 Commonwealth Prize for Best Book in Canada and the Caribbean. His essay "Bhoot Ki Kahanian" appeared recently in the anthology, *AIDS Sutra: Untold Stories from India*.

John Vigna is an advertising copywriter who lives in Richmond, B.C., with his wife, the writer Nancy Lee, and his dog, Jaine, who keeps a wary eye on him. His writing has appeared in numerous publications, including *Grain, Event, sub-Terrain, The Antigonish Review*, the *Vancouver Sun*, the *Georgia Strait*, and *Exact Fare 2: Stories of Public Transportation*. He is the recipient of the Dave Greber Award for Freelance Writers, winner of the *sub-Terrain* Lush Triumphant fiction contest, and finalist for a Western Magazine Award, the *Event* creative non-fiction contest, and the CBC literary non-fiction contest.

Jeff Warren is the author of *The Head Trip: Adventures on the Wheel of Consciousness*, a delirious neuro-romp through the sleeping, dreaming, and waking mind. He is a freelance producer for CBC Radio's *Ideas*, a former producer at *The Current*, a graduate of McGill University, a resident of Toronto's Kensington Market, a frequent consumer of soup-filled Kaifeng buns, and an undisciplined reader of the mystic, the cryptic, and the scientific. He is currently working on a book about the evolution of consciousness, a manual for a bonkers mechanical device called the Dream Director that remixes dreaming, and a "Mind Circus" theatrical extravaganza that will dazzle audiences around the world should he ever complete it, which is unlikely.

Margaret Webb's "Johnny Flynn's Oysters" grew up into the book *Apples to Oysters: A Food Lover's Tour of Canadian Farms* (Penguin Canada, 2008), shortlisted for a 2009 Evergreen Award. Margaret grew up on a farm near Barrie, Ontario, became a senior editor at several city and national magazines then a multi-tasking writer. Her articles have appeared in *Saturday Night*, *Toronto Life*, *Chatelaine*, and *Canadian Geographic*; her poetry and fiction have been published in two anthologies and numerous journals. She won a Walt Disney Screenwriting Fellowship and has written four optioned screenplays. She lives in Toronto and dreams of farming.

Andrew Westoll is an award-winning narrative journalist and internationally published author specializing in science, travel, conservation, and culture. A former biologist and primatologist, his first book, *The Riverbones*, is a travel memoir set deep inside the jungles of Suriname, where he once lived as a monkey researcher. Andrew writes regularly for many of Canada's premier venues, including *The Walrus*, *explore*, and *Canadian Geographic*. He lives in Toronto, and online at www.andrewwestoll.com.

Megan Williams is a writer and journalist based in Rome, Italy. Her radio reports can be heard regularly on CBC and other public broadcasters around the world. She has won numerous awards, her favourite being the Golden Grape Award for a documentary on a cous-cous cook-off in Sicily. Megan has written for many newspapers and magazines, including *The Globe and Mail*, *The Toronto Star*, *Star-Ledger*, *South China Morning Post*, *Salon.com*, *The Walrus*, and *Nature*. She's a graduate of Columbia University School of Journalism, where she was awarded a Pulitzer Fellowship. Her most recent book is the story collection *Saving Rome*.

General
Editors

Moira Farr has been on the faculty of the Rogers Literary Journalism program at The Banff Centre for the Arts since 2001 and was co-editor with Ian Pearson of *Word Carving: The Craft of Literary Journalism* (The Banff Press, 2002). Her essays, reviews, and features have appeared in *The Walrus, More, Toronto Life, Ottawa, The Globe and Mail, Canadian Geographic, Chatelaine,* and many other publications. Her book *After Daniel: A Suicide Survivor's Tale* (HarperFlamingo) was shortlisted for the Pearson/Writers' Trust Prize for Non-Fiction and was *The Edmonton Journal*'s top pick for non-fiction in 1999. She is an instructor in magazine writing at Carleton University's School of Journalism in Ottawa.

Ian Pearson is a veteran Toronto writer, editor, and radio producer. He has worked as an editor at *Maclean's, Toronto* magazine, and *Saturday Night*. His articles have appeared in most major Canadian magazines, winning five National Magazine Award nominations. He was books producer for CBC Radio's *Morningside* for three seasons and was a contributing editor of *Saturday Night* during the 1990s. He was an editor in the Banff Centre's Literary Journalism program from 2001 to 2008 and is the proprietor of the Zedtone record label.